CHRISTI

John Young

TEACH YOURSELF BOOKS

Dedication

To
Barbara, Carolyn and Sharon
and to the
Ecumenical 'One Voice' committee
With warmest thanks

For UK orders: please contact Bookpoint Ltd, 39 Milton Park, Abingdon, Oxon OX14 4TD. Telephone: (44) 01235 400414, Fax: (44) 01235 400454. Lines are open from 9.00 – 6.00, Monday to Saturday, with a 24 hour message answering service. Email address: orders@bookpoint.co.uk

For U.S.A. & Canada orders: please contact NTC/Contemporary Publishing, 4255 West Touhy Avenue, Lincolnwood, Illinois 60646-1975, U.S.A.. Telephone: (847) 679 5500, Fax: (847) 679 2494.

Long-renowned as the authoritative source for self-guided learning – with more than 30 million copies sold worldwide – the *Teach Yourself* series includes over 200 titles in the fields of languages, crafts, hobbies, business and education.

British Library Cataloguing in Publication Data
A catalogue record for this title is available from the British Library

Library of Congress Catalog Card Number: On File

First published in UK 1996 by Hodder Headline Plc, 338 Euston Road, London, NW1 3BH.

First published in US 1997 by NTC/Contemporary Publishing,
4255 West Touhy Avenue, Lincolnwood (Chicago), Illinois 60646-1975 U.S.A.

The 'Teach Yourself' name and logo are registered trade marks of Hodder & Stoughton Ltd.

Copyright © 1996 John Young

Typeset by Transet Ltd, Coventry, England.
Printed in Great Britain for Hodder & Stoughton Educational,
a division of Hodder Headline Plc, 338 Euston Road, London NW1 3BH
by Cox & Wyman Ltd, Reading, Berkshire.

Impression number   12 11 10 9   8   7   6   5   4   3
Year   2004 2003 2002 2001 2000 1999   1998

CONTENTS

Acknowledgements

On reflection, I am surprised at just how many people have been involved in producing one book of modest size. This is mainly because different people agreed to read drafts of different chapters.

I am extremely grateful to them all for so many valuable suggestions, and I hope they will not be embarrassed at being publicly associated with the finished work: Dr David Barrett, Dr Peter Brierley of *Christian Research*, Fr Cyril Brooks OSB, Pastor Iain Collins, Rev Dr Bill East, Nicky Enticknap, Nigel Forde, Rev Dr Michael Frost, Rev Christopher Idle, Brother Patrick Moore FSC, Rev David Mullins, Rev Linda Norman, Rev Professor John Polkinghorne, Fr Stephen Robson, David and Sheena Steels, Dr Alison Wray and Chris Woodcock.

My special thanks are due to three friends who agreed to write specific chapters and then bravely submitted themselves to my editorial control:

The Revd Canon John Cockerton, Chapter 7
The Revd Canon Dr John Toy, Chapters 12 and 19
The Revd Dr Peter Williams, Chapters 15, 16, 17 and 18

Above all, to Barbara Thompson, Carolyn Prestwich and Sharon Winfield – the trio to whom this book is dedicated and upon whom I came to depend for endless drafts and carefully researched information – one immense THANK YOU.

The author and publishers would like to thank the following for their kind permission to reproduce extracts from copyright material:
The Central Board of Finance of the Church of England for *The Mystery of Salvation*, Church House Publishing, 1995; HarperCollins Publishers Ltd for *School for Prayer* by Archbishop Anthony Bloom, and *Surprised by Joy* by C S Lewis; Hodder and Stoughton Ltd for *With Hope in Our Hearts* by David Sheppard and Derek Warlock; Newspaper Publishing Plc for an article by William Rees-Mogg, *The Independent*, 21 December 1992; Oxford University Press for *The Oxford Dictionary of Saints* edited by David Hugh Farmer, 3rd edn. 1992; SCM Press Ltd for *Our Faith* by Emil Brunner, 1936, and *Introducing the Christian Faith* by A M Ramsey, revised edn 1970; Times Newspapers Limited for 'Odds on God's fine tuning' by Clifford Longley, *The Times*, 13 April 1991 © Times Newspapers Limited, 1991.

Cover: Ronald Sheridan (The Ancient Art and Architecture Collection).

PREFACE

Anyone who attempts to write a survey of Christianity in one volume is open to the charge of arrogance, ignorance or folly. Is he not aware that the Christian faith has generated thousands of books, because it has influenced almost every corner of life over two millennia?

That was my first response on being invited to write this volume for the *Teach Yourself* series. But I was pleased to accept, because I am aware that there are certain crucial facts and key events which deserve to be more widely known. My judgement as to what these are (see the topics included or omitted) is certainly open to question. Another author would have tackled the task differently.

Throughout this volume I am as concerned with *feel* as with fact. What is it about the Christian faith that attracts people? Why do so many people, more today than ever before, respond to the invitation of Jesus of Nazareth to 'Come, follow me'?

There has been, and is, much that is shameful in the life of the Church. It is not surprising that many turn away. But I hope that by the end of this book, readers will have a clearer idea as to why millions continue to embrace the Christian way of being human.

How to use this book

To some, this will be obvious. They will start at Chapter 1 and read one chapter each day for three weeks. However, others may choose to tackle the book differently. For example, some readers may be particularly interested in a survey of Church History and will begin at Chapter 15. Others might omit the historical chapters (15–18) altogether. Whatever their particular interests, it is my hope that *all* readers will tackle chapters 1, 2, 3, 6 and 21, together with pages 254–7. These passages attempt to give some idea of the significance for Christians of Jesus Christ, and to provide a glimpse of what it means to be a Christian today.

Throughout the book I have given Bible references. Those who wish to look these up are advised to use a good modern translation. I would recommend the *Revised English Bible*, the *Jerusalem Bible* (an official Roman Catholic translation) or *The New International Version* (NIV). Most Bible quotations in this book are taken from the NIV.

An attempt has been made to explain technical terms in the text itself. Reference has also been made to other chapters which refer to related issues. But there is a short **Glossary** at the end of the book (terms included in the glossary are in bold text).

I have used a wide range of books and I am grateful for permission to quote from several. At the end of the book there is a **Recommended Reading** list for those who wish to read more widely. On some topics in this book I have written elsewhere (especially in *The Case Against Christ* and *Know Your Faith* – both published by Hodder & Stoughton) and I have drawn from these books at certain points.

1
JESUS CHRIST

The impact of Jesus

Professor Hans Küng, a leading Christian scholar, makes the following points about Jesus Christ and the faith which bears his name:

> 'None of the great founders of religions lived in so restricted an area. None lived for such a terribly short time. None died so young. And yet how great his influence has been . . . Numerically, Christianity is well ahead of all world religions.' (*On Being a Christian*, Collins)

This is not quoted in a spirit of competitive superiority; it is nothing more nor less than a statement of significant fact. In considering the Christian faith, we are studying the largest movement in history. Christianity has exercised tremendous influence (for good and ill) upon our world.

Jesus has been the focus of more study, more controversy and more art than any other figure. He is the one who has 'chopped history in half: BC = *before Christ*; AD = *in the year of our lord* (or CE = *Common Era*). In today's world, millions of people, from every continent and nearly every country, claim some allegiance to him. Christians make up about one-third of the world's population.

Ralph Waldo Emerson, the American essayist, summed up the significance of Jesus when he said that his impact has not so much been *written on,* as *ploughed into,* the history of the world. All this is remarkable enough. But when we consider the short and rather obscure life of Jesus, it becomes extraordinary. However, according to the Bible, there were clear indications of his greatness even before his birth.

The life of Jesus

According to St Luke's **Gospel**, the story began in the district of Galilee in Israel. A young woman, betrothed but not yet married to a man called Joseph, was visited by the angel Gabriel. He announced (hence *The Annunciation*) that she had been chosen by God to give birth to a son who was to be called Jesus. Troubled as she was by this ('How will this be, since I am a virgin?') she declared herself ready to do God's will: 'I am the Lord's Servant.' (Luke 1:38)

The child was due to be born at the time of a Roman census. For Mary and Joseph, this entailed a journey of about 70 miles from Nazareth to Bethlehem near Jerusalem. The baby was born in Bethlehem and he was visited by local shepherds and wise men from eastern lands; a choir from heaven celebrated the birth. King Herod, on hearing from the eastern travellers of the birth of 'a king', tried to kill the infant Jesus. But Mary, Joseph and Jesus ('the holy family') escaped to Egypt and so fulfilled a prophecy (Matthew 2:15). Eventually they returned to Nazareth, where Joseph earned his living as a carpenter – a craft which he taught his son.

THE BIRTH NARRATIVES RAISE QUESTIONS

Why do only two of the four Gospels (see Chapters 4 and 5) carry these narratives?

And why are these two accounts so different: one focusing on Mary, the other on Joseph?

Are we intended to read these accounts of the birth of Jesus as history?

Or are they a particular kind of story, alerting readers to the fact that *this* child is very special indeed?

We are told little about the early years of Jesus, apart from one visit to Jerusalem when he was 12 years old. On that occasion Jesus went to the **Temple** where he listened to the teachers and asked and answered questions: 'Everyone who heard him was amazed at his understanding and his answers'. (Luke 2:47)

We learn nothing more for nearly 20 years, when Jesus was baptised by his cousin John ('the Baptist') in the river Jordan. At his baptism, a voice from heaven declared, 'This is my Son, whom I love; with him I am well pleased.' (Matthew 3:17) Then Jesus was led by God's Spirit into the desert where he fasted and wrestled with the devil for 40 days. This time of temptation was to fashion the shape of his ministry. Now he was ready.

After spending a night in prayer, Jesus called 12 disciples and set out on his travels around his small country. He began his ministry in his home area in the north, in the towns, villages and countryside around the Lake of Galilee. The four Gospels record some of his deeds and words. Jesus healed people with a wide range of diseases: a paralysed man, a man with leprosy, a woman who suffered from excessive bleeding, a man possessed by a demon. He even raised the dead (Luke 7:15; John 11:43).

He also showed power over nature; for example, he stilled a storm, and fed a huge crowd from five loaves and two fish. Jesus became known as a powerful and controversial teacher, who was willing to challenge the established traditions. All this made him famous and popular. Time for rest, solitude and prayer was limited but he 'often withdrew to lonely places and prayed.' (Luke 5.16)

——— The teaching of Jesus ———

Christianity is based not only on ideas, but on events. At its centre we do not find a theory, but *a person*: Jesus Christ. Many people have a sentimental picture of Jesus. They view him as a rather anaemic character, more interested in flowers, birds and children than in the harsh world of adult reality. How different is the towering figure of the New Testament. We see there:

- a man marked out as a dangerous rebel by the authorities
- a man who drew great crowds

- a man who inspired others
- a man who took the uncompromising road to martyrdom
- a man of deep passion and decisive action

The Gospels assure us that Jesus *was* interested in children and in nature. And with the down-trodden he was very gentle. But the world he inhabited was a harsh world of hatred, intrigue, brutality and revenge. The Gospels portray a dynamic figure who waged war against evil with the weapons of love, openness, honesty and forgiveness. His honesty was fearless. Against those greatest sins of pride, hypocrisy and indifference, his attack was blistering and devastating.

Jesus did not set out to be an 'original' teacher. As a Jew he stood in a tradition which was steeped in the Hebrew Scriptures (known to Christians as the *Old Testament*). He drew on those Scriptures and

---

THE SERMON ON THE MOUNT

Jesus' Sermon on the Mount (Matthew 5–7: see page 10) starts with a series of Beatitudes:

Blessed are the poor in spirit for theirs is the kingdom of heaven.
Blessed are those who mourn for they shall be comforted.
Blessed are the meek for they will inherit the earth.

The Sermon also contains:

- a breathtaking call to love and forgiveness: '*But I tell you: Love your enemies and pray for those who persecute you . . . For if you forgive men when they sin against you, your heavenly Father will also forgive you.*' (Matthew 5:44; 6:14)

- an encouragement to faith in God: '*So do not worry, saying, "What shall we eat?" or "What shall we wear?" . . . your heavenly Father knows that you need them.*' (Matthew 6:31)

- an encouragement to pray: '*Ask and it will be given to you; seek and you will find; knock and the door will opened to you* '. (Matthew 7:7)

- an uncompromising call to accept Jesus' teaching: '*But everyone who hears these words of mine and does not put them into practice is like a foolish man who built his house on sand.*' (Matthew 7:26)

his central demands – that we should love God with all our heart and our neighbour as ourselves – link two separate Old Testament texts (Deuteronomy 6:5; Leviticus 19:18). This was his genius: to make new connections, to bring fresh emphases, to take old ideas and give them new content, to reveal the deeper meaning which was latent within them.

The Kingdom of God

Jesus spoke frequently about 'the Kingdom of God' or 'the Kingdom of heaven'. This idea is certainly found in the Jewish Scriptures. But Jesus put it at the *centre* of his teaching and illustrated (but never defined) its meaning with a series of brilliant, yet often puzzling, pictures and parables. In this way he made his hearers, and now his readers, think very hard.

> *The kingdom of heaven is like treasure hidden in a field. When a man found it, he hid it again, and then in his joy went and sold all he had and bought that field. Again, the kingdom of heaven is like a merchant looking for fine pearls. When he found one of great value, he went away and sold everything he had and bought it.'* (Matthew 13:44–46)

Jesus made it clear that his notion of God's kingly rule was very different from the popular views of his time. His country was under enemy occupation. The hated Romans were in charge and there were many Jews who looked for armed revolt. Their nation had a famous history of success on the battlefield; perhaps this teacher would be the new military leader? To those who wanted to go down that road, Jesus was a great disappointment: 'My kingdom is not of this world.' (John 18:36) In *his* Kingdom, his followers would turn the other cheek and leadership must be characterised by humble service.

Miracles of the Kingdom

Many miracles are recorded in the Gospels, showing Jesus' power over sickness, sin, nature, demons and death. When his enemies accused him of healing by Satan's power he replied, 'But if I drive out demons by the finger of God, then the kingdom of God has come to you.' (Luke 11:20)

God's kingly rule was present because Jesus was present. But his ministry was also the sign of a future in which God's kingly rule would be fulfilled and consummated. One day the '**Son of Man**' will come 'in his Father's glory with the holy angels'. (Mark 8:38) *Now* and *not yet* are held in balance.

Parables of the Kingdom

Jesus became famous for his stories or parables. A parable is a story which works on two levels. It is 'an earthly story with a heavenly meaning'. At one level it is an interesting tale with strong human interest. But the story has a deeper meaning and a personal application. Jesus' hearers are usually left to work this out for themselves. Some parables convey the notion of *growth*. Others convey a sense of *crisis*: a decision must be made, sides must be chosen. Jesus' stories are usually about people:

- a woman who lost a coin (Luke 15:8)
- a woman who badgered a Judge for justice (Luke 18)
- a man who built a tower (Luke 14:28)
- a farmer who scattered seed (Mark 4:3)
- a Samaritan traveller who cared for a man who was mugged and robbed (Luke 10:25)
- a young man who left home and squandered his money (the Prodigal Son) before returning to a father who forgave him and a brother who resented him (Luke 15:11)

Best known are *The Good Samaritan* and *The Prodigal Son*. The former isn't just an exhortation to compassion and kindness (though it is that). It is a strong attack upon racism and bigotry. Samaritans were widely despised by Jews and vice-versa. Jesus was taking a huge risk in making a *Samaritan* the hero, in contrast to the establishment figures of his own race and religion. Here were the seeds of conflict with the authorities which would end in his death by crucifixion.

'The teaching of Jesus stands on an Everest alone. No other teaching has had the same impact and influence, in countless lives and diverse cultures. No other teaching has provoked so much change, or stirred so much debate. (Professor Sir Norman Anderson)

'With every sceptical faculty alive and kicking I do believe that nearly 2000 years ago, in the land we today call Israel, the "word" . . . was made flesh and dwelt in a Galilean Jew called Jesus . . . for a brief moment in history there was magic in the air. The sick were healed, men and women caught a glimpse of heaven, all too good of course to last. (Ian Wilson)

Alec McCowen, the British actor, set out to memorise St Mark's account of the ministry and death of Jesus – as a hobby! To his surprise, large audiences around the world wanted to hear his recitation of the life of Jesus, taken straight from the Bible. When asked what he made of the story he replied: 'Something absolutely marvellous happened in Palestine 2000 years ago.'

The anguish of the *Prodigal Son* is captured vividly by the sculptor Rodin, whose bronze figure of the Prodigal can be seen in London's Tate Gallery. Archbishop Desmond Tutu describes the significance of this story with typical vigour and enthusiasm:

'What a tremendous relief . . . to discover that we don't need to prove ourselves to God. That is what Jesus came to say, and for that he got killed . . . The Good News is that God loves me long before I could have done anything to deserve it. He is like the father of the prodigal son, waiting anxiously for the return of his wayward son . . . That is tremendous stuff – that is the Good News. Whilst we were yet sinners, says St Paul, Christ died for us. God did not wait until we were die-able for He could have waited until the cows come home'. (Hope and Suffering, Collins)

The parable of the Prodigal Son could equally well be entitled *The Forgiving Father*. Again, the notion of God as Father was familiar to Jesus' contemporaries. But he underlined its importance, stressing both the *rule* and the *love* of God. He emphasised his own close relationship with God and taught that discipleship cannot be reduced to a set of rules. At its centre is a relationship with the living God, who is 'your Heavenly Father' – to be loved and trusted. But a loving father is not a doting uncle. Much of Jesus' teaching is uncompromising in its moral and spiritual demands.

- Turn the other cheek (Matthew 5:39)
- Go the extra mile (Matthew 5:41)

- Judge not or you will be judged (Matthew 7:1)
- Forgive seventy times seven (Matthew 18:22)
- Sell your possessions and give to the poor (Mark 10:21)

His teaching makes intellectual demands too. Jesus did not spoonfeed his largely uneducated audience; he respected their intelligence. He often said things that he did not mean! By exaggeration and paradox Jesus left, and leaves, his hearers thinking furiously, 'He can't really mean *that*. So what *does* he mean . . .':

- let the dead bury their dead (Matthew 8:22)
- become like a little child (Matthew 18:3)
- cut off a foot rather than allow it to lead to sin (Mark 9:45)
- hate your father and mother (Luke 14:26)
- you must be born again (John 3:3)

A father's love includes discipline as well as encouragement. Hence Jesus taught us to *trust* God, to *love* God and to *fear* God – to hold him in respect and awe, for God *is* GOD. He emphasised that prayer, forgiveness, honesty, humility and generosity are all involved in accepting God's kingly rule in our lives. All this is summed up in the world's most famous prayer, given by Jesus in response to his disciples' request, 'Lord teach us to pray':

> *Father, hallowed be your name,*
> *your kingdom come.*
> *Give us each day our daily bread.*
> *Forgive us our sins, for we also*
> *forgive everyone who sins against us.*
> *And lead us not into temptation.*
> (Luke 11:2; see Matthew 6:9–13)

EARLY CHRISTIAN TESTIMONY TO JESUS

Inevitably, it fell to the followers of Jesus to write about his life, his death, and his remarkable impact. This need not detract from the reliability of these accounts. Many of the finest, most detailed studies of great people have come from their friends or followers (Boswell on Johnson, for example). Of course we make allowances for bias. But we also recognise that close friends are the only people who have detailed, accurate information.

The four Gospel writers are called Evangelists because that word means 'bringer of good news'. They do not claim to be objective reporters. They are convinced of the immense significance of Jesus and want to convince others. St John makes this quite clear when he disarmingly admits that 'these (signs) are written that you may believe that Jesus is the Christ, the Son of God, and that by believing you may have life in his name.' (John 20:31)

At the same time they insist that they are recording the truth about Jesus. There was no need to exaggerate, because Jesus was big enough already! Of course, they didn't have cassette-recorders. They were dependent upon memories, stories and records. But Middle-Eastern memories were good (and still are: many Muslims today can recite the entire *Qur'an* from memory). And there were enough eyewitnesses to act as a check on wild exaggeration.

There is lively debate among scholars concerning the way in which the first Christians regarded Jesus of Nazareth. To cite one celebrated theological question: is the 'Jesus of history' the same as the 'Christ of faith'? Some scholars believe that the early Christians used Jesus' teaching freely, adapting it to their own purposes; even inventing sayings of their own. Others are convinced that the first believers treated his teaching with great reverence and took trouble to remember and record it accurately (see page 65). They also point out that it would take someone of the stature of Jesus to invent the teaching of Jesus!

'The gospels (we are told) are faith-documents: therefore, they are not about history. The gospels are the product of long theological reflection: therefore, they are not biographies. The first thing to be said to this is that these are false alternatives ... the theological reflection which they offer is emphatically Jewish. Like Jesus himself, they wear their Jewish ancestry on page after page. And the great thing about first-century Judaism ... was its concentration on history.' (Who Was Jesus? N T Wright, SPCK)

——— The authority of Jesus ———

'. . . *the crowds were amazed at his teaching, because he taught as one who had authority, and not as their teachers of the law.*' (Matthew 7:28–29) Jesus quickly established himself as a popular, unconventional and controversial teacher. As a result, many members of the established leadership felt threatened. No doubt this striking authority had its roots in his dynamic personality. But it was emphasised by the *content* of his teaching.

The Temple and the Sabbath

These were two of the foundation stones of Jewish society at the time of Jesus. He challenged the traditions which had grown up around them. It was Jesus' dramatic action in overturning the tables of the money-changers in the Temple precincts that led to his crucifixion, according to the influential American scholar E P Saunders. Jesus claimed to be greater than the Temple itself (Matthew 12:6), and greater than some great Old Testament characters, such as the prophet Jonah and King Solomon (Matthew 12:41–42). And he caused controversy by healing on the Sabbath. This drew the accusation that he disregarded the religious laws, because the Sabbath was a day of rest and healing the sick was regarded as work. In response, Jesus reminded his hearers that he was 'Lord even of the Sabbath'. (Mark 2:28)

The Sermon on the Mount

At the beginning (see page 4) Jesus declares a blessing on anyone who is persecuted 'for my sake'. In the middle he considers some important moral issues: murder, adultery, divorce, honesty, revenge and love. He refers to the established interpretation of the Jewish law ('you have heard that it was said to the people long ago') before giving his own interpretation ('. . . but I tell you': with the stress on the 'I'). In this way Jesus claims to be *the* authoritive interpreter of the sacred Law. Even more startling, on the final *Day of Judgement* people will address Jesus as 'Lord, Lord' and he will judge the nations. The sermon ends with a vivid picture of two men: one wise, the other foolish. What is the difference between them? The wise man 'hears these words of mine and puts them into practice.'

The Last Supper

The supper which Jesus ate with his disciples (page 20) just before his arrest and crucifixion, has been painted by countless artists – most famously by Leonardo da Vinci. At this meal Jesus instituted a new covenant 'in my blood'. 'Covenant' is an important biblical term. It describes an 'agreement' between unequals: God and his people. God was faithful *to* them; he required faithfulness *from* them. But the nation had failed and a new covenant was needed. Six hundred years before Jesus sat down to eat the Last Supper with his disciples, the prophet Jeremiah promised that God would make a new, more glorious covenant. By his words and actions, Jesus indicated that the great day had arrived at last – and that he, Jesus, was the central figure.

Relationship with God

In a beautiful and gentle passage, Jesus asserts that he alone knows God and that he alone can reveal God (Matthew 11:25–29). He frequently speaks of the Kingdom of God; occasionally he refers to it as 'my kingdom' (Luke 22:30; John 18:36).

A puzzle

Here is a puzzle indeed! Jesus taught humility. He associated with and served ordinary people. He chose fisherman for his close companions. He lived a simple, rough life, and befriended outcasts such as prostitutes and tax-collectors who collaborated with the hated Romans. Yet in an unassuming way, he made explosive claims. The New Testament scholar Bishop John Robinson summed up: *'He steps in the eyes of his contemporaries into the space reserved for God . . . It is impossible to escape the conclusion that he went around not just talking about God (that would not have provoked the reaction he did) but standing in God's place, acting and speaking for him.'* (*Can we trust the New Testament?*, SCM)

To find such a humble man saying the sort of things which Jesus claimed for himself is puzzling, even shocking. It is to that puzzle that we turn on page 13.

EARLY NON-CHRISTIAN REFERENCES TO JESUS

As far as the Roman authorities were concerned, Jesus was a small-time trouble maker. They were forced to revise their opinion when the movement which bore his name grew rapidly – after his death. His followers were accused of many things: *cannibalism* because they spoke of feeding on the body and blood of Christ in Holy Communion (see Chapter 8); *atheism* because they did not accept the Roman gods.

- TACITUS, a Roman historian born in AD 56, describes (in his *Annals*) how the Emperor Nero blamed Christians for the burning of Rome. *'Therefore, to scotch the rumours, Nero substituted as culprits, and punished with the utmost cruelty, a class of men, loathed for their vices, whom the crowd styled Christians. Christus, the founder of the name, had undergone the death penalty in the reign of Tiberius, by sentence of the procurator Pontius Pilate.'*

- PLINY THE YOUNGER (Roman Governor of Bithynia, AD 110–113) complained of the problems caused by Christians who sang *'a hymn to Christ as to a god.'*

- JOSEPHUS was a Jewish historian who defected to the Romans in the Jewish-Roman war which began in AD 66. He affirmed that Jesus was 'the Christ' who rose from the dead. There is no textual evidence against Josephus' remarkable testimony to Jesus. But many scholars assume that some key words were inserted later, because they cannot believe that Josephus could have written so positively about him.

- The Jewish TALMUD (an ancient commentary on Jewish teaching) acknowledges Jesus as a Jew. His miracles, his teaching and his disciples are referred to, and he is described as a false teacher who was executed.

RECENT TESTIMONY TO JESUS

- MAHATMA GANDHI, the great Hindu: 'I believe that Jesus belongs not only to Christianity but to the entire world, to all races and people.'

- MILAN MACHOVEC, a Czech Marxist, wrote a book entitled *A Marxist looks at Jesus*. He acknowledged that Jesus *'set the world on fire'*, and he explains why: *'. . . he himself was the attraction. They saw in him a man who already belonged to this coming Kingdom of God; they saw what it meant to be "full of grace" . . .'*

- MARTIN BUBER, the influential Jewish teacher: *'From my youth onwards I have found in Jesus my great brother . . . I am more than ever certain that a great place belongs to him in Israel's history of faith and that this place cannot be described by any of the usual categories.'*

- GEZA VERMES, another Jewish scholar, warmly acknowledges Jesus as a fellow Jew who was *'an unsurpassed master of the art of laying bare the inmost core of spiritual truth.'*

- H G WELLS the early science fiction writer, was not a Christian; nor was he a natural ally of the Christian Church. But his admiration for Jesus was boundless. In his *Outline of History* he wrote several fine pages on the impact of Jesus, including these sentences: *'He was too great for his disciples . . . He was like some terrible moral huntsman digging mankind out of the snug burrows in which they had lived hitherto . . . Is it any wonder that men were dazzled and blinded and cried out against him? Is it any wonder that to this day this Galilean is too much for our small hearts?'*

—— Jesus: More than a Man? ——

All the New Testament writers assert the human nature of Jesus. Like us he got hungry, thirsty, and tired. He experienced the full range of human emotions, including joy and sorrow. But attend a church service which includes the Nicene **Creed** and you will hear the congregation recite or sing these astonishing words:

> *We believe in one Lord, Jesus Christ,*
> *the only Son of God,*
> *eternally begotten of the Father.*
> *God from God, Light from Light,*
> *true God from true God,*

> *begotten, not made,*
> *of one Being with the Father.*
> *Through him all things were made.*
> *For us men and for our salvation*
> *he came down from heaven;*
> *by the power of the Holy Spirit*
> *he became incarnate of the Virgin Mary,*
> *and was made man.*
> *For our sake he was crucified . . .*

This Jesus, a real human being, is the focus of Christian worship. Such worship contrasts sharply with all other great world religions. In speaking about Sikh attitudes to their Gurus in *Teach Yourself Sikhism* (Hodder & Stoughton) Owen Cole writes: 'This can be summed up in one brief statement; profound respect falling well short of worship.' The same is true for the Muslim attitude to Muhammad. He is a great prophet, a key figure. But he is not to be worshipped. So Muslims dislike being called 'Muhammadens'. In contrast, Christians rejoice at the fact that their title links them so closely with Jesus Christ, whom they honour as 'my Lord and my God!'. (John 20:28)

The language of worship and praise is found throughout the New Testament. Even great words like Prophet and Messiah aren't big enough for Jesus. The writers stretch language to its limits with terms like Son of God, Light of the World, Lord, Saviour, Emmanuel, the Word made Flesh, Lord and God. All this raises three immense questions.

1 Where did these ideas come from?

The first disciples of Jesus were God-fearing Jews; strict **monotheists**. Frequently they recited the *Shema*: 'Hear, O Israel: the Lord our God is one Lord' (Deuteronomy 6:4). Notice: *one* Lord. Most Jews refused to embrace the Roman gods or to acknowledge the Roman emperor as divine, for that would deny their belief in *one* God. So we can sympathise with those Jews who objected to the exalted view of Jesus which came to be held by his followers. The notion that a man could be divine held no great problems for Gentiles. But for Jews it was unthinkable. *Yet some of them came to think the unthinkable. At the same time they insisted that they were monotheists*, who continued to be loyal to the one true God.

In a remarkably short space of time, the early Christians came to the startling conclusion that Jesus was *divine* as well as *human*. This resulted partly from their belief in his resurrection (see Chapter 3). But their conclusion finds its seeds in the teaching of Jesus himself: in his teaching about authority and the Temple and the New Covenant which we noted earlier. Of course Jesus did not go around saying, 'I am God.' Indeed, he joyfully acknowledged his dependence upon God his 'heavenly Father'. He was no usurper. *But he did claim a unique relationship with God; he did claim a unique mission from God; and he did claim that he, and only he, was able to do things which it was proper only for God to do.*

In this way Jesus himself laid the foundations for the kind of language used about him in the New Testament and (later) in the Nicene and other Creeds. As the New Testament scholar Professor C H Dodd put it: *'His words carried divine authority and his actions were instinctive with divine power.'* Over the years the distinctive Christian view of God emerged. He is three 'Persons' in one God: Father, Son and Holy Spirit. This doctrine of **The Trinity** was not invented by the early Christians; it has its seeds in the teaching of Jesus himself. Those seeds can be seen in bloom on other pages in the New Testament.

- *'He is the image of the invisible God, the firstborn over all creation. . . all things were created by him and for him.'* (Colossians 1:15–16)

- *'May the grace of the Lord Jesus Christ, and the love of God, and the fellowship of the Holy Spirit be with you all.'* (2 Corinthians 13:14)

- *'Your attitude should be the same as that of Christ Jesus:*
  Who, being in very nature God,
  did not consider equality with God
  something to be grasped' (Philippians 2:5,6)

- *'Thomas said to him (Jesus), "My Lord and my God!".'* (John 20:28)

At the same time, the New Testament writers held that Jesus was *a real human being*. Their concern was to declare that God reveals himself through Jesus Christ – not to speculate on the innermost nature of God. Such speculation came later, as Christians pondered the relationship between Father, Son and Holy Spirit. The result of this mature consideration can be seen in the Nicene and other Creeds (pages 13, 216–7 and 287).

2 How can Christianity relate to other faiths?

We live in a multi-faith world. Tragically, this sometimes leads to strife, even war. For religious faith is a passionate business. It *matters* to those who practise it; it matters a lot. And of course, over the centuries, the world's religions have become linked to particular cultures and nations. So people fighting over territory or language or history or other issues, sometimes seem to be fighting about religion – and sometimes *are*, of course.

One of the most important questions facing the modern world is: How can adherents of the great religions live together in harmony? Christians are called by Jesus to be *peacemakers* (Matthew 5:9) and many wish to contribute actively to establishing good inter-faith relationships. This does not mean surrendering or 'fudging' distinctive beliefs. Dialogue is at its healthiest when the differences between faiths, as well as the similarities, are openly recognised.

At the theological (as distinct from a social) level, inter-faith dialogue raises sharp issues for Christians. For if Jesus Christ is the *Son of God*, the *Light of the world* and the *Word made flesh*, what are they to make of other faiths? Can other religions be regarded as equally valid vehicles of God's revelation? We shall consider this key question later. (see Chapter 14)

3 'Who do you say that I am?' (Mark 8:29)

Any study of Christianity is bound to focus on Jesus Christ. And any study of Jesus leaves each of us with a personal challenge. It is impossible to understand Christianity from a Christian perspective, without experiencing this challenge.

Jesus continues to issue his gentle invitation, which is also a stern command: 'Come, follow me.' Michael Ramsey, one hundredth Archbishop of Canterbury, expressed this challenge with powerful simplicity, as he described some of the claims of Christ which we have considered and drew out their implications.

> *'Perhaps you are trying the line that you welcome Christ's moral teaching and admire it: but reject his own claims. It seems to me a most unconvincing line. The moral teaching and the claims are woven in one, for both concern the reign of God. I see no escape*

from the dilemma: either Jesus is fraudulent, or his claim is true: either we judge him for being terribly amiss, or we let him judge us. That was, in fact, the dilemma that cut through the consciences of his contemporaries.' (Introducing the Christian Faith, SCM)

JESUS IN OUR IMAGE

It is moving to find African artists painting an African Jesus, Indian artists painting an Indian Jesus, and English artists painting an English Jesus. For they are claiming that Jesus is one of them. *He came for all people; he transcends cultures and nations.* Jesus came not primarily as a first-century Jew *but as a human being.* He is able to cut through cultural differences; he shows us what it means to be truly human.

But **Incarnation** – the belief that in Jesus Christ, God became a human being – carries with it the necessity of particularity. In one sense, no one man can be universal. He must belong to *one* period in history, to *one* nation, to *one* culture, to *one* family. Jesus, in his particularity, was a first-century Palestinian Jew. In this sense he is, for most modern Western people, an uncomfortable figure, not easy to fathom. Perhaps too often, however, he is all too easy to understand. So we feel the force of Mark Twain's quip: 'It's not the parts of the Bible which I can't understand that bother me, it's the parts that I *can* understand'!

Conclusion: Jesus our contemporary

'Christianity is Christ'. That statement sums up the Christian view of Jesus of Nazareth. Hans Küng expresses the challenge of Jesus for his disciples like this: *'A real Christian is not only a good and well-intentioned person but a man or woman for whom Jesus Christ is ultimately decisive; for whom Jesus – not Caesar, not another god, not money, sex, power, or pleasure – is Lord.'*

David L Edwards made the same point: *'There are many ways of defining what a Christian is. The best one is this: a Christian is one who takes orders from Jesus Christ as Lord.'*

But this figure who challenges us at every turn is also the source of all comfort. The Lutheran pastor Dietrich Bonhoeffer spoke strongly against 'cheap grace'; he insisted that Christian discipleship is costly and challenging. He demonstrated this during his years in a Nazi concentration camp, and by his execution just before the end of the Second World War. But throughout those long difficult months, he felt the comfort and encouragement of Jesus. In one of his prison letters he wrote:

> *'All we may rightly expect from God, and ask him for is to be found in Jesus Christ . . . If we are to learn what God promises . . . we must persevere in quiet meditation on the life, saying, deeds, sufferings, and death of Jesus . . . it is certain that in all this we are in a fellowship that sustains us . . .'*

This then is the Jesus of the New Testament, the Jesus of history and the Jesus for today – whenever *our* 'today' might be. He comes to us with tough demands – calling us to serve a troubled and divided world in his name and with his strength. He comes, too, with unutterable comfort.

To a world beset by problems he comes as guide. In a world where many are lonely, he comes as friend. To a world which often seems to lack meaning, he brings understanding. For a world tempted to despair, he provides the ground for hope. Over a world where dying is the single certainty, he sits enthroned as the conqueror of death.

The words of Jesus as recorded in St John's Gospel have been tested and proved in countless lives: *'I am the light of the world. Whoever follows me will never walk in darkness, but will have the light of life.'* (John 8:12)

2
CRUCIFIED SAVIOUR

The final week

Near the end of his three years in the public eye, Jesus faced a crucial decision. Should he return home, to the safety of Galilee? Or should he go on to Jerusalem and to conflict? In his Gospel Luke tells us that 'Jesus resolutely set out for Jerusalem.' That decision led to his death.

In Mark's Gospel we find a refrain on Jesus' lips: 'The Son of Man must suffer.' And in John's Gospel, Jesus refers to his death as his 'hour'. Everything he taught and did led up to his climactic death. This is seen most clearly in the dramatic events of the last week of his life.

The week began with his entry into Jerusalem. Jesus timed this to coincide with the great Jewish festival of Passover, when Jerusalem was teeming with pilgrims. His reputation ensured a large crowd. He rode on a humble donkey, fulfilling the prophecy of Zechariah 9:9.

> *Rejoice greatly, O Daughter of Zion!*
> *Shout, Daughter of Jerusalem!*
> *See, your king comes to you,*
> *righteous and having salvation,*
> *gentle and riding a donkey....*

Here was no worldly king, coming in glittering style to impress and command. Here was the Prince of peace, riding in great humility. The crowds greeted him with shouts: 'Hosanna', which means '*Save Now*'. They scattered coats and palm branches on the road (hence

Palm Sunday). As he approached Jerusalem, Jesus wept bitterly over the city. For some days, he taught in the precincts of the Temple – a fabulous building erected by King Herod 'the Great', who had tried to kill him as a baby. Jesus made a direct attack on the attitudes and practices of many of the leaders of his people. He even drove out those who were trading in the Temple precincts. *'It is written'*, he said to them, *'My house shall be a house of prayer, but you have made it a den of robbers.'* (Luke 19:46)

To mark the annual Passover festival, Jewish people gathered in homes to eat a celebration supper – a practice which continues today. This was the last meal which Jesus ate with his disciples; it was to become the most celebrated meal in history. As the meal ended, Judas, one of the 12 disciples, left the room and betrayed Jesus to the Jewish authorities. He was rewarded with 30 silver coins. They plotted to arrest Jesus by night, away from the crowds. Although the other disciples swore undying allegiance, Jesus warned that they too would abandon him. His prophecy was fulfilled.

After their meal, they sang a hymn and walked to a garden called Gethsemane on the Mount of Olives. Jesus knew what was coming. He prayed with deep emotion, asking that he might be spared the dreadful suffering which the next few hours would bring. But his prayer ended with these famous words, *'. . . yet not my will, but yours be done.'* (Luke 22:42) Shortly after this, Jesus was arrested and interrogated through the night by hastily convened Jewish and Roman courts.

Rabble-rousers stirred up the people. No longer did the crowds cry 'Hosanna!' and 'Welcome!' Now they shouted 'Crucify!' Pontius Pilate, the Roman Governor of Judea from AD 26–36, wanted to release Jesus but gave way to the popular outcry. To distance himself from this decision he washed his hands in public. (Matthew 27:24)

Jesus was stripped. Nails were driven through his hands and feet. The cross was raised, and he was left hanging between two criminals. Soldiers gambled for his single worldly possession: a seamless robe. Later, his side was pierced with a spear to ensure that he was dead. As he was dying, Jesus uttered seven sentences which are recorded in the four Gospels. Among these is this astonishing prayer: *'Father, forgive them, for they know not what they are doing.'*

JESUS' WORDS FROM THE CROSS

- 'Eloi, Eloi, Lama Sabachthani? – My God, my God, why have you forsaken me?' (Matthew 27:46; Mark 15:34, from Psalm 22:1)

- 'Father, forgive them, for they know not what they are doing.' (Luke 23:34)

- 'I tell you the truth, today you will be with me in paradise.' (Luke 23:43)

- 'Father, into your hands I commit my spirit.' (Luke 23:46 from Psalm 31:5)

- 'Dear woman, here is your son... Here is your mother.' (John 19: 26–27)

- 'I am thirsty.' (John 19:28)

- 'It is finished.' (John 19:30)

A startling contrast

Blandina was a Christian who had the misfortune to live in Lyons in Gaul (modern France) in 177 AD. The authorities wished to stamp out the Church. The job was straightforward; they had to persuade the Christians to disown their God and swear by the pagan idols.

Eusebius, an early historian, recorded these events. Blandina, he reported, wore out her tormentors with her endurance. So they put her back in prison. Later, they brought her into the arena, together with a 15-year-old boy called Ponticus. After he had been killed, they put Blandina in a net and presented her to a bull. 'And so', wrote Eusebius, 'she travelled herself along the same path of conflicts as they (her fellow martyrs) did, and hastened to them rejoicing and exulting in her departure.'

The peace and serenity, and the sense of the *presence* of God, displayed by Blandina, is characteristic of the Christian martyrs since the time of Stephen (Chapters 9, 11 and 15). *It is in sharp contrast to the death of Jesus himself*. In the Passion Narratives in the Gospels (eg Mark 14:32 – 15:47)

- We find a *lack* of serenity: 'He began to be deeply distressed and troubled.'
- We find a *lack* of peace: 'My soul is overwhelmed with sorrow.'
- We find a *desire for escape*: 'Abba, Father, everything is possible for you, take this cup from me.'
- We even find a *sense of abandonment* by God, as Jesus quotes the opening line of Psalm 22: 'My God, my God, why have you forsaken me?'

Jesus was no less courageous than the martyrs who followed him. He could have escaped to safe obscurity. Instead, he pressed on to Jerusalem, to his fatal confrontation with the authorities. But the striking contrast remains: *for those who died for Jesus Christ – a constant sense of the presence of God; for Jesus as he died – a sense of abandonment by God and of utter loneliness. The martyrs faced death willingly; Jesus shrank from it.*

Add to this, the fact that those who followed Jesus to martyrdom drew *their* inspiration from *his* death, and we have a remarkable puzzle. It is a puzzle to which the New Testament gives a solution. The answer given there is that, for Jesus, there was *an extra factor*. The martyrs suffered *physically*; Jesus suffered physically *and spiritually*, as he experienced separation from God the Father for the first time in his life.

The martyrs bore *pain* for him; he bore *sin* for them: not only their sin but the sin of the whole world. And it is sin which separates from God – hence the cry of abandonment from the cross. All this was summed up by John the Baptist when he referred to Jesus as, 'the Lamb of God, who takes away the sin of the world.' (John 1:29)

The Mediator

For there is one God, and one mediator between God and men, the man Christ Jesus . . . (1 Timothy 2:5)

We cut ourselves off from other people when we turn our backs on them, or when we relate to them only at a superficial level. Christians believe that we human beings have cut ourselves off from God through disobedience and indifference. To bring two separated parties together, a mediator or *trouble-shooter* is sometimes required. To be a mediator can be dangerous, for it might mean getting involved in the dispute. This is what Jesus did. According to the New Testament, he became the Mediator between God and humanity – at the cost of his life. The apostle Peter conveys this with great power: 'He himself bore our sins in his body on the tree . . . by his wounds you have been healed.' (1 Peter 2:24)

Many people know what it is to experience a sense of alienation, lostness, guilt and meaninglessness. The New Testament writers see the death of Jesus Christ as *the* solution to this dilemma. It is for this reason that they give such emphasis to this event and so much space to exploring its significance. This same emphasis has been maintained within the Christian community over the centuries. The cross has become *the* central symbol of Christianity.

Not only do we find a cross or crucifix within most churches, but many church buildings are designed in cruciform style (Chapter 19). The two great sacraments of the Church focus on the cross (Chapter 8). *Baptism* is 'into Christ', and especially into his death and resurrection. In the *Holy Communion* or *Eucharist*, the bread and wine refer to the broken body and shed blood of Jesus.

——— Light from a dark place ———

The death of Jesus Christ takes us to the heart of the Christian understanding of **salvation**. It is, according to St Paul, of 'first importance' (1 Corinthians 15:3). John Polkinghorne, former Professor of Mathematical Physics at Cambridge University, sums it up:

> *'In that lonely figure in the dark, in the spent force of a deserted man dying on a cross, they see not the ultimate triumph of evil or futility but the only source of hope for mankind. "God was in Christ reconciling the world to himself" (2 Corinthians 5:19) . . . The crucifixion was not something which got out of hand, a tragic mistake which marred an otherwise wonderful life. On the contrary, it was the inevitable fulfilment of the life, purposed by God.'*

> (*The Way the World Is*, SPCK).

Why it was necessary for Jesus to die to win our salvation, is a deep mystery. Indeed, St Paul admits that the notion that a man dying on

> **W**e all have to choose between two ways of being crazy; the foolishness of the gospel and the nonsense of the values of this world.' *Jean Vanier*

a cross might save the world, appears very foolish (1 Corinthians 1: 18–25). It cannot be fully understood: it can only be proclaimed – and believed or denied. But this mystery sheds light upon, and brings meaning to, countless lives. The New Testament probes the significance of the death of Christ at many points: we may attempt to sum up its significance under four headings.

The cross reveals the depth of human sin

It was pride which opposed Jesus; it was greed which betrayed Jesus; it was jealousy which condemned Jesus. Cruel men flogged and mocked him. Then they led him out to die a shameful death in a public place called Golgotha, which means 'The Place of the Skull'.

As Jesus died, the land was covered in daytime darkness. '*At the birth of the Son of God there was a brightness at midnight, at the death of the Son of God there was darkness at noon.*' (Douglas Webster) It was as though heaven itself was saying: *this* is the most dreadful day of all. But Christians believe that God took those evil actions and attitudes and used them as the raw materials from which to quarry our salvation.

The Cross reveals the depth of God's love

Rather than using his power to dominate, Jesus chose to submit himself to human wickedness. So the power of God is seen in symbols of weakness: a borrowed manger for his birth and a wooden cross at his death. Here is power kept in check; power handed over; power utterly controlled by love. Jesus' body was broken like bread and his life was poured out like wine, for the forgiveness of sins. One of the most famous of Bible verses begins: 'For God so loved the world that he gave his only begotten Son . . .' (John 3:16)

The Cross reveals the way back to God

In the temple in Jerusalem, a large curtain hung between the Most Holy Place and the rest of the building. It was a symbol of the separation between the Holy God and the human race, resulting from our sin. As Jesus died, that curtain was torn in two from top to bottom. It was a dramatic sign of new access into the presence of God. On the cross Jesus cried out: 'It is finished.' The Greek word ('*tetelestai*') carries a triumphant ring. Not 'It's all over' but '*It is accomplished.*' According to the Bible, only his death, the death of the Son of God, could break down the barriers of rebellion and indifference which separate us from God and from one another. So we call that terrible day *Good Friday*. The day was terrible, but the fruit of the day is beautiful.

The Cross reveals the demands of Christian discipleship

'Follow me', said Jesus. Then he took the road to crucifixion. As baptism indicates (Chapter 8), following Christ always involves a sort of death. It means trying to hold Christian standards in a world which often rejects those standards. It means following Jesus in a world which is often indifferent towards him. Jesus summed up like this: 'If anyone would come after me, he must deny himself and take up his cross and follow me.' (Mark 8:34)

Paradoxically, Jesus insists that the cross is also about *life*. He goes on to say; 'For whoever wants to save his life will lose it, but whoever loses his life for me and for the gospel will save it.'

Lord George McLeod founded the modern Iona Community in Scotland. His words remind us that the crucifixion of Jesus is not just a terrible but fascinating incident in history, nor a puzzle in theology, nor even an object for adoration and art. It is a constant challenge to all who seek to follow the crucified Christ.

'*I simply argue that the cross be raised again at the centre of the marketplace as well as on the steeple of the church. I am recovering the claim that Jesus was not crucified in a cathedral between two candles, but on a cross between two thieves; on the town garbage heap; at a crossroads so cosmopolitan that they had to write his title in Hebrew and Latin and in Greek . . . at the kind of place where cynics talk smut, and thieves curse, and soldiers gamble. Because this is where he died. And this is what he died about. And that is where churchmen ought to be and what churchmen should be about'.*

—— Painting pictures with words ——

The second of the Ten Commandments tells us that the early Israelites were forbidden to make graven images (Exodus 20). It was an essential instruction for a people surrounded by pagans (people who fashioned images and worshipped idols). As a result of this prohibition, painting was an art form which did not flourish in ancient Israel. But other art forms did, especially music, architecture and literature – including poetry.

Much of the Bible is rich in pictorial language and many of the great Bible themes paint pictures on the mind. For example, in the Psalms God is seen as a shepherd, king, judge, rock, fortress, etc. To make good sense of this we need to be aware of the way in which such images 'work'. Calling God a rock does not mean that he is lifeless; it does mean that he is utterly dependable. One image needs to be balanced by another.

Bible language about salvation is highly pictorial too: from death to life; from darkness to light. The word 'salvation' is dramatic, suggesting rescue from danger. So is the word 'atonement', which means 'at-one-ment' or reconciliation with God.

So it is no surprise to find that the language concerning the death of Jesus – of which there is a great deal in the Bible – is full of verbal images or pictures. Dr Colin Morris put it like this:

'The writers of the New Testament ransacked language to find some way of conveying the sense of what had happened to Jesus on Calvary. They used the jargon of the law courts and the slave galleys and the slaughter house to get across the meaning of his death . . .'

Consideration of some of these great images helps us to understand the significance afforded to the crucifixion in the Bible:

Ransom St Mark records these words of Jesus: 'The Son of Man came not to be served, but to serve, and to give his life as a ransom for many.' (Mark 10:45) A slave in the ancient world could be redeemed (set free) by a ransom price paid on his behalf. The Bible teaches that every person, regardless of culture, background, virtue or vice, can be set free ('redeemed') from sin, fear, guilt and death, by the death of Jesus.

Reconciliation The Christian gospel is about reconciliation (2 Corinthians 5:19, 20). The death of Jesus built bridges across apparently unbridgeable gaps. To change the image, it knocked down two dividing walls (Ephesians 2:14):

● between the Holy God and sinful human beings
● between Jews and Gentiles (non-Jews)

Elsewhere, the New Testament is even bolder. Christ's death brings together *all things* previously fragmented. Nature itself will be redeemed. (Colossians 1:20; Romans 8:20–22)

The idea of atonement for sin runs throughout the Bible. In the Old Testament we find an elaborate set of rituals based on the **tabernacle** and the Temple. These found their focus in animal sacrifices. Those ancient practices have no practical significance for Christians today. They were the shadow; the death of Jesus was the substance – the fulfilment and summation of the entire sacrificial system. For on the cross, Jesus became the *one perfect sacrifice* and the *one true* **High Priest**. This is spelt out in detail in the New Testament *Letter to the Hebrews*. The way back to God is open; through Jesus we may come to God the Father with confidence. (Hebrews 10:19; Ephesians 3:12)

Suffering Servant The prophet Isaiah wrote about the *Servant of the Lord*. He was the *suffering* Servant. The earliest Christians made the connection: *Jesus was that Servant*. Indeed, Jesus saw his own ministry like that: '. . . the Son of Man . . . came to serve.' (Mark 10:45) This servant identified himself with the poor, the powerless, the stranger, and the marginalised: 'Whatever you did for one of the least of these brothers of mine, you did for me.' (Matthew 25:40)

This emphasis is particularly important for our century, when more people have suffered in wars than in all previous centuries put together. It helps as we face the sharpest of all questions for those who believe in a loving God. Where is God when we suffer? Where was he in the Nazi concentration camps and the Soviet labour camps? Where is he in the sweat shops of our world? Where is he when people suffer illness, torture, drought and famine?

This question was addressed powerfully by the German theologian Jürgen Moltmann. His answer was that *God in Christ is there in the anguish*, sharing the bitter pains of a suffering world. The crucifixion assures us that God does not sit on the side-lines; he gets involved. The Son of God did not only suffer *for* us; he suffers *with* us. In this way, he brings redemption and shows his love. The Bible does not offer us a theoretical solution to the question, 'Why does God allow suffering?' Instead, it offers us a God who suffers with us, and who redeems us through the cross.

'God was in Christ reconciling the world to himself' (2 Corinthians 5:19). It was God in Christ who died a degrading death. It was God in Christ who hung naked, exposed and helpless. *This is the message of the cross. All this leads to a gospel of hope. Christians are confident that we human beings are not on our own in a cold, heartless universe. At the centre of all things is the crucified God – who brings life out of death, as the resurrection shows.* Indeed, the most anguished and problematic words in the whole Bible point to this conclusion. 'My God, My God why have you forsaken me?' cried Jesus from the cross, quoting Psalm 22:1. Rabbi Hugo Gryn alleges that the opening line of a Psalm represents the whole Psalm to a devout Jew. And Psalm 22 ends in confidence and faith. Even the desolation, though desperately real, is shot through with hope.

—— 'A theory of the atonement'? ——

None of this amounts to one definitive 'theory of the atonement'. Just *how* the death of Jesus on the cross saves us is not spelled out in detail in the Bible. Ultimately it is a deep mystery – a mystery of love which conveys life and light. Throughout Christian history, theologians have tried to explain this mystery. They set several ideas before us, based upon Bible images. Jesus is seen as:

- the perfect Penitent
- the Victor over the powers of darkness

- the One who paid the ransom to set us free
- the Substitute who died in my place
- the Representative who died for all humanity
- the perfect Sacrifice for sin
- the One whose death satisfies the demands of holy justice
- the One who delivers us from a guilty verdict in a court of law
- the supreme Example of self-giving love
- the One whose death moves and inspires us to acts of loving service

Each of these helps us to understand; none contains the whole truth. So it is not surprising that no single account has been adopted by the Church as *the* 'official theory' of the atonement. Indeed, the term 'theory' is often criticised as being inappropriate for this great act of passion, love and sacrifice. Perhaps in the end, the death of Jesus can best be understood through pictures, parables and stories.

One such story is *The Long Silence* (author unknown). It is set on Judgement Day, when people who have suffered terribly, complain that 'God leads a pretty sheltered life.' To qualify as Judge, they say, God should be sentenced to live on earth as a man.

'Let him be born a Jew and let the legitimacy of his birth be questioned. Let him be doubted by his family and betrayed by his friends. Let him face false charges and be tried by a prejudiced jury in front of a hostile crowd. Let him be tortured to death – and as he dies, let him feel abandoned and alone.'

When this judgement was pronounced, there was a long silence. Nobody moved. For suddenly all knew that God had already served his sentence.

— The cross through the centuries —

'He who did not spare his own Son, but gave him up for us all – how will he not also, along with him, graciously give us all things?' (St Paul: Romans 8:32)

'Like a sheep to the slaughter he humbled himself, and by his death delivered us from the peril into which our sins had put us.' (Origen: c185–254)

'Then the young Hero – it was God Almighty –
strong and steadfast, stripped himself for the battle;
he climbed up on high gallows, constant in his purpose.'
(Anglo-Saxon: Anon)

'Where is the strength of Christ? . . . Surely his strength is in his
hands, for his hands were nailed to the arms of the cross . . . O hidden
strength! A man hanging on a cross lifts the weight of eternal death; a
man fixed on wood frees the world from everlasting death. O hidden
power!' (Anselm: c1033–1109)

'Thus naked am I nailed? O man, for thy sake
I love thee, then love me. Why sleepest thou? Awake!'
(Medieval: Anonymous)

'. . . his most dreadful cry, which at once moved all the powers in heav-
en and earth, 'My God, my God, why hast thou forsaken me?' Weigh
well that cry, consider it well, and tell me if ever there were cry like to
that of his. Never the like cry, and therefore never the like sorrow.'
(Lancelot Andrewes 1555–1626)

'And where pride and envy and hatred, etc., are suffered to live, there
the same thing is done as when Christ was killed and Barabbas was
saved alive.' (William Law 1686–1761)

'Thomas, be not faithless, but believing. Christ shall show you his
hands and his feet. He is the same now as He was yesterday, full of love
and graciousness to self-condemned sinners. That you may experience
the full power and efficacy of the Redeemer's blood is the ardent prayer
of, dear Thomas, your sincere friend, George Whitefield.' (1714–1770)

– 1 –

Am I a stone, and not a sheep,
  That I can stand, O Christ, beneath Thy cross,
  To number drop by drop Thy blood's slow loss,
And yet not weep?

– 2 –

Not so those women loved
  Who with exceeding grief lamented Thee;
  Not so fallen Peter weeping bitterly;
Not so the thief was moved;

– 3 –

Not so the Sun and Moon
  Which hid their faces in a starless sky,
  A horror of great darkness at broad noon –
I, only I.

– 4 –

Yet give not o'er,
  But seek Thy sheep, true Shepherd of the flock;
  Greater than Moses, turn and look once more
And smite a rock.

(*Christina Rossetti 1830–1894*)

'On June 7th, 1917, I was running to our lines half mad with fright . . .
being heavily shelled. As I ran I stumbled and fell over something. It
was an undersized, underfed German boy, with a wound in his stomach

and a hole in his head . . . Then there came light . . . It seemed to me that the boy disappeared and in his place there lay the Christ upon his cross, and cried, "Inasmuch as ye have done it unto the least of these my little ones ye have done it unto me." From that moment on I never saw a battlefield as anything but a crucifix. From that moment on I have never seen the world as anything but a crucifix.' (G A Studdert-Kennedy: 1883–1929)

'The Cross of Christ is the reality to which we must continually return. For this is the light in which all our values are to be seen. Our understanding of the good and the true and the beautiful is to be jarred and rejigged by the divine humility.' (Bishop Richard Harries)

'I could never myself believe in God, if it were not for the cross . . . In the real world of pain, how could one worship a God who was immune from it?' (John Stott)

I spoke recently with a woman whose child had died. One saying of Jesus had helped her more than any other. It wasn't his affirmation of victory over death ('I am the Resurrection and the life'). It wasn't his promise of strength ('I am with you always'). It was his cry of dereliction: 'My God, my God, why have you forsaken me?' She felt that Jesus understood her suffering.

The power of the cross

'Jews demand miraculous signs and Greeks look for wisdom, but we preach Christ crucified: a stumbling-block to Jews and foolishness to Gentiles . . . For the foolishness of God is wiser than man's wisdom, and the weakness of God is stronger than man's strength.' (1 Corinthians 1:22–25)

The apostle Paul wrote these words after his conversion to Jesus Christ. At one time he had persecuted the Church of Christ. In those days he *knew* that the Christians were wrong, because he knew the Hebrew Scriptures. Deuteronomy 21:22–23 is clear: 'anyone who is hung upon a tree is under God's curse.' Jesus had been crucified – hung upon a tree – therefore he was accursed. So he could *not* be the Messiah, as his followers claimed. This was the logic which motivated Saul.

Later, the apostle came to see that the cross was indeed the place of a curse. But the curse which Jesus bore was *ours*, not his. For he took upon himself the curse of human sin. So Paul could write: 'Christ delivered us from the curse of the law, having become a curse for us.' (Galatians 3:13)

So it was that Paul discovered and described the power of the cross in this vivid, almost shocking, way. Throughout the next 20 centuries, countless individuals would come to find its power by one route or another. This is captured by the historian G Kitson Clark, who ends his book *The Kingdom of Free Men* (CUP) with these words:

> *'So we have reached the end of our journey, and we have arrived at no pleasant place. It is in fact a place of public execution. Yet all human roads lead here in the end. This is the capital of the kingdom of free men and there, ruling from the gallows, is the King.'*

3
RISEN LORD

The Acts of the Apostles describes a visit made by the apostle Paul to Athens. As he spoke, some local philosophers asked, 'What is this babbler trying to say?' They were told that he seemed to be speaking about foreign gods, 'because Paul was preaching the good news about Jesus and the resurrection.' (Acts 17:18) As they half-listened, Paul's hearers thought that he was talking about two gods (*Jesus* and *Anastasis* – the Greek Word for resurrection), because they heard these two words so frequently linked together.

This stress on Jesus and his resurrection is found throughout the New Testament. *The Letters* were written in the conviction that Jesus is alive. The *Acts of the Apostles* contain sermons which declare that God raised Jesus from the dead. The *Gospels* end, not with the death and burial of Jesus, but with stories about the way in which he appeared to his disciples.

POST-RESURRECTION APPEARANCES OF JESUS

- Two Marys encounter the risen Lord (Matthew 28:1–10)
- The risen Christ commissions the 11 disciples (Matthew 28:16–20)
- Three women are bewildered and afraid at the empty tomb (Mark 16:1–8)
- Jesus appears to two disciples on the road to Emmaus (Luke 24:13–35)
- Jesus eats with his disciples (Luke 24: 36–39)

- Mary Magdalene encounters Jesus at the tomb (John 20: 10–18)
- Thomas doubts until he meets Jesus (John 20:24–29)
- A miraculous catch of fish followed by breakfast (John 21:1–14)
- Jesus encourages and commissions Peter (John 21:15–23)
- Jesus appears for 40 days before ascending to heaven (Acts 1:3–11)
- Saul has a vision of the risen Lord on the Damascus Road (Acts 9:1–9)
- Jesus appears to more than 500 people (1 Corinthians 15:3–8)

The different situations in which Jesus appeared, and the different people to whom he appeared, is striking. This can be viewed as a problem: can these appearances be harmonised into one coherent narrative of events? Or it can be seen as a strength. If the first disciples had invented the resurrection, surely they would have made a tidier presentation?

We will consider just one of these stories: the appearance of Jesus to Mary Magdalene. St John tells us (John 20:1) that Mary went to the tomb very early on the first day of the week, only to find the stone removed from the entrance. She alerted two disciples who inspected the empty tomb and then returned home.

Mary remained and encountered an angel and a man. Thinking that the man was the gardener, Mary asked if he had moved the body. But according to the fourth Gospel, Mary was not talking to a gardener – she was talking to a carpenter. It was Jesus himself, risen from the dead. Jesus addressed Mary by name and she recognised him. He instructed her to tell his followers ('my brothers') about their meeting. Mary went to the disciples with her exciting news: 'I have seen the Lord.'

This story focuses on two important features which occur frequently in the Gospels:

- the tomb was empty
- the risen Lord appeared to one (sometimes more than one) of his followers

The centrality of resurrection

The resurrection of Jesus Christ is not just one aspect of Christianity. We cannot remove a portion of the Christian jigsaw labelled 'resurrection' and leave anything which is recognisable as Christian faith. Subtract the resurrection and you destroy the entire picture. Indeed, without the resurrection of Jesus from the dead, it is unlikely that we would have a trace of his teaching, or anything else in the New Testament.

In the early Church there was no preaching about Jesus except as risen Lord. Nor could there be. For without the apostles' conviction that they had seen Jesus alive again after his crucifixion, there would have been no preaching at all. There would have been deep mourning for a lost friend and great admiration for a dead hero. No doubt his profound teaching would have been remembered and cherished by his small, loyal circle of followers. But when they died, he would have been forgotten. Significantly, the early Christian preachers were less concerned to expound his teaching, than to declare his death and resurrection.

The central Christian claim that God raised Jesus from the dead has been carefully examined and vigorously debated. Nobody disputes that the first Christians made this extraordinary claim but various alternative explanations have been put forward – and vigorously dismissed by others. The scholar-bishop John Austin Baker sums up the Christian position like this: *'It is still very important, in a sceptical and often hostile culture, that the Easter story should stand up to attack – no easy matter at a distance of almost 2000 years. But stand up it does.'*

Some have gone even further. Lord Darling, a former Lord Chief Justice of England, asserted that: 'There exists such overwhelming evidence, positive and negative, factual and circumstantial, that no intelligent jury in the world could fail to bring in the verdict that the resurrection story is true.'

—— Approaching the evidence ——

Christian scholars vary in their approach to the resurrection. Some, observes Pinchas Lapide (a *Jewish* scholar), appear to be embarrassed by the material nature (the 'facticity') of the resurrection. So they make assertions such as:

- 'Easter means: The cause of Jesus goes on.' (Willi Marxsen)
- 'Jesus has risen into the Kerygma.' (i.e. the preaching of the Church) (Rudolph Bultmann)
- 'To believe in the resurrection of Jesus means to undertake the surprising risk to reckon with Jesus Christ as a present reality.' (Meinrad Limbeck)

Other scholars, such as Lapide, feel that this is far too cautious. It is, he says, 'all too abstract and scholarly to explain the fact that the solid hillbillies from Galilee who, for the very real reason of the crucifixion of their master, were saddened to death, were changed within a short period of time into a jubilant community of believers. Such a post-Easter change, which was no less real than sudden and unexpected, certainly needed a concrete foundation which can by no means exclude the possibility of any physical resurrection.' (*The Resurrection of Jesus*, SPCK)

The assertion that a man who was dead and buried has been raised up from the grave is breath-taking: those who make such a claim must give their reasons. In this chapter, some important facts will be set out and their possible implications discussed. Readers may consider the evidence to be strong or weak. Certainly it is not overwhelming. Always there are some who will assert that something as extraordinary as resurrection simply could *not* have happened, however strong the evidence might appear to be.

The Gospel accounts of the post-resurrection appearances of Jesus are striking in this regard. They provide readers with space in which to doubt, to question and to explore. For they freely admit that the disciples themselves found the whole thing very difficult to accept. St Matthew tells us that at the end of the 40 days during which Jesus appeared, 'some doubted' (Matthew 28:17). St Luke tells us that even with the risen Lord present, the disciples 'disbelieved for joy' (Luke 24:41). It was simply too good to be true! The burning conviction which runs throughout the New Testament did not come easily.

In any case, evidence can take us only so far. We may sympathise with 'doubting Thomas' who reserved his judgement until he received convincing proof. But when he received the evidence which he requested, he did not simply say, 'So it *is* true.' Rather, he acknowledged the risen Christ as 'My Lord and my God!' (John 20:28) For Thomas, fact and evidence were followed by faith and commitment. With this in mind, we turn to ten significant facts which cry out for adequate explanation.

Fact 1   No-one produced the body

The Church began, not primarily by the spreading of ideas, but by the proclamation of a *fact*. Something has *happened*, said the apostles: God has raised Jesus from the dead. Those who wanted to discredit the apostles – and the Jewish leaders wanted to do that very much indeed – had only to produce one piece of evidence. *All they had to do was to produce the body of Jesus. If they had done so, we would never have heard of him or his followers. There would be no New Testament and no Church.*

It is very significant that they did not do this. If the authorities had taken the body, or discovered it still in the tomb – because the disciples had lied, or gone to the wrong grave – they would have produced the corpse. This would have silenced all talk of resurrection. Instead, the authorities imprisoned, threatened, and beat the disciples. And they circulated the report that the disciples had stolen the body. It is clear that the Jewish and Roman leaders had no idea what had happened to Jesus. Yet the stubborn fact remains: his body had gone.

Fact 2   The tomb was not venerated

The empty tomb is strongly supported by the fact that the grave of Jesus did not become a place of pilgrimage. Tomb veneration was common at the time of Jesus; people would often gather at the grave of a prophet – as they do today. In surprising contrast, the earliest Jewish Christians did no such thing. 'No practice of tomb veneration, or even of meeting for worship at Jesus' tomb is attested for the first Christians,' writes Professor James Dunn in *The Evidence for Jesus* (SCM). (The practice of venerating Jesus' tomb did start 200–300 years later, and it persists today. But it is the *risen* Lord who is worshipped there.)

That the tomb of Jesus did not become a place of pilgrimage for the first Christians, has only one satisfactory explanation. As Professor Dunn puts it: *'The tomb was not venerated, it did not become a place of pilgrimage, because the tomb was empty!'* The focus of attention was not on the tomb but on Jesus who was gloriously alive, according to the growing band of believers.

Fact 3   The movement almost died

The Christian faith shares some common features with other great world religions. In particular, it looks back to a charismatic founder whose teaching is central for all his followers. In this it is like Buddhism, which traces back to Guatama the Buddha; and Islam, which owes so much to the energy, vision and inspiration of Muhammad, the Prophet of Allah. But when all the similarities have been noted, the *differences* between Jesus and other great religious leaders are startling and puzzling. Three in particular are relevant to this chapter.

● Jesus died very young (Guatama died c483 BC, aged 80; Muhammad died in 632 AD, aged 62; Jesus died c33 AD, in his 30s).
● Jesus spent no more than three years in the public eye.
● When Jesus died, the movement which he founded was in rapid decline.

Movements can and do grow and develop after the founder's death; we have ample evidence of this. It happens when the founder leaves a growing movement. And it happens when the founder's followers are in a buoyant frame of mind, because everything depends on their 'get-up-and-go'. When Jesus died, these factors were conspicuously absent. His followers were dwindling in number; those who remained were dispirited and afraid.

Yet somehow this demoralised, dispirited group experienced a remarkable turn-around. Within a few weeks they were full of creative energy. They launched the biggest movement the world has ever seen, and one of the eventual fruits of this remarkable turn-around was the New Testament. *In other words, it was the resurrection of Jesus which gave the teaching of Jesus to the world. No resurrection; no record of his teaching.* His disciples gave two reasons for their remarkable transformation, and these reasons have been celebrated ever since, in two great Christian festivals:

Easter The first disciples claimed that God had raised Jesus from the dead. Because this happened on a Sunday, they transferred their 'special' day from the traditional Jewish Sabbath (the last day of the week) to the first day. This change is in itself a remarkable fact, requiring adequate explanation. For Christians, *every* Sunday is a 'mini-Easter'.

Pentecost (sometimes called Whitsun) The first disciples claimed that God had given them the gift of his **Holy Spirit**. They affirmed that it was God's Spirit who gave them boldness, joy and insight.

Those who deny the resurrection of Jesus, must find a satisfactory alternative explanation for the beginnings of the Church in such unlikely circumstances.

Fact 4   The disciples suffered for their preaching

'Then all the disciples deserted him and fled.' In this short sentence, Matthew describes the behaviour of the disciples of Jesus following his arrest. He goes on to tell of the way in which Peter, for all his earlier boasting, denied all knowledge of Jesus. In the circumstances such behaviour was completely understandable. But a few weeks later those men were out in the streets, preaching that God had raised Jesus from the dead. These were the same men who had deserted him. They were the same men who had been shattered by his crucifixion. But as the Acts of the Apostles makes very clear, they were very different same men!

In place of bitter disappointment there was joyful confidence; in place of fear there was boldness. Instead of thinking gloomily that their leader was dead, they proclaimed that he had conquered death. In other words, they were transformed. The question is: what transformed them? They claimed that it was their experience of the risen Lord. Were they right? Were they mistaken? Or were they guilty of the most successful fraud in history?

An invention?

From time to time during his ministry, Jesus spoke about his future death and resurrection. Perhaps his disciples embellished this idea into a sequence of stories about appearances by Jesus after his death?

This possibility is undermined by one significant fact: history and human psychology teach us that people will suffer for deeply held convictions. But nobody is prepared to suffer for an invention. We tell lies to get *out* of trouble, not to get *into* it. The whip and sword soon uncover fraud. Besides, liars don't usually write high-calibre moral literature like the New Testament.

In any case, if they *were* inventions they weren't all that good. A shared, deep conviction about Jesus' resurrection is clear from the Bible, but the details of his appearances vary considerably from Gospel to Gospel. It is unlikely that a conspiracy would have given rise to so many puzzles. It is even less likely that inventors would have given so much prominence to the testimony of women, for in ancient Jewish culture such evidence carried little weight.

We note too that the Bible gives no description of the resurrection itself. Nobody witnessed that holy moment when God raised Jesus from the dead. Perhaps no human being could have withstood such as outpouring of love and power. But whatever the reason, the records freely admit that nobody was there: the accounts start with the empty tomb and the appearances of the risen Lord. It is quite likely that inventors would have attempted a description of the resurrection itself. And it is unlikely that inventors would have given such emphasis to the fear, bewilderment and doubt (page 36) which were such a central feature of the experience of the first disciples. Christians believe that the Gospel accounts carry 'the ring of truth.'

Did Jesus really die?

The willing suffering of the disciples also rules out the 'swoon' theory. On this view, Jesus didn't die on the cross. Despite terrible wounds, he recovered in the tomb and escaped. The disciples nursed him back to health, or tried to and failed.

This theory bristles with problems. Roman soldiers knew when a man was dead; and there was a guard on the tomb. But if we allow that somehow the disciples overcame these problems, the events which follow simply don't fit. Jesus would have *cheated* death; he would not have *conquered* it. No doubt the disciples would have been delighted. But they would have kept the whole thing very quiet. *Publicity and preaching would have been fatal*, for these would have resulted in a search. The authorities would not have made a second mistake.

Besides, to preach that God had raised Jesus from the dead – which is exactly what they *did* preach – would have been a lie. We are back where we started. The lash, the dungeon and the sword would soon have loosened their tongues. People will suffer and die for their *convictions*, but for not their *inventions*. A handful of frightened men would not preach boldly about the resurrection to the very people who had killed their leader – especially if they knew that it wasn't true! This would be far too risky. People do not behave like that *unless something tremendous happens to drive away the fear and disappointment.*

Fact 5   Hallucinations need certain conditions

One thing is certain. The first disciples passionately *believed* that God had raised Jesus and that Jesus had appeared to them. Were they mistaken? Perhaps they saw a ghost, or suffered from hallucinations?

If it was a vision or ghost which appeared to them, it spent a lot of time and energy trying to persuade them that it wasn't! The risen Lord had extraordinary powers of appearance and disappearance. But he convinced the disciples that it was *in his body*, albeit remarkably transformed, that he came and went. He ate with them and he encouraged Thomas to touch him: they concluded that God had raised Jesus from the dead.

Perhaps the disciples were suffering from hallucinations? At first sight this is a stronger possibility. However, when we compare the factors involved in hallucinations with the appearances recorded in the Gospels, they don't fit either. For one thing, hallucinations happen to individuals. Several people in a group – under the influence of drugs, for example – might hallucinate together, but they will experience *different* hallucinations, arising from the unconscious mind. And every individual's subconscious is as personal as his or her fingerprints.

In his book *Jesus Christ: the Witness of History*, Professor Sir Norman Anderson examined this possibility in some detail. He discussed five factors which count against the likelihood of hallucinations:

1 People from a wide range of personality types claimed to see Jesus
2 1, 2, 7, 10, 11 and 500 people are unlikely to experience the same fantasy

3 There was deep mourning at Jesus' death, but no strong sense of wishful thinking or expectancy about his resurrection

4 The outward circumstances (timing and setting) varied

5 Hallucinations, if repeated, usually continue for a considerable period. The appearances of Jesus all occurred within 40 days, then stopped abruptly (apart from very occasional subsequent visions of Christ which were of a different order)

We are forced to consider another possibility: perhaps the disciples were telling the truth. In the words of Cambridge scholar John Robinson: *'HE came to them . . . Jesus was not a dead memory but a living presence, making new men of them.'*

Fact 6   They preached resurrection, not resuscitation or survival

Professor James Dunn underlines this point: throughout history, including Jewish history, extraordinary happenings have convinced some people about life after death. For example, ancient Jewish literature speaks of people seeing visions of their dead heroes, such as Abel and Jeremiah. But as Professor Dunn says, 'In no other case did the ones seeing the vision conclude: "This man has been raised from the dead."'

It is true that many Jews believed in resurrection. But this belief was about the resurrection of *all people* on the 'last day' – not of *one man* in the middle of history. Nothing in the thought-forms of the day led the disciples to expect the resurrection appearances of Jesus to occur in the way in which the New Testament describes them. Like so many other factors surrounding Jesus, the events are unique and unexpected.

Fact 7   Eyewitnesses were available

Around AD 55, the apostle Paul wrote what has become a classical passage about resurrection (1 Corinthians 15). In this he writes: *'For what I received I passed on to you as of first importance: that Christ died for our sins according to the Scriptures, that he was buried, that he was raised on the third day according to the Scriptures, and that he appeared . . .'* Scholars have detected an early Christian creed attesting faith in the resurrection, embedded in this passage (hence the word 'received'). Some date this creed within three to eight years of the crucifixion.

Paul goes on to list various eyewitnesses – people who had seen the risen Lord, who were still alive when he wrote and who could be questioned. This list includes a crowd of 'more than 500.' Free invention for purposes of propaganda could have been checked and contradicted.

Fact 8   Jesus is called Lord

As we noted in Chapter 1, the early disciples were Jews – devout monotheists who frequently recited the Shema: 'The Lord our God, the Lord is one.' (Deuteronomy (6:4) Then they met Jesus or heard about him in sermons and conversations.

At no point did they abandon their belief in the One God. It would have been unthinkable for them to become 'bi-theists' (believers in two gods). Yet their concept of God was greatly enlarged as a result of their contact with Jesus. So, while continuing to assert that God is *One*, they began to speak of God the Father and God the Son. Indeed, shortly after his death they had firmly placed Jesus, the man from Nazareth, on the *Godward* side of that line which divides humanity from divinity. They did not doubt that he was truly human, but they offered him their worship (see page 14).

How can this amazing shift in attitude be explained? How can we account for the fact that those Jewish men and women (some of whom knew Jesus personally, and all of whom knew that he was a man who sweated and wept) addressed him as *Lord*?

Jewish men and women would have been incapable of deciding to use the word 'Lord' in that way. Their entire upbringing was against it, because it carried a huge risk of being blasphemous. No, it was *forced* upon them – partly by the teaching of Jesus but mainly by their conviction that God had raised Jesus from the dead. They quickly came to realise that if Jesus was Lord over death, he was quite simply . . . 'LORD'.

Fact 9   Christ's continuing presence

One surprising feature of the reported resurrection appearances is that they were confined to a period of six weeks. After that they stopped abruptly. Yet the first disciples continued to speak and behave as though Jesus were still with them – not physically, but by his Spirit. Even more remarkable is the fact that this conviction came to be shared by others – at first by hundreds, then thousands, then millions – who had never seen Jesus, before or after his crucifixion.

This evidence is not confined to the past. Thousands of men and women continue to experience a new power, and a continuing 'presence' in their lives. Although of differing backgrounds, cultures, ages and temperaments, they put it down to the same cause: the risen Lord is alive and at work in our world and in our lives.

Fact 10   Significant witnesses endorse it

In a court of law, expert and surprising witnesses are sometimes called: those with special expertise in the subject under consideration, or people whose background and insights might lead the jury to expect them to come down on the opposite side. Two such witnesses in this investigation are *Jewish* scholars with no Christian axe to grind. We might expect them to reject the Christian claim, but Dr Geza Vermes of Oxford University wrote this about that first Easter morning:

'First, the women belonging to the entourage of Jesus discovered an empty tomb and were definite that it was the tomb. Second, the rumour that the apostles stole that body is most improbable. From the psychological point of view, it is likely that they would have been too depressed and shaken to be capable of such a dangerous undertaking. But above all, since neither they nor anyone else expected a resurrection, there would have been no purpose in faking one.' (Jesus the Jew, Collins). Rabbi Pinchas Lapide, another Jewish scholar (page 36), goes even further: 'I accept the resurrection of Jesus not as an invention of the community of disciples, but as an historical event.'

But perhaps the weightiest witnesses of all are those who have experienced the transforming power of the resurrection in a profound way. Many people whose lives were in a mess (such as drug addicts and criminals) are now living stable, honest lives. They deny that it was a question of turning over a new leaf or pulling up their socks, because they say that they lacked the moral vision and spiritual strength to put their own lives in order. Rather, they claim to have 'met' the risen

Lord. They talk of finding a new sense of direction and a new source of energy (Chapter 6). Such testimony is not easily discounted.

After reviewing the cumulative evidence for the resurrection of Jesus from the dead, Professor C F D Moule of Cambridge put this searching question:

'If the coming into existence of the Nazarenes (i e the Christian Church) . . . rips a great hole in history, a hole of the size and shape of Resurrection, what does the secular historian propose to stop it up with?'

Implications

Christians believe that the resurrection of Jesus from the dead has enormous implications. The New Testament sees it as a great new act of creation by God. It is 'a primal act of God, unimaginable and indescribable, like the creation, with which it is sometimes compared' (C F Evans). At least two implications are clear, and extremely practical.

▶ Death is dead

We shall consider this more fully in Chapter 9. At this point we simply note the fact that our mortality exercises a profound influence upon our lives – producing a range of responses from fear to curiosity. Most reflective people occasionally feel the need to consider the fact that they will die, and the related need to attempt to make sense of life in the light of this inevitable but awesome fact.

The words of Jesus, as recorded in the fourth Gospel, are breathtaking in their sweep: *'I am the resurrection and the life. He who believes in me will live, even though he dies; and whoever lives and believes in me will never die. Do you believe this?'* (John 11:25,26) Here is the highest arrogance and folly, or the most profound truth. Which of these alternatives is true, depends upon the truth or otherwise of the resurrection of Jesus himself.

In a moving passage, the Venerable Bede (c673–735) reports that Edwin, King of Northumbria, gathered his warriors to listen to the missionary Bishop Paulinus. As Paulinus urged them to accept his teaching, a bird flew through the hall and out into the darkness. One of the nobles commented:

'The life of man is as if a sparrow should come to the house and very swiftly flit through. So the life of man here appears for a little season, but what follows or what has gone before, that surely we know not. Wherefore, if this new learning has brought us any better tidings, surely methinks it is worthy to be followed.'

▶ Jesus is alive

As we have noted, countless believers from all cultures and personality types testify to a sense of being
'accompanied' through life by a 'presence' which, though unseen, is very real. This presence, they affirm, is a Person – the risen Christ. They claim that he challenges, guides, encourages, inspires and renews them. Their experience is captured in a paragraph by the great (and controversial) Albert Schweitzer (1875–1965), a famous theologian and brilliant musicologist. He abandoned his outstanding academic career to train as a doctor, to go to West Africa as a missionary. Albert Schweitzer wrote:

'He comes to us as one unknown, without a name, as of old by the lakeside He came to those men who knew Him not. He speaks to us the same word: "Follow thou me!" and sets us to the tasks which He has to fulfil for our time. He commands. And to those who obey Him, whether they be wise or simple, He will reveal himself in the toils, the conflicts, the suffering which they shall pass through in His fellowship, and, as an ineffable mystery, they shall learn in their own experience Who He is.' (The Quest of the Historical Jesus, SCM)

4

THE BIBLE: CONTENTS

— The Bible in the modern world —

For some years, **Jonathan Edwards** was a good athlete. In 1995 he became a *great* athlete, breaking the world triple jump record three times and becoming the first man in history to jump over 60 feet. Frequently interviewed, he is open about his Christian faith. Jonathan speaks of the Bible as the 'Word of God'. With his family, he reads it regularly: drawing strength, gaining inspiration and seeking direction for their lives. In this, he is not alone in the sporting community. *Christians in Sport* is a fellowship of sportsmen and women, many of whom testify to the importance of the Bible for their lives.

Brian Redhead was a popular British broadcaster. To prepare for a BBC series entitled *The Good Book* he read the Bible from cover to cover and commented:

> *'It's really a journey through life. It makes sense of the universe we find ourselves in. The story line is tremendous. It just is* the *greatest document of the lot, and once you've read it, your life is never the same.'*

Howard Marshall is Professor of New Testament Exegesis at Aberdeen University. He immerses himself in the Greek and Hebrew Scriptures and is aware of keen debate about all aspects of the Bible. He ended one of his books with this moving testimony:

> *'So the Christian is faced by the authority of Scripture as the*

Word of God in its written form . . . It is through the Bible that I know of the God who has declared his salvation in the life, death and resurrection of Jesus, and with deepest thankfulness I embrace that saving truth and stake my life on it.'

We turn now to consider this all-time best seller, written by numerous people (many of them unknown) over a time span of more than 1000 years. As we do so, we recognise the immense impact it has had, and continues to have, on nations and on individuals. For many people in the modern world this ancient book is also a living book, providing direction and encouragement, correction and challenge, puzzlement and mystery, inspiration and joy. To use word pictures for the Bible itself, the Word of God is:

- sweeter than honey (Psalm 19:10)
- a lamp which gives light to our path (Psalm 119:105)
- a fire burning in our hearts (Jeremiah 20:9)
- a hammer which breaks rocks in pieces (Jeremiah 23:29)
- sharper than a two-edged sword (Hebrews 4:12)

Before Christ: the Hebrew Scriptures

The Hebrew Scriptures are called the *Old Testament* by Christians. These writings describe God's dealing with the Jewish people over the centuries before Christ. But they begin with an account of Creation through the command and will of God. Running through the first chapter of the first book of the Bible (*Genesis*) are two refrains.

- 'And God said.'
- 'And God saw that it was good.'

In the beginning God created the heavens and the earth. Now the earth was formless and empty, darkness was over the surface of the deep, and the Spirit of God was hovering over the waters. And God said, 'Let there be light,' and there was light. God saw that the light was good, and he separated the light from the darkness. (Genesis 1:1–4)

Genesis does not attempt to give a scientific account of the creation of the universe, for it was written in a pre-scientific age. The focus of attention is not upon the 'mechanics' (the *how*) of creation, but upon the central fact that our universe was made, and is sustained, by the creative power of God. *We are not here by chance.* Further, these early chapters underline our responsibility as *God's stewards* of the natural world.

In Chapter 3 of Genesis we read of the temptation of Adam and Eve, their disobedience and the entry of disharmony, pain and toil (*the Fall*). Thus we find a recognition by the biblical writers of a world which is both beautiful and unpredictable, exciting and terrifying. In the following chapter of Genesis we find an account of the murder of Abel by his brother Cain. This story of jealousy and violence would be at home in our newspapers. History as we know it had begun.

This is typical of the Bible. *It is consistently realistic, reflecting real life with all its glory and its degeneration.* It refuses to whitewash even its heroes. This realism is one factor which gives the Bible its enduring validity. In some ways the gulf in outlook and experience between ourselves and those men and women is immense. But the Scriptures deal with the 'constants' in human life – with anguish and joy, with personal relationships, with our need to make sense of life.

These ancient writings tell us about men and women who worked, worried, fell in love, laughed, suffered, married, grew old and died. They are about people like us. The Bible considers the great and abiding issues of life and death, sensitively and profoundly. It illuminates the human condition with deep insight and enduring wisdom. As Queen Elizabeth the Queen Mother put it:

'*Men turn this way and that in their search for new sources of comfort and inspiration, but the enduring truths are to be found in the Word of God.*'

Judgement and Exodus

In Chapter 6 of Genesis, we encounter God's judgement on human sin and arrogance. Only Noah and his family, together with a multitude of animals, escape a great flood. At the end of this famous story, God points to the rainbow as a sign of his covenant of faithfulness (Genesis 9:16). In their pride men seek to build a tower to heaven and

God scatters them throughout the earth. He 'confused the language of the whole world' (Genesis 11:9) – hence the 'tower of Babel.'

The small group which escaped the flood became numerous and the history of the nation of Israel began with Abraham, Isaac and Jacob (the *Patriarchs*). Following a widespread famine, the Hebrews were enslaved and oppressed in Egypt. After many years, they escaped from the Egyptian Pharaoh under the leadership of Moses. This escape became known as *The Exodus* and it is celebrated today by Jews everywhere, in the Passover meal.

Moses insisted that this escape was due to the LORD (Yahweh or Jehovah), who is not a local god but the Creator of heaven and earth. God chose this relatively small nation, but not because it had intrinsic merit. Rather, because it was small and vulnerable compared with the surrounding super-powers, Israel was an ideal vehicle to demonstrate God's power and love. Throughout the Bible there runs a reminder that God is saving them, but not simply for their own sake; they are to be a blessing to *all* the nations. This idea was often resisted by the people and their leaders. Prophets made themselves unpopular by reminding them of this abiding truth.

Conquest and Exile

Following their escape from Egypt, the people grumbled against their leaders and spent 40 years as nomads in the desert. Eventually they conquered Canaan and settled in the land which we know as Israel. The Bible gives an action-packed account of the fortunes of the nation: its rise to power under Kings David and Solomon (c1000 BC) and its conquest by mighty empires like Assyria and Babylon. Often the nation seemed doomed but God remembered his covenant of faithfulness. Despite disobedience by kings, leaders and people, the authentic voice of faith was kept alive by a series of prophets and poets, and by ordinary people with extraordinary vision and courage.

The prophets preached and wrote powerful condemnations of the way in which their nation was served by its leaders. They spoke out against injustice and foreign treaties made in desperation, which showed a lack of faith. They warned of God's judgement but spoke words of hope too. The prophet Jeremiah bought a field at the very moment when his nation was conquered and many were exiled to Babylon. It was Jeremiah's way of expressing his God-given conviction that, in course of time, God would restore the nation.

Over the centuries, key institutions developed. These included:

- the **SABBATH** as a day without work, because God rested after creating the world

- **CIRCUMCISION** of male children on the eighth day

- the **TEMPLE** in Jerusalem

- **SYNAGOGUES** in every town

Gifted poets expressed the anguish and joy of the nation in a series of Psalms or songs. The Bible contains 150 of these, varying considerably in length and style. The Hebrew Scriptures contain three major sections: *the Law*, *the Prophets* and *the Writings*. The Psalms fall within *the Writings*. So does the book of *Job*, a profound exploration of suffering, and the much pithier book of *Proverbs*. We also find there a tender celebration of erotic love entitled *The Song of Solomon* (or *Song of Songs*).

During times of oppression and disappointment the people looked for – longed for – a great leader who would rescue and redeem his people. He would be anointed by God. In the Hebrew language the *anointed one* is the *Messiah*. In Greek, it becomes *Christ*. So when we refer to Jesus of Nazareth as Jesus Christ we are acknowledging that, for some of his fellow Jews, Jesus fulfilled that longing and that prophecy – even though others did not recognise him. The New Testament is written by those who joyfully accepted Jesus as the Son of God (Mark 1:1).

'Whoever made this book made me; it knows all that is in my heart.' (A Chinese reader of the Bible)

'The Bible is the cradle in which Christ is laid.' (Martin Luther)

'For Christians, the Bible centres on Christ – the New Testament being explicitly about him, the Old foretelling him.' (Professor Ninian Smart)

One Bible, two Testaments

The Christian Bible is divided into two unequal parts. The New Testament (or Covenant) contains 27 'books'; the Old Testament contains 39 books and is far longer. It is highly significant that on accepting Jesus as the great new act of God, the early Christians did not feel that the Hebrew Scriptures were redundant. They had been *fulfilled*, not replaced.

The Old Testament contains a rich variety of styles: story, history, law, poetry, reflection . . . The New Testament writers drew frequently from these older writings, especially the prophets and the psalms. Among Old Testament passages which are especially loved by Christian believers are Psalm 23 and Isaiah 53. The first Christians viewed the latter as a highly significant passage pointing to, even describing in detail, the crucifixion of Jesus (Acts 8:26–35).

The Old Testament prophets spoke about a *New Covenant* yet to come (Jeremiah 31:31). At the Last Supper which Jesus ate with his disciples, he made it clear that the New Covenant was about to be sealed in the terrible events to follow. Thus, for Christians, the two sections are held together: the Old pointing forward to the New; the New fulfilling the Old. It is also true that the New Testament marks a radical new beginning. There is *contrast* as well as *continuity*.

'The Lord is my shepherd, I shall not want . . .

Surely goodness and love will follow me all the days of my life, and I will dwell in the house of the Lord for ever.' (Psalm 23:1,6)

'But he was pierced for our transgressions, he was crushed for our iniquities; the punishment that brought us peace was upon him, and by his wounds we are healed. We all, like sheep, have gone astray, each of us has turned to his own way; and the Lord has laid on him the iniquity of us all.' (Isaiah 53:5,6)

'The time is coming,' declares the Lord, 'when I will make a new covenant with the house of Israel and with the house of Judah. It will not be like the covenant I made with their forefathers when I took them by the hand to lead them out of Egypt, because they broke my covenant, though I was a husband to them,' declares the Lord. (Jeremiah 31:31,32)

The Apocrypha

Pick up a modern Bible and it might contain a section between the Old and New Testaments entitled *The Apocrypha*. This term refers to texts which were included in the ancient Greek translation of the Jewish Scriptures (known as the Septuagint or LXX) but not in the Hebrew Scriptures. These texts (sometimes referred to as deutero-canonical) are accepted by the Roman Catholic and Eastern Orthodox Churches as Holy Scripture. Protestant Churches regard them as helpful in that they cast further light upon Bible times, but not on a level with the 39 Old Testament and 27 New Testament books.

The four Gospels

The New Testament contains not one, but four, summaries of the life, teaching, death and resurrection of Jesus. The first three Gospels are often referred to as the *Synoptic Gospels*, which literally means 'with one viewpoint'.

This draws attention to:

- the many similarities to be found between Matthew, Mark and Luke
- the different approach taken by John as he paints his pen-portrait of Jesus

Mark is widely regarded as the earliest Gospel, although it is placed after Matthew in the Bible. It was probably completed around 65 AD, some 30 years after the death of Jesus. (Some scholars give it an earlier completion date). Written in fairly rough Greek, it breathes dynamic action: 'Immediately' is one of Mark's favourite words. He includes some Aramaic words (Chapter 5) and takes care to explain Jewish customs for Gentile readers. Jesus is seen as the One who has authority over sickness, sin and chaos. A quarter of Mark's 16 chapters focus on the death of Jesus. He also describes the beheading of John the Baptist, whose work of preparation for Jesus is recorded in all four Gospels. This Gospel ends on an enigmatic note, with the women visiting the tomb in which Jesus was laid. The tomb is empty and they are over-awed by forces and events which are beyond their understanding.

Because Mark's Gospel is probably the first, and as Christianity is the largest movement in all history, Lord Blanch (a former Archbishop of York) described this short Gospel as 'the most important document in the history of the world.'

Matthew This is a longer account than Mark's, written from a clearly Jewish perspective. The writer gathers the teaching of Jesus into five sections, consciously echoing *the Pentateuch* – the five books of 'the law of Moses' at the beginning of the Bible.

The first of these blocks of teaching is the *Sermon on the Mount*, which begins with the *Beatitudes* (see page 4). Matthew records other beautiful, gentle words of Jesus: 'Come to me, all you who are weary and burdened, and I will give you rest . . . ' (11:28–30). But from the same pen we read words of fierce judgement and the refrain: 'Woe to you . . . ', spoken against hypocrites. (Matthew 23).

Jesus is seen as a new and greater Moses. But despite his Jewish background and emphasis, Matthew records the visit of the Wise Men from the East to the infant Christ. In this way he makes it clear that Jesus is the Saviour of the *whole world*, not just the Jewish people.

Luke, probably a Gentile (non-Jewish) doctor, picks up this theme of the universal significance of Christ. In a song often used in Christian worship (the Nunc Dimittis), Luke records the response of an old man (Simeon) to the infant Jesus in the temple in Jerusalem. Simeon describes him as *'a light to lighten the Gentiles and the glory of his people Israel.'* (Luke 2:32) Luke underlines the concern of Jesus for the poor, for the marginalised and for women. He stresses the importance of prayer and the activity of the Holy Spirit. The scholar Ernest Renan described St Luke's account as 'the most beautiful book ever written.'

John It is widely agreed that the fourth Gospel was written last. A reflective account of the impact and importance of Jesus, this Gospel revolves around certain miracles of Jesus, described by John as *signs*. These are linked with *discourses* which highlight the significance of Jesus through a sequence of 'I am' sayings. Thus the healing of a blind man is linked with, 'I am the light of the world.' The raising of Lazarus from the dead is linked with Jesus' statement, 'I am the resurrection and the life.' In the same way, Jesus is seen as 'the door', 'the way, the truth and the life,' 'the vine' and 'the bread of life.' **Eternal life** is a frequent 'Johannine' phrase. This term means everlasting life; it also carries the meaning of a new quality of life in *this* world, given to all who put their trust in Jesus Christ.

In the fourth Gospel the enormous significance of Jesus is underlined. John makes it clear that Jesus breaks through and transcends all the usual categories. Even great words like teacher, prophet and messiah are not significant enough to capture him. He is Lord, God and the Word made flesh. Yet John shows Jesus as a real human being. He thirsts, grows tired and experiences deep emotions, including sorrow and joy. 'Jesus wept' (John 11:35) is the shortest, and possibly the most poignant, verse in the Bible.

Here in the Gospel narratives we find the foundation stones for key Christian doctrines, the *Incarnation* and the *Trinity*, which would develop over the centuries.

E V Rieu, was invited to translate the Gospels for *The Penguin Classics*. After doing so, he wrote:

- They are full of quiet humour. The crowds must often have laughed.
- Superimposed on all my previous impressions is one of power, tremendous power, utterly controlled.
- It was his (Jesus') eyes that seem to have impressed his followers most deeply. Of the other features of his face they have left no record.
- Of what I have learnt from these documents in the course of my long task, I will say nothing now. Only this, that they bear the seal of the Son of Man and God, they are the Magna Charta of the human spirit.

— Other New Testament writings —

Well before these four celebrated Gospels were completed, other Christian pens had been at work.

Letters

There are 21 letters (epistles) in the New Testament, written by a range of authors. Although they stand after the four Gospels in the

Bible, many of them were written before the Gospels were completed. Some are very brief; others are more comprehensive. Several bear the names of, or are linked with, apostles: Peter (two letters); John (three letters); James (one letter); Jude (one letter). One lengthy letter is anonymous (the letter to the Hebrews).

Paul wrote most of the letters. Following his conversion on the Damascus road (see Chapter 15), he poured his vision and energy into planting churches in the countries surrounding the Mediterranean. He regarded the preaching of the good news of Jesus Christ and the formation of Christian communities as events of enormous, cosmic significance. Paul believed that God was creating nothing less than a new humanity.

Yet he was well aware of the fragility of the whole enterprise. Professor David Ford has calculated that the number of early Christians in Corinth was about 50. They were surrounded by powerful pagan influences which many converts continued to find attractive. Paul knew that the enterprise was secure; ultimately it was God's work and Paul had unshakeable faith in 'the God and Father of our Lord Jesus Christ.' (2 Corinthians 1:3)

But on another level, he realised that these churches and individual Christians were very vulnerable. So he wrote letters in which he challenged, encouraged and argued, displaying intense passion and great tenderness.

He dealt with *doctrinal questions* such as the importance of 'justification by faith' (see Chapter 17), and the cosmic significance of Christ. He dealt with *ethical questions*, seeking to strengthen ties of faith, love, family life and Christian fellowship. Paul was a trained Jewish scholar who employed the Hebrew Scriptures in the service of Christ, boldly and creatively.

Frequently he focused on the significance of the death of Jesus, the implications of the resurrection of Jesus and the power of the Spirit of Jesus. His thought is complex but if there is a single key it is this: 'God was in Christ reconciling the world to himself.' (2 Corinthians 5:19) This theme of reconciliation is vital for an understanding of the Christian faith. According to Paul, through Jesus God knocked down all the barriers which divide, especially:

- the barriers which sin erects between disobedient humanity and the holy God
- the barriers between races, social classes and the sexes

The Acts of the Apostles

Following the four Gospels there is a fast-moving 'book' of 28 chapters, which describes the expansion of the Christian church, following the death and resurrection of Jesus. This account is written as a sequel to his Gospel by Luke, who focuses on certain key individuals: Peter, Stephen, Philip, Barnabas, Silas, Lydia, Priscilla and Aquila, Timothy and Paul . . .

Acts is dedicated to someone called 'Theophilus' and seeks to give an orderly account of recent extraordinary events. *The* key event occurs in Acts Chapter 2 when, at the Jewish Festival of Pentecost in Jerusalem, God's Holy Spirit came upon the disciples in power (see Chapter 15).

Peter is centre-stage for the first few chapters but after Paul's conversion (page 210), Luke focuses on him. His three great missionary journeys – full of action and incident – are described in detail. As he seeks to take the gospel to Jews and Gentiles, Paul is knocked about, imprisoned and opposed, but nothing is able to suppress him. At certain points Luke writes in the first person plural (the 'we passages'), for he was one of Paul's travelling companions. Friendship and mutual support were key factors in the spread of the gospel.

In a telling phrase in Acts, Luke informs us that in his Gospel he outlined 'all that Jesus *began* to do and teach.' (Acts 1:1) With this phrase, Luke affirms his faith that Jesus *continues* to be active in and through his followers, by his Spirit. They do not worship a dead hero; they are inspired, guided and empowered by a living Presence.

Revelation

The Bible ends with a remarkable book, cast in the form of a series of visions or revelations experienced by St John the Divine in exile on the Isle of Patmos. (This John is probably not the author of the fourth Gospel. John, like Mary, is a very common name in the New Testament!)

Written when the Church was being persecuted, it belongs to a genre of writing called apocalyptic. *'Revelation belongs to the literature of protest and religious revolt.'* (John Court) This book encourages embattled Christians by:

- pointing to Jesus, the Lamb upon the Throne
- assuring them that God will ultimately judge and overthrow the persecuting powers
- reassuring them that perseverance will result in victory and glory

Written in a kind of code, its meaning is not always transparent to the modern reader. This book has become a key text for some sects and cults, who claim to be able to work out from its pages the precise date and programme for the end of the world.

Revelation and, therefore, the entire Bible, ends with John's vision of 'a new heaven and a new earth.' A moving passage, often read at Christian funeral services, contains these beautiful words:

> *'And I heard a loud voice from the throne saying, "Now the dwelling of God is with men, and he will live with them. They will be his people, and God himself will be with them and be their God. He will wipe every tear from their eyes. There will be no more death or mourning or crying or pain, for the old order of things has passed away."'* (Revelation 21:3–4)

The Bible is a great love story. It describes how, despite our disobedience and indifference, God persevered with the human race. Indeed, 'God loved the world so much that he gave his only Son.' (John 3:16) The Bible is also a book about a battle: it describes a cosmic struggle between good and evil. That great struggle finds its focus in Jesus Christ. We read that darkness and light, love and hatred, compassion and indifference have contended and that he – Jesus – is Victor, Lord and King.

We find too, that at a more modest level we are all caught up in that same struggle. The Bible assures us that eternal issues are at stake, as it challenges us with this central question: will we follow 'the true light' (John 1:9) or do we 'love darkness rather than light.' (John 3:19)?

5
THE BIBLE:
QUESTIONS

—— Remembering and recording ——

Jesus of Nazareth and his first disciples (all Jews) were conscious of standing in a long and noble tradition. It was a tradition in which the Scriptures had a central place. In his Gospel Luke tells us that Jesus went into the **Synagogue** in his home town of Nazareth, where the people had gathered for worship on the Sabbath. He took a scroll of Hebrew Scripture and read from the prophet Isaiah:

> *'The Spirit of the Lord is upon me, because he has anointed me to preach good news to the poor. He has sent me to proclaim freedom for the prisoners and recovery of sight for the blind, to release the oppressed, to proclaim the year of the Lord's favour.'* (Luke 4:18,19)

Jesus returned the scroll to the official and declared: *'Today has this prophecy been fulfilled in your hearing.'*

Jesus constantly drew on the Hebrew Scriptures, bringing out deeper meanings, making new connections and – astonishing to his hearers – claiming to be the One to whom the Hebrew prophets pointed. This notion of Jesus fulfilling the rich promises and prophecies scattered throughout the Old Testament, became a key theme for the writers of the New Testament.

Scrolls represented weeks of careful work by authors or scribes. The development of the *codex* (a book with a spine) by the fourth century would bring a minor revolution, but *scrolls* carried the first written accounts of the good news about Jesus Christ.

Many scrolls were communal property which were read out to the assembled company. In addition, unrecorded stories were passed on by word of mouth. This is how the stories about Jesus, and accounts of his teaching, circulated in the days of his ministry and in the months and years following his death. Teaching, preaching, story-telling; hearing, remembering, repeating: these were crucial elements in the spread of the message of Jesus and his early followers. The oral and the written accounts intermingled at an early stage.

Which languages?

Eventually the first disciples grew old, or their lives were in danger from persecution. The need for a written record of the actions and teaching of Jesus became urgent. In a remarkably short time, the four Gospels which stand at the beginning of the New Testament came into being – written in Greek.

Jesus and his first disciples were almost certainly tri-lingual. They spoke Aramaic and a few Aramaic words are scattered throughout the New Testament. They understood Hebrew, the language of their own Jewish Scriptures. But to communicate widely they also needed Greek, the language spoken and written throughout the Roman Empire. This is the language of the New Testament.

From God or men?

These Greek accounts of the activity and teaching of Jesus have been studied more closely than any other document. Scholars continue to be fascinated by the relationship of one Gospel record to another.

- Which came first?
- Were sections from one copied into another?
- If so, why are there so many puzzling differences?
- Do they give a reliable account of events and teaching?
- How many years elapsed between the events which they record and the written accounts?

The Christian Church has, by and large, welcomed this scholarly scrutiny.

The Church accepts and rejoices in the authority of the New Testament as sacred Scripture, inspired by God's Spirit and authoritative for Christian living. But its inspiration by God's Spirit (or more accurately its 'expiration': the Greek word is *God-breathed* – 2 Timothy: 3:16) subtly blends with the personalities and outlook of the human authors. (2 Peter 1:20,21 – see page 69).

The *Catechism of the Catholic Church* (1994) sums up like this: 'God inspired the human authors of the sacred books. To compose the sacred books, God chose certain men who, all the while he employed them in this task, made full use of their own faculties and powers so that, though he acted in them and by them, it was as true authors that they consigned to writing whatever he wanted written, and no more.'

In this regard the Christian view of the Bible is different from the Muslim view of the *Qur'an* or the Mormon view of *The Book of Mormon*. These books are believed by the adherents of those faith communities to have been dictated by the angel Gabriel and sent from heaven on golden plates, respectively. Human involvement in the production of their sacred books is minimal, according to Muslims and Mormons. In contrast, the strong human involvement in the production of the Christian Scriptures is to be expected and welcomed in a faith which centres on Incarnation – God becoming a human being.

Why these books?

The first few Christian centuries gave rise to a considerable volume of literature. So the question arises: why did these particular 27 books come to be included in the New Testament?

In the early Church, the term 'Scripture' usually referred to writings from the Old Testament. But the second letter of Peter refers to Paul's letters as Scripture and very soon Christian writers, such as Justin Martyr c100–165, were referring to 'the New Testament'. For some time there was debate about whether certain books should be included (for example, hesitations were expressed about Hebrews, 2 Peter and Jude). In the Armenian Church, the inclusion of Revelation was resisted until the 12th century.

Some other early writings, such as the *Didache* and the first letter of Clement, were serious contenders for inclusion. There was also some disagreement about the order of the books. The four Gospels and Paul's letters were settled by the end of the second century. In AD 367, Bishop Athanasius wrote a letter in which he listed the 27 books of the New Testament as being canonical, i.e. official scripture.

Which criteria were used in deciding which books should be included in the **canon** of the New Testament? Presumed authorship by an apostle was one strong reason for including some books; but not, for example, the Gospels of Mark and Luke. Apostolic authorship of some of these documents would be questioned by some biblical critics, several centuries later. Dr Alister McGrath helpfully sums up: *'The basic principle appears to have been that of the* recognition *rather than the* imposition *of authority. In other words, the works in question were recognised as already possessing authority, rather than having an arbitrary authority imposed upon them.'*

APOCRYPHAL GOSPELS

'At the age of five, Jesus fashioned 12 sparrows from clay on the Sabbath day. This was reported to Joseph who asked, "Why are you doing these things which ought not to be done on the Sabbath?" Jesus clapped his hands and called out to the sparrows, "Be off!" At this the birds flew away chirping.'

This story comes from the *Infancy Gospel of Thomas*. It reminds us that the four Gospels in the Bible were not the only early documents about Jesus. Other non-biblical writings include *The Gospel of Nicodemus, The Acts of Pilate, The Gospel of Peter* and *The Gospel of Thomas.*

The last is the best known. This fourth-century Coptic document was discovered near Nag Hammadi in Upper Egypt in 1946 and contains 114 sayings attributed to Jesus. Some are similar to those in the New Testament Gospels; others not so. A few sayings give a flavour of this document which was used by a Gnostic community (see Chapter 15).

'These are the secret words which Jesus, the living one, spoke and Didymus Judas Thomas wrote down . . .

- And he said: "Whoever finds the interpretation of these words will never face death."
- Love your brother as your own soul; guard him like the apple of your eye.
- Split the wood; I am there. Lift up the stone and you will find me there." '

The Apocryphal Gospels may contain some authentic material but they were written much later than the New Testament Gospels and have few roots in history.

Biblical criticism

We turn now to examine some of the tools and approaches which scholars employ in their study of the Christian scriptures.

The word 'criticism' has two meanings. In everyday speech, to criticise is to say something negative (however constructive the outcome may be). In the Arts, however, it is a neutral term. Film critics are not always critical. They may say that a film is poor *or* superb, and go on to give their reasons: such critics are simply using their critical faculties. Whether they praise or condemn, they are seeking to make a careful analysis leading to an informed judgement.

Biblical 'critics' do not stand in judgement on the Scriptures. Rather, they seek to deepen understanding by bringing knowledge and discernment. Indeed, *all* who read the Bible seriously find themselves involved in this enterprise. Sooner or later we are bound to ask such questions as:

- Why does Luke include the shepherds in his birth narratives but not the visit of the wise men (included only in Matthew)?
- Why does Matthew have a *Sermon on the Mount* and Luke a *Sermon on the Plain*?
- Why do different evangelists record different post-resurrection appearances of the risen Lord?

We are intrigued by the possible reasons for these and other differences, which engage our critical faculties. In pursuing such questions, scholars have developed many tools and we shall look briefly at six different kinds of Biblical criticism.

Textual criticism

This activity is designed to establish, as closely as possible, what those who wrote the biblical texts actually recorded on their scrolls. Textual critics work with the numerous early copies available to them. They note and seek to resolve differences, and attempt to provide translators with accurate Hebrew and Greek texts. This is sometimes called *Lower Criticism*, not because it is an inferior form of activity, but because it lays the foundation for all Bible study and translation. All other kinds of biblical criticism taken together are called *Higher Criticism*.

Source criticism

This was first applied to the *Pentateuch* (the first five books in the Old Testament) in the 18th century. Later it was applied to the New Testament, especially the Gospels. The things which Jesus said and did were remembered and passed on by word of mouth: some material was written down. In course of time, the Gospel writers (Evangelists), drew on a variety of oral and written sources, none of which has survived in its own right. Many scholars have tried to unravel this process in an attempt to discern the various sources which fed into the completed Gospels. Two questions are of particular interest:

• Was there a document (now lost) containing collected sayings of Jesus? (Scholars refer to this as Q, probably from 'Quelle', the German word for *Source*).

• What is the relationship between the three Synoptic Gospels? For centuries it was thought that Mark abbreviated Matthew's Gospel, but most modern scholars believe that Matthew and Luke drew on Mark's Gospel.

Form criticism

Form critics are concerned with the various forms of material in the Bible, for example, miracle stories and sayings of Jesus. They are also concerned with the 'sitz im leben' (*situation in life*) of the various units. In the fourth Gospel, we read that Jesus said and did far more than could be recorded. Why then was *this* episode recorded but not *that*?

And why does Luke (for example) include material omitted by Mark? Possibly because one writer had access to different information about Jesus, from another. Possibly because they had different interests. Possibly too, because the communities for which the different authors originally wrote, had particular concerns. (Hence 'sitz im leben': a consideration of the circumstances of the early Christian communities for which the Gospels were first written.) If Jesus addressed issues of importance to these churches, it would be natural for the evangelists to record those particular words and deeds.

Form criticism flourished in Germany in the Middle of the 20th century and some form critics were very radical – assuming that the early church would readily invent sayings which they attributed to Jesus. Other scholars disputed this. John Robinson spoke for these when he wrote:

> *'There seems to have been a reverence for the remembered speech and acts of Jesus which provided an inbuilt resistance to the temptation to make him merely their mouthpiece or puppet.'*

Redaction criticism

This was a reaction against methods based on analysis and dissection. True, the evangelists used a range of sources, but they did not 'cut and paste.' *Selection is interpretation* and they were skilful editors (i.e. *redactors*) and purposeful theologians. The four evangelists were highly creative – weaving their sources into genuine works of art. Redaction criticism considers the complete text, the particular concerns of each writer and the emphases which he wished to make.

Narrative criticism

This is concerned with the Bible as a sequence of stories within an overall Story. It takes seriously the universal appeal of the story, in all its various forms. (Those who wish to read further might try *Why Narrative?* S. Hauerwas and G. Jones (Eds): Eerdmans.)

Canonical criticism

This emphasises the final form of the biblical text. It is less concerned with stages in the development of the text; more interested in asking what it means to honour a text as sacred Scripture. The Church has received this text as canonical. What are the implications of this? The next question is but a short step away: just what is the Bible saying to the living community of faith *today*?

> '**H**owever much Christianity has to update itself and adapt to circumstances, it can never cut adrift from the spirit of Jesus, whether he suits us or whether he does not. And the New Testament, honestly read and studied, is the one place you can face that bit of reality.' (Professor Leslie Houlden)

Reliable manuscripts?

Existing ancient documents have survived a hazardous journey down the centuries. They were written and copied by hand (a slow and laborious process) and were liable to damage or destruction by fire, water, rough usage or simple neglect. So it comes as no surprise to learn that the world's museums and libraries contain only:

- eight ancient copies of *Thucydides' History*
- ten ancient copies of *Caesar's Gallic War*
- two ancient copies of the *Histories of Tacitus*

By ancient copies we mean that there is a gap of about 1300, 900 and 700 years respectively, between the originals of these famous historical documents and the copies which have survived. In contrast, hundreds of ancient copies of the Gospels can be found in the world's museums and libraries. So it is evident that there is a rich harvest of ancient biblical texts for scholars to work with.

> *'The wealth of manuscripts, and above all the narrow interval of time between the writing and the earliest extant copies, make it by far the best-attested text of any ancient writing in the world.'* (John Robinson)

> *'The New Testament manuscripts in our possession are much closer in time to the original writings, more numerous and in closer agreement with each other than any other ancient book.'* (Hans Küng)

In the end, of course, we weigh all the available evidence and decide to trust the records – or not, as the case may be. Professor David Ford puts the Christian position with great clarity:

> *'The Gospels are testimony. Because we cannot re-run historical events, you either have to trust or not trust some of the people who were there. It is important that we as Christians are part of a community that did decide early on to trust certain testimonies. That does not rule them out from cross-examination. But we can be absolutely confident that in terms of the testimony of Jesus, there is no disproof of the main thrust of that testimony.'*

Hundreds of early copies of parts of the New Testament are available to scholars. Two complete copies of the New Testament are dated around AD 350 – less than 300 years after the original. One is in the Vatican Library; the other in the British Museum. The latter was bought from the Soviet Government on Christmas Day 1933 for £100,000. The earliest undisputed find, a fragment from St John's Gospel, is dated around 130 AD and is held in the John Ryland's Library in Manchester.

The Dead Sea Scrolls

From time to time an archaeological find, or a new theory, makes headlines because it gives rise to sensational claims which appear to disprove established ideas. One famous example is the Dead Sea Scrolls. These scrolls were from the library of a Jewish community based at Qumran on the north-western shore of the Dead Sea, between 150 BC and 68 AD. Their discovery in 1947 was described by Professor W F Albright as 'the greatest manuscript discovery of modern times.'

Wild claims were made for the Scrolls. In particular, a few writers suggested that there were strong similarities between Jesus and the original leader (*The Teacher of Righteousness*) of the community which wrote and preserved the scrolls. It was argued that

Christianity had its roots in the teaching of this Jewish sect, which flourished before Jesus was born. A group of scholars working on the Scrolls denied this. They issued a statement asserting that: 'Nothing that appears in the scrolls hitherto discovered throws any doubts on the originality of Christianity.' The *contrast* is marked between:

● The Community at Qumran (where the scrolls were found) *and* the early Christians
● The Teacher of Righteousness *and* Jesus

This contrast was later confirmed by two Jewish scholars: Geza Vermes and Yigael Yadin. The position is summed up by the British archaeologist, Alan Millard: *'The differences between the Teacher of Righteousness and Jesus are huge.'*

Of course, this does not detach Jesus from his culture. There are similarities between Jesus and other Jewish teachers of his day. As we have seen (Chapter 1), Jesus was unique in approach and stature but he did not set out to be 'original'. He gladly accepted many of the rich traditions of his nation and was aware of standing within the flow of its history.

Pursuing links between Jesus and the Teacher of Righteousness may have ended in a cul-de-sac, but the Dead Sea Scrolls do have some bearing upon the Bible: both Old and New Testaments.

The Scrolls increase our confidence in the text of the Old Testament. At least part of every Old Testament book (except *Esther*) has been found in the Scrolls. They are about 1000 years older than any other text of the Hebrew Scriptures so far discovered. Careful comparison shows just how successful Jewish scribes were, over the centuries, in their desire to pass on faithful and accurate copies of the Scriptures. Magnus Magnusson rightly speaks of 'the essential integrity of the scribal tradition.'

The Scrolls illuminate the world of the New Testament, for they were written between 150 BC and 68 AD. Before the Scrolls were discovered, some scholars believed that John's Gospel was a free composition, written in the second century under Greek influence. If so, it had no strong roots in history. But when we put the Dead Sea Scrolls alongside the fourth Gospel, we see how very *Jewish* St John's work is. Contrasts like 'light and dark', 'life and death' which abound in

John, were thought to be Greek in origin. The Dead Sea Scrolls show that these contrasts are at home in first-century Jewish thought. So the fourth Gospel fits clearly into the Jewish background which it describes; it has a secure basis in the history of that period.

The Word of God?

For centuries, belief in the inspiration of Scripture by God was uncontroversial and widespread. Just what was meant by such phrases as the *Word of God* and *inspired Scripture* was not a real issue, until Enlightenment thinking (see Chapter 18) gave rise to biblical criticism. In today's Church, various views are held concerning the precise nature of divine inspiration. Debate centres around questions such as:

- What does the Bible teach about itself?
- How did Jesus view and use the Hebrew scriptures?
- How did the New Testament writers use the Old Testament?
- Does inspired necessarily mean 'infallible'?
- Does inspired mean 'inspiring'?
- Did God inspire the writers and/or the text itself; does his Holy Spirit also inspire the reader to understand the true meaning?
- Should we refer to the Bible *as* 'the Word of God'? Or does it *contain* the Word of God?

In this regard, two important Bible verses are:

- *'All Scripture is inspired (literally "breathed") by God and profitable for teaching, for reproof, for correction, and for training in righteousness.'* (2 Timothy 3:16–17) This indicates the *practical* nature of the Bible. It is recorded for our guidance and obedience. God's word speaks to our condition; it speaks in a dark world which desperately needs light. The concept of *revelation* (self disclosure by God) is vital to Christianity. Christians believe that the Bible reveals otherwise hidden truths about God, about life, and about the way of salvation. '"Revelation" does not mean merely the transmission of a body of knowledge, but the personal disclosure of God within history.' (Alister McGrath)

- *'No prophecy ever came by the impulse of man, but men moved by the Holy Spirit spoke from God.'* (2 Peter 1:20–21) This shows that inspiration by God does not rule out full human participation in the communication of his message. Debate about the precise nature of inspiration continues. But all churches believe that they are called to live under the Bible's authority. Interpretation and application can and do vary, but the Bible is – or should be – decisive for Christian belief and behaviour.

> *Blessed Lord,*
> *who caused all holy Scriptures*
> *to be written for our learning:*
> *help us so to hear them,*
> *to read, mark, learn, and inwardly digest them*
> *that, through patience, and the comfort*
> *of your holy word,*
> *we may embrace and for ever hold fast*
> *the hope of everlasting life,*
> *which you have given us in our Saviour Jesus Christ*
> (Collect for the Second Sunday in Advent)

Inspiring?

'Inspired' does not always mean *inspiring*. Some of the Bible is intrinsically boring! Tables of family names, and detailed rules and regulations for sacrifices to be offered in tabernacle and temple do not make exciting reading! Nor is every part of equal importance. Some of the rules for worship in the Old Testament have no authority over Christians, because those rules have been fulfilled and superseded by Jesus Christ.

But these passages are necessary if we are to understand the overall message. And of course some passages are wonderfully inspiring. Who cannot be stirred by the storm scenes in the book of Acts? Who can fail to be moved by the suffering servant in Isaiah 53, the passion narratives, and the great hymn about love in 1 Corinthians 13? Who is not comforted by Psalm 23? Whose heart is not lifted on hearing the *Sermon on the Mount*? Whose will is not challenged by the call to forgiveness in the *Lord's Prayer*?

Some passages which seem, at first sight, to be of little direct relevance, contain underlying principles with universal application. For example, few Western Christians face the question of 'meat offered to idols' discussed by the apostle Paul (Romans 14). But the need for empathy, mutual support and consideration of the effects of our behaviour on others, are never out of date. These issues are at the heart of that debate.

It is because the Bible *'speaks'* to us that it is read at the bedsides of the sick and dying and on occasions of great joy such as weddings. And many Christians meditate upon a Scripture passage daily and find with the psalmist that it is 'sweeter than honey.' To use another image from the Bible itself, it is a lamp which gives light to their path through life – encouraging, inspiring and challenging by turns.

— Why so much sex and violence? —

The Bible takes the form of a *history*, not a treatise. This is why it contains so much sex and violence, for all real history does! We learn from this that God is concerned with the world *as it really is*. The ancient world was certainly very violent. Fighting between nations was widespread, and Israel was no exception. Many battles are described in the Bible, and the Jewish people prayed for God's help as they fought.

But the Israelites were different from many of their neighbours in various ways. They knew that certain forms of violence were forbidden by God – human sacrifice for example. And their teachers and prophets emphasised the importance of offering care and hospitality – especially to orphans, widows, and foreigners within their borders.

Two further points are relevant. First, the Bible is an honest book. It tells the truth about its heroes – even when this is painful. Peter's cowardice in denying Jesus just before his crucifixion is not hushed up (Matthew 26:70). Nor are King David's murder of Uriah and seduction of Bathsheba (2 Samuel 11), Abraham's deception (Genesis 12) or the psalmist's desire for revenge (Psalm 137).

These things are recorded, not because they are uplifting but because they happened. They show us real human beings with all their glory and shame – not plaster saints. Their deception, cowardice and violence are condemned by the very Scriptures which describe these human failings with such honesty. In this way, they help us to understand our own motives and actions. *Above all, they illuminate God's grace, mercy and transforming power. And they challenge us to repentance, faith and obedience, as they invite us to become part of the ongoing story.*

We note too that the Bible shows moral and spiritual development. We do not find a smooth progression over the centuries, from violence to love. The upward path was very uneven, and some Old Testament characters were streets ahead of many in the New Testament, or in the modern world. But development there is. Slowly, through many years and even more hard lessons, God taught the people of Israel more and more about love and forgiveness. The climax came when Jesus told his astonished hearers, 'Love your enemies.' He put his own teaching into practice. On the cross he prayed for his torturers: 'Father, forgive them, for they do not know what they are doing.'

Active today?

As we draw to the end of a chapter of thorny issues, we need to ask the question: so what? A study of the Bible raises questions which send us to scholars and source books. But it continues to speak to ordinary people, with no great learning. Numbers of people testify to the power of the Bible to alter the course of their lives.

For the Olympic medal winning athlete **Kriss Akabusi**, the Bible was the way into the Christian faith. During the 1986 Commonwealth Games in Edinburgh, he found a modern translation of the New Testament in his hotel room. He read it from cover to cover. 'There was a guy in there,' he said, referring to Jesus. 'I'd used his name before, but I never realised he actually lived. I thought he was like the Tooth Fairy or Father Christmas.' That Bible pointed that athlete to Jesus Christ, whom he accepted as Teacher, Lord and Saviour.

Jon Jeffery found himself in hospital following a bad 'fix'. It looked as though he would lose his arm. The doctor who treated him gave him a Bible, although he would have preferred a cigarette! But he flicked through the New Testament and two sentences registered:

- Fear not, for I am with you.
- If the Son shall set you free, you shall be free indeed.

In the event the surgeon was able to save his arm, although two fingers had to be amputated. Jon was sent to prison for drug offences and he linked up with the Prison Christian fellowship. As a Jew he knew the Old Testament well and 'made a nuisance' of himself by asking difficult questions. But eventually, in his prison cell on Christmas Day 1978, Jon put his faith in Jesus Christ. Today he is off drugs and happily married with two sons. He has a fulfilling job with the *Bible Society* – very fitting for a man who probably owes his life to the power of the ancient Scriptures to speak in the modern world.

Translations

One verse in the Bible (John 3:16) has been translated into more than 2000 languages. Here are eight of them:

ENGLISH

For God so loved the world that He gave His only begotten Son, that whoever believes in Him should not perish, but have everlasting life.

RUSSIAN

Ибо так возлюбил Бог мир, что отдал Сына Своего единородного, дабы всякий, верующий в Него, не погиб, но имел жизнь вечную.

SINHALESE

මක්නියාද දෙවියන්වහන්සේ සව කීය ඒකජාතක පුතුයාණන් දෙත තරම් ලෝකයාට ප්‍රේම කළ සේක. එසේ කළේ උන්වහන්සේ කෙරෙහි අදහා ගන්ත සැමදෙනම විතාශ තොවී සද කාල ජීවිතය ලඛත පිණිසය.

SPANISH

Porque de tal manera amó Dios al mundo, que ha dado a su Hijo unigénito, para que todo aquel que en él cree, no se pierda, mas tenga vida eterna.

SWAHILI

Kwa maana jinsi hii Mungu aliupenda ulimwengu, hata akamtoa Mwanawe pekee, ili kila mtu amwaminiye asipotee; bali awe na uzima wa milele.

SWEDISH

Ty så älskade Gud världen, att han utgav sin enfödde Son, på det att var och en som tror på honom skall icke förgås, utan hava evigt liv.

TAMIL

தேவன், தம்முடைய ஒரேபேறான குமாரனை விசுவாசிக்கிறவன் எவனோ அவன்கெட்டுப்போகாமல் நித்தியஜீவனை அடையும்படிக்கு, அவரைத் தந்தருளி, இவ்வளவாய் உலகத்தில் அன்புகூர்ந் தார்.

WELSH

Canys felly y carodd Duw y byd fel y rhoddodd efe ei unig-anedig Fab, fel na choller pwy bynnag a gredo ynddo ef, ond caffael ohono fywyd tragwyddol.

Source: *Reproduced by kind permission of Gideons International*

An estimated 5000 languages and major dialects are spoken around the world. But many of these are spoken by minority groups who are often competent in at least one other mainstream language. In 1994, the number of languages with a translation of at least one book from the Bible, reached 2092. The complete Bible was available in 341 languages and the New Testament was available in a further 822. This means that at least part of the Bible is available to the vast majority of nations, tribes and clans. The present rate of translation is around four whole Bibles and 18 New Testaments per year.

The first book to be printed using moveable type was the *Gutenberg Bible* in 1456. This was the Old Latin edition by Jerome (342–420) called the *Vulgate*. The world's presses continue to print hundreds of thousands of copies of the Bible, which continues as the world's best seller (even though copies are often given away free of charge!). English translations abound; among the most famous are:

- The *Geneva Bible* which was dedicated to Queen Elizabeth I who came to the throne in 1558. This Bible introduced the verse numbers which are now in universal use. Before this, only chapter divisions had been available.

- The *Authorised Version* (or *King James Version*) of 1611 which established itself as *the* English edition for 300 years. It is still in use but many regular Bible readers use modern editions. These are easier to understand and based on more numerous and accurate sources (see Preface).

Moving stories are told of churches where Bibles are scarce. The Scriptures are treasured, memorised, copied and circulated with great care and love. By their commitment these believers declare with the Psalmist that:

'The ordinances of the Lord are sure
and altogether righteous.
They are more precious than gold,
than much pure gold;' (Psalm 19:9, 10)

6

CHRISTIAN EXPERIENCE OF GOD

———— Starting with the Bible ————

The Bible is full of people who claim to have experienced God. Celebrated examples in the Old Testament are:

- Abraham who heeded a call from God to leave his home in order to 'go to a land which I will show you.' (Genesis 12:1) This is frequently recalled throughout the Bible as a key example of obedience and trust.

- Moses who encountered God in a burning bush, where God revealed himself as 'I am who I am.' (Exodus 3:14)

- Isaiah who received a vision of the blazing holiness of God, in the Temple in Jerusalem. He had a deep sense of his own unworthiness, and received a call from God to be a prophet to his people. (Isaiah 6)

As with the Old Testament, so with the New. Its pages describe numerous examples of people encountering God – sometimes with joy, often in awe and fear.

- At the first Christian Pentecost, the Holy Spirit came in power upon 120 followers of Jesus (Acts 2). They became bold and were able to communicate with those who had gathered in Jerusalem for the Festival, even though the visitors spoke a wide range of languages.

- The apostle Peter, a devout Jew, was wrestling with the question of Gentiles (non-Jews) and the gospel. Was it possible that they could be welcomed as full members of the Church without first becoming Jews? As he was praying, Peter had a vision in which he was commanded by God to eat food which was 'impure' according to the Jewish law. He protested but a voice replied, 'Do not call anything impure that God has made clean.' (Acts 10:15)

  Peter came to realise that he had the answer to his problem: the gospel was for *everyone*, regardless of race. That realisation by one praying man was a defining moment for the history of the world.

- St John, the author of *Revelation*, was in exile on the Isle of Patmos when he had a vision of the risen and ascended Christ. So awesome was the sight that he 'fell at his feet as though dead.' Jesus encouraged him with words of gentleness and an instruction to 'write what you have seen.' (Revelation 1:17–19)

Somewhat similar experiences have been recorded throughout Christian history. Some have become famous; others are known to only a few. In this chapter we shall consider a tiny sample, to illustrate the breadth of the Christian experience of God.

Conversion

'The human heart is heavy and hardened. God must give a man a new heart. Conversion is first of all a work of the grace of God who makes our hearts turn to him . . . God gives us the strength to begin anew.' (Catechism of the Catholic Church: 1994)

St Augustine was born in Algeria to a pagan father and Christian mother. He wrestled with the Christian faith for many years. In AD 386 he was in his garden when he heard a child singing the words, 'Take up and read.'

He picked up the Scriptures and read these words from Paul's letter to the Romans '. . . *not in sexual immorality and debauchery, not in dissension and jealously. Rather, clothe yourselves with the Lord Jesus Christ, and do not think about how to gratify the desires of the sinful nature.'* (Romans 13:13–14) That moment was a turning point for Augustine, and for the Church. From then on, he employed his formidable intellect in the service of Christ.

Much more recently the American **Charles Colson** had a somewhat similar experience. He was deeply involved in President Nixon's infamous Watergate scandal, but he encountered the living Christ who gave him fresh values and a new direction. He has written about this in *Born Again* – a title taken, not from a revivalist rally, but from his wife's Roman Catholic hymn-book! Charles Colson now has an international Christian ministry, and he shows particular concern for prisoners.

In his early 20s, **David Greaves** found himself in a British prison for a violent offence. He read about Nicky Cruz, the leader of a ruthless gang in an American city, who was dramatically converted to Christ. On leaving prison David met a friend who, like Nicky Cruz, had experienced an outpouring of God's love.

David continues:

> 'God had forgiven him, so that night I just thought to myself: "Surely if God is real and he loves people and he can forgive, if I pray and ask him then he'll do it for me." So I prayed a simple prayer for forgiveness and as I prayed I didn't experience fireworks, but I felt a real cleanness come inside and all the guilt, shame and sin just washed away. And then a peace – and then joy, purpose and meaning put back in.'

Malcolm Worsley had a similar background to David. On the day of yet another release from prison, a prison officer remarked, 'You'll be back, Worsley.' That officer was right; Malcolm did return, but as a member of staff! For like David, Malcolm was converted to Christ. He trained to be a probation officer, and is involved in helping people who are dependent on drugs. In July 1996, Malcolm was ordained as a Minister in the Church of England.

Archbishop Anthony Bloom was different from David Greaves and Malcolm Worsley in almost every way: education, personality, upbringing and culture. In turn he became a surgeon, a member of the resistance movement in the Second World War and leader of the Russian Orthodox Church in Britain. He too had a remarkable experience which gave shape and direction to his future life.

As a teenager he wanted to prove to himself that Christianity was untrue, so he read St Mark's Gospel. (He chose St Mark because it is the shortest, and he did not want to waste time on the exercise!) He wrote:

> 'Before I reached the third chapter, I suddenly became aware that on the other side of my desk there was a presence. And the certainty was so strong that it was Christ standing there that it has never left me. This was the real turning point. Because Christ was alive and I had been in his presence I could say with certainty that what the Gospel said about the crucifixion of the prophet of Galilee was true, and the centurion was right when he said, "truly he is the Son of God."' (School for Prayer: DLT)

Hugh Montefiore, Anglican Bishop of Birmingham from 1978–1987, had a somewhat similar experience. He grew up in a Jewish family and went to Rugby School. One wintry afternoon, as a teenager alone in his room, he became aware of a figure in white. In his autobiography he writes, 'I heard the words "Follow Me." Interestingly, I knew that this was Jesus, heaven knows how: I knew nothing about him.' He goes on to say that this was 'an indescribably rich event that filled me afterwards with overpowering joy. I could do no other than follow those instructions . . . it shaped the whole of my future life.' (Oh God, What Next? Hodder & Stoughton)

There are two further points to note about conversion. First, the phrase 'conversion of life.' Many writers on spirituality insist that conversion is *a process. Every day* we need to do battle with temptation and turn to Christ. Second, Christian discipleship does not depend upon dramatic experiences. From the New Testament it seems likely that Timothy (a younger colleague of the apostle Paul), came to faith gradually through the influence of a Christian home (2 Timothy 1:5; 2 Timothy 3:15). Research suggests that a minority of Christians have a dramatic conversion experience. The way into faith is less important than the outcome. David L Edwards, a former Chaplain to the House of Commons, made this point clearly and helpfully:

> 'That is why everyone is challenged to respond to God through Jesus Christ in a personal turning (which is what the word "conversion" means). You have to meet Jesus yourself, and to accept him as your friend and as your Lord . . . In many Christian lives, this turning or conversion reaches a climax which can be dated.

People can remember the exact time when they accepted Jesus Christ as Lord and Liberator, often after intense struggles to escape from the pressure of his love. But it is not necessary to be able to date your conversion like that.

What is essential is that everyone should have his or her personal reasons for being a Christian. You cannot inherit Christian faith as you can inherit red hair or a peculiar nose. You cannot copy Christian faith as you can copy hairstyle or an accent. And you cannot get it completely out of books, as you can get a knowledge of history. Your faith, to be authentic, to guide your life, must be your own. Your very own experience, whether it is dramatic or quiet, long or short, must lead you to know Jesus Christ as your personal liberator.' (What Anglicans Believe, Mowbray)

If David Edwards is right, then the phrase 'born again Christian' must be used with care. It is true that Jesus told Nicodemus, a Pharisee, that 'no-one can see the kingdom of God unless he is born again.' (John 3:3) And, of course, conversion experiences do give a dramatic sense of new beginnings: people like St Augustine and Malcolm Worsley have indeed been 'born again.' The danger is that those who come to faith more slowly and less dramatically can feel themselves to be inferior. Another translation of that phrase is 'born from above' (i.e. by the Holy Spirit). In this sense, *all* who put their trust in Jesus Christ are 'born again Christians', whether they turn to him in an instant or gradually over a period of time. But however it starts, this turning to Christ must continue throughout life.

Guidance

Michael Bourdeaux is an Anglican clergyman who speaks fluent Russian. He is Director of the Keston Institute, a research unit which, during the years of the Cold War, devoted its resources to helping believers in Communist lands. The way in which he was 'directed' into this work is striking. In 1963 he received a letter, via Paris, in semi-literate Russian. The letter was not addressed to him personally, but it described the fierce persecutions under Khruschev, including the confinement of active Christians in psychiatric asylums.

The following year Michael went to Moscow. He set out to visit the Church of St Peter and Paul, only to find that it had been destroyed by order of the authorities. As he looked at the rubble, two elderly women were doing the same. They talked, and to his astonishment he found that these two strangers had written that all-important letter. Those women had travelled 700 miles and its recipient had flown from Britain. They would not have met if either of them had arrived at the site of the demolished church an hour earlier or later. The women spoke for Michael as well as themselves when they said, 'God sent you to meet us.'

We begin to see what Archbishop William Temple meant when he commented that when he stopped praying, coincidences stopped happening! Following their plea for help, Michael Bourdeaux launched his life's work: careful research into the facts concerning life for believers (Jewish, Muslim, Christian, Buddhist and others) in Communist lands.

Frances Young is a university teacher and a mother. She teaches theology, and returns home to a severely handicapped son. Frances is a radical, probing theologian, who knows that there are no knock-down arguments for the existence of God. Yet she speaks with deep conviction of her own faith, and about certain experiences which convince her of the reality of a personal God.

One day she was sitting in a chair when she had a 'loud thought.' It was as though a voice said to her, 'It doesn't make any difference to Me whether you believe in Me or not!' Later, when driving her car, she had another 'loud thought' telling her to be ordained. She can't remember the journey itself ('I must have been on automatic pilot or something!') but she remembers the experience very clearly. ' *I had the whole of my life laid out in front of me; and all its peculiar twists and turns which hadn't seemed to make very much sense suddenly fell into a pattern, as though this was all leading up to that moment and that conclusion. It was quite dramatic in its way.'* Frances was ordained as a minister in the Methodist Church on 3rd July, 1984.

Alexander Solzhenitsyn, the Russian author, also believes that he received a commission from God for his life's work. As a young dissident he was imprisoned by the Soviet authorities. In his memoir *The Oak and the Calf* he describes his despair at being told that, because of cancer, he had only three weeks to live. He had so much to tell the world and he feared that the Soviet authorities would discover and destroy his writings.

Desperately he hid his work (in champagne bottles!). That was in 1953. In 1970 he won the Nobel Prize for literature! He commented,

'With a hopelessly neglected and acutely malignant tumour, this was a divine miracle; I could see no other explanation. Since then all the life that had been given back to me has not been mine in the full sense: it is built around a purpose.'

— Prayer, protection and reassurance —

A remarkable example of God apparently answering prayer, has been recounted by the Russian poet Irina Ratushinskaya. Irina spent four years in Soviet prisons and labour camps for her literary and human rights activities, before being released in 1986. In a poem, Irina describes herself as 'a huddle by an icy wall.' This gives a sense of the biting cold, the inadequate clothing and the poor diet. But she testifies to two kinds of warmth which she sometimes experienced: the inner emotional warmth of joy *and* a physical warmth throughout her body, despite the freezing conditions. It is her conviction that these phenomena (experienced by other prisoners, too) were a direct answer to prayer, as this extract from one of her poems shows.

> Believe me, it was often thus
> In solitary cells, on winter nights
> A sudden sense of joy and warmth
> And a resounding note of love.
> And then, unsleeping, I would know
> A-huddle by an icy wall:
> Someone is thinking of me now,
> Petitioning the Lord for me.
> from: *Pencil Letter* (Hutchinson)

Gerald Priestland was a distinguished BBC Foreign Affairs correspondent. Following a breakdown, he underwent psychoanalysis and moved from atheism to belief in God. He became a Quaker. Gerald once said, 'I hope I believe. I know that I trust.' His faith, his doubts and his questions were essential tools for his next job as BBC Religious Affairs correspondent.

In 1991 Gerald suffered a stroke. In one of his last broadcasts, his voice marked by a slur resulting from the stroke, he spoke these moving words:

'I have had the feeling of being crushed under a rock till I could see only one crack of light, and that was the love of God, the absolute certainty, when everything else had been taken from me, that God loved me.'

Mysticism

Can the above experiences properly be described as 'mystical'? Professor Owen Chadwick defines mysticism as 'an experience of direct communication with God. It is not, for example, reading about Jesus and saying that is what God must be like: but kneeling down to say a prayer and suddenly feeling God there, facing you or beside you or in you.' He goes on to say that while people often attempt to describe such experiences, they all acknowledge the inadequacy of words to capture them. Other writers point out that while such experiences can be accompanied by a sense of ecstasy, this is not always the case. It is clear, therefore, that most of the experiences described above could be called 'mystical' – although the people involved might not wish to use that term. Such phenomena have been experienced by Christians throughout the centuries and some have become famous. Three examples are given below:

Mother Julian of Norwich (c 1342–1414)

Julian was an anchoress who chose to live in a sealed cell in Norwich, where she gave herself to prayer and meditation. In May 1373 she received a series of 16 revelations or 'shewings.' Her book *Revelations of Divine Love* has become a classic and is widely read today. The revelations were centred on the Holy Trinity and the suffering (the Passion) of Jesus. She held a hazel nut in her hand and took it to represent the whole world. *'In this little thing I saw three properties. The first is that God made it, the second that God loves it, the third that God keeps it.'*

Despite being confined to a cell, she was visited by many people, for she became famous as a spiritual counsellor. Her direct experiences of God gave Mother Julian a deep sense of peace and assurance, as her most famous utterance shows: *'all shall be well, and all shall be well, and all manner of thing shall be well.'*

Blaise Pascal (1623–1662)

A mathematician and scientist of great stature, he is as famous for his theological writing as for his scientific work. In particular, his *Pensées* (*Thoughts on Religion and Some Other Subjects*) are still read today. On a 'Night of Fire' he experienced the reality of 'the God of Isaac, of Abraham and Jacob' (as opposed to the 'First Cause' God of the philosophers). He describes this in a series of vivid words: *'Fire . . . Certainty . . . Peace . . . Joy, tears of joy.'* He wrote, *'the heart has its reasons, of which reason knows nothing.'*

John Wesley (1703–1791)

As a student at Oxford he engaged vigorously in religious activities and was a member of the 'Holy Club', whose members came to be called Methodists. He was ordained as an Anglican priest and travelled to Georgia in America as a missionary. This was an unhappy and unsuccessful venture and Wesley sailed home. On this dangerous journey he was deeply impressed with the strong faith, in the face of death, of a group of Moravians.

On 24th May, 1738 he attended a Moravian meeting in London's Aldersgate Street, where he felt his 'heart strangely warmed.' This gave him assurance of salvation and a renewed desire to preach. Throughout a long life, he travelled thousands of miles on horseback, preached thousands of sermons (often in the open air) and founded the Methodist Church. His last known letter was to William Wilberforce, encouraging him in the campaign against slavery.

As we saw at the beginning of this chapter, such experiences are not confined to the past. Nor are they confined to Christian believers. The eminent zoologist Sir Alistair Hardy set up a research centre to investigate such phenomena. As a result, a remarkable number of people have recounted experiences of this kind.

Such experiences can lead to dramatic changes in life style and attitude.

But not always. In his autobiography, the art critic Lord Clark wrote: *'I had a religious experience . . . for a few minutes my whole being was irradiated by a kind of heavenly joy.'* This presented him with a dilemma; should he respond to this revelation by repentance and faith? Kenneth Clark could not face such an upheaval. He continues, *'I was too deeply embedded in the world to change course. But that I had felt the finger of God I am quite sure, and, although the memory of this experience has faded, it still helps me to understand the joys of the saints.'* (*The Other Half: A Self Portrait*) Shortly before he died, Lord Clark was received into the Roman Catholic Church.

Daily life

As already indicated, the experiences outlined above are not confined to a few 'super-saints.' Large numbers of Christians could describe dramatic, 'out of the blue' spiritual experiences which have made a tremendous difference to the quality and direction of their lives. Sometimes they are life-transforming; frequently they leave the person involved with a quiet certainty about the reality and love of God.

But many other believers, probably the majority, do not have experiences of this kind. As a result, some feel 'second-class' in comparison. This is sad, for it is possible to have a strong faith in God without experiencing anything 'dramatic'. For some, the main pointer to the reality of God is a quiet confidence that they are 'accompanied', 'helped' and 'directed' through life by an unseen Presence – and challenged too, to acts of love and service.

In a famous sentence, Jesus promised his disciples that *'where two or three come together in my name, I am there in the midst of them.'* (Matthew 18:20)

Millions of ordinary believers, who have never had a 'special' encounter with God, testify that these words of Jesus sum up their experience. They affirm that they meet for prayer, worship and fellowship, not to remember a dead hero, but to meet – and to be met by – a living Person. Their testimony is impressive.

The importance of such *un*dramatic experiences of God is captured by Cardinal Basil Hume, the leader of Britain's Roman Catholic community:

'Holiness involves friendship with God. God's love for us and ours for him grows like any relationship with other people. There comes a moment, which we can never quite locate or catch, when

an acquaintance becomes a friend. In a sense, the change from one to the other has been taking place over a period of time, but there comes a point when we know we can trust the other, exchange confidences, keep each other's secrets. We are friends. There has to be a moment like that in our relationship with God. He ceases to be just a Sunday acquaintance and becomes a weekday friend.' (To Be a Pilgrim, SPCK)

Discipleship

As we have seen, powerful life-changing experiences are described on the pages of the Bible. And words of emotion, such as *joy* and *fear*, are often found there too. In the light of Christian beliefs about the resurrection of Jesus and the activity of the Holy Spirit, it is not surprising that experiences of God (whether gentle or dramatic) continue to be widespread. But all Christians would agree that the *quality of our discipleship* matters more than any particular spiritual experience.

What *really* counts is the response of the individual believer. Such experiences are 'given' for practical purposes: to broaden our understanding, to deepen our faith, to enlarge our compassion and to secure our obedience.

C S Lewis became a leading Christian 'apologist' (defender of the faith), part of whose story was told in the film *Shadowlands*. He was Professor of Medieval Literature at Oxford University who wrote a series of famous children's books, including *The Lion, the Witch and the Wardrobe*. He also wrote science fiction, as well as many books about Christianity. He was converted from atheism after a long period of mental wrestling. C S Lewis described one striking experience in his autobiography *Surprised by Joy* (Collins):

'I was going up Headington Hill on the top of a bus. Without words and (I think) almost without images, a fact about myself was somehow presented to me. I became aware that I was holding something at bay, or shutting something out. Or, if you like, that I was wearing some stiff clothing, like corsets, or even a suit of armour, as if I were a lobster. I felt myself being, there and then, given a free choice. I could open the door or keep it shut; I could unbuckle the armour or keep it on. Neither choice was presented

as a duty, no threat or promise was attached to either, though I knew that to open the door or to take off the corset meant the incalculable. The choice appeared to be momentous, but it was also strangely unemotional.'

C S Lewis wrote a great deal about Christian faith, religious experience and obedience. He believed that God is often most obvious to the emotions and senses at the *beginning* of our Christian pilgrimage, to help get us started on our journey of faith. And he argued that Christians sometimes make greater progress during periods when they have *no direct sense* of the presence of God. For only then are they really living 'by faith, not by sight.' (2 Corinthians 5:7); – learning to trust the promises of God found in the Bible, 'not in the teeth of reason, but in the teeth of lust, and terror, and jealousy and boredom and indifference.'

For Lewis, the *truth* of Christianity is everything. We are called to follow Jesus Christ whether we experience his presence or not, because he is 'the Way, the Truth and the Life.' (John 14:6) He summed up his position like this:

'Christianity is a statement which, if false, is of <u>no</u> importance, and if true, of infinite importance. The one thing it cannot be is moderately important.'

7

PRAYER AND WORSHIP

Christian prayer is characteristically offered to God the Father, through Jesus Christ, under the leading of the Holy Spirit. To use a traditional term, it is 'trinitarian' in form. This is no accident of history. It springs from the nature of God's revelation, the supreme moment of which is the life, death and resurrection of Jesus Christ.

Christian prayer is offered on the basis that Jesus cleared away the 'road-blocks' between God and human beings, for on the cross he endured and overcame the alienation caused by our sin. And it is offered in full recognition that what Christ did was the work of God, on behalf of the human race and the whole creation. This work was devised by God and carried through by him out of sheer love and compassion.

Christian prayer also recognises that the Holy Spirit is the member of the Trinity who enables us to approach God as **Abba, Father**. God's Spirit can be regarded as the bond of love between the Father and the Son. The Spirit guides and intercedes for us because we do not know what to pray for, or how to pray (Romans 8:15,26). But the trinitarian shape of Christian prayer is also seen in the fact that, because Christianity holds Jesus Christ and the Holy Spirit to be fully divine, prayer is addressed:

(a) *to God the Father*. Most notably in *The Lord's Prayer*, the prayer which Jesus taught his first disciples, beginning 'Our Father in heaven . . .' (page 8). It is God the Father who is most commonly addressed in prayer, through Jesus Christ, in the power of the Holy Spirit.

(b) *to Jesus Christ the Son.* A remarkable fact, when we recall that the first disciples were Jews who believed that 'the Lord our God, the Lord is One.' (Deuteronomy 6:4; see page 14)

(c) *to the Holy Spirit.* In the form of invocation as in the ancient hymn, 'Come Holy Ghost, our souls inspire.' (Which has the Latin title *Veni Creator.*)

> *Thanks be to thee, my Lord Jesus Christ,*
> *For all the benefits which thou hast given me,*
> *for all the pains and insults which thou hast born for me.*
> *O merciful Redeemer, Friend and Brother;*
> *may I know thee more clearly, love thee more dearly*
> *and follow thee more nearly, day by day.* Amen
> (St Richard of Chichester: 1197–1253)

Doing God's will

Christianity is deeply concerned with the world as it is. Christians are called to live in the 'here and now.' But they live and pray out of the inspiration gained by *looking back* and *looking forward*. The events of the life, death and resurrection of Jesus Christ are seen as fully relevant at all times. Indeed, he himself is believed in as the ever-living and ever-contemporary Lord. Christians believe that what happened 2000 years ago affects the whole world, since God then set in motion a new order. God will eventually bring this to perfection when he makes 'all things new.' (Revelation 21:5)

So there is for Christians a backward look and a forward look, reminding them that all history is in the hands of God. This is why Christian prayer seeks to 'key in' to the will and work of God, who is leading his creation towards a future of restoration, renewal and glory. *Prayer is not a matter of persuading God to do things which he might not want to do. Rather, it is a matter of aligning ourselves with his purpose.* Even when (as is often the case) his will in detail is far from clear, the desire of the praying person is to bring his or her will into conformity with God's will; to want *his* will to be done.

The Khouds of North India have a prayer which reads: *'Lord, we don't know what is good for us. You know what it is. For it we pray. Amen'.* It is a prayer of confidence in God, a prayer which rests in his perfect, loving will. But what if we fear that we don't really want God's will to be done in some particular situation? Writers on prayer tell us that our 'fear' shows that we *ought* to want it. So they encourage us with the thought that God, who knows our hearts, mercifully accepts our *wanting to want it* and gently leads us into a fuller desire for it.

Jesus Christ taught his followers to pray to the Father, '*May your will be done on earth as it is in heaven.*' (Matthew 6:10) From this we understand that the very best that could happen 'on earth' at any time, is that God's will should be done. Furthermore, the Holy Spirit is always at work, guiding those who genuinely want the will of God to be done. The confidence that God is active in the world (and will one day make all things new, permeating every part of his new creation with his glory), spurs the believer on to pray and work to make this world a better and a fairer place. This is in anticipation of the future consummation of God's Kingdom. So prayer is best thought of as an active response to the will of the God of history.

In the Bible Abraham and Moses prayed, so did Naomi and Hannah, David and Elijah, Jonah and Daniel, Elizabeth and Mary. Jesus prayed. His disciples asked him to teach them, and he did. He emphasised privacy, trust, honesty, brevity and forgiveness. Most churches regularly use *The Lord's Prayer.*

If any part is harder than the rest, it must be the words about forgiveness. Jesus developed this great theme in parable and instruction – and by example.

Aspects of prayer

Prayer takes a number of forms:

Adoration

The wonder of God's being and character brings adoration. He is beyond our understanding; but he has revealed himself, supremely in Jesus Christ. God is seen as the One before whom heart and mind must bow, because in him is all perfection and beauty. Prayer may be expressed in words; but sometimes it goes beyond words into an attitude of silent and word-less devotion. A great medieval theologian,

Thomas Aquinas, when at prayer in front of a crucifix heard a voice saying, 'You have written well of me. What reward would you like to have?' He replied, 'No reward, but you yourself, Lord.'

Thanksgiving

This is clearly related to adoration. We reflect on everything which enriches our lives, sometimes giving thanks to God for specific blessings. But it does not stop there, for the *whole* work of God, past and present, occasions thanksgiving.

> *Almighty God, Father of all mercies,*
> *we your unworthy servants give you*
> *most humble and hearty thanks*
> *for all your goodness and loving kindness*
> *to us and to all men.*
> *We bless you for our creation, preservation*
> *and all the blessings of this life*
> *but above all for your immeasurable love*
> *in the redemption of the world by*
> *Our Lord Jesus Christ*
> *for the means of grace, and for the hope of glory . . .*

From a *General Thanksgiving* by Bishop Edward Reynolds (1599–1676)

Confession

This begins with an awareness that nobody is without sin in God's sight. In addition to 'sinfulness' (a shared failure to love God wholeheartedly and our neighbour as ourselves) there are particular sins of thought, word and deed to be acknowledged and repented of, if God's forgiveness is to be received and a fresh start made. While it is undesirable to 'rummage' in our lives to try to uncover every fault (as if this could be done), confessing particular known sins is important and can be therapeutic. However, in the course of Christian worship (ie worship in a Christian congregation) the prayer of confession must necessarily be general in character. The brief and beautiful 'Jesus Prayer' from the Eastern Orthodox tradition is used by many Christians: *'Lord Jesus Christ, Son of God, have mercy on me, a sinner.'*

Many people find it helpful to share with another human being, in strict confidence, those things which are burdening their conscience. Some Christian traditions (such as Roman Catholic and Orthodox) commend the practice of personal confession to God in the presence of a priest. Some believers find that they come to an assurance of divine forgiveness more readily, when they hear a declaration of that forgiveness from an authorised representative of the Church.

Intercession

This looks out at the world. It is the prayer of concern for individual people, groups of people, causes and events. Since God, in his love, wants the best for his whole creation, the intercessor prays with confidence, asking that God's perfect will may be done. Intercession is based on whatever information is available. The blessing asked for is what seems to the intercessor to be needed, but the prayer is offered essentially as a contribution (itself God-inspired) to the realisation of God's will. Just why God should wish to involve us in his purpose through prayer is a mystery. But, encouraged by Jesus' example and teaching about prayer, Christian believers gladly accept it as a mystery of love – and as a great privilege.

Petition

The Bible encourages us to make specific requests to God. There are three important considerations:

1 As the Lord's Prayer shows (page 8) the prayer of asking is meant to bind us ever more closely to God in our daily lives. We come to recognise that we are entirely dependent on him for everything.

2 Jesus taught his disciples to pray for things *in his name*: that is, to pray as he would pray. This prevents petition from becoming a selfish kind of prayer. As always, we pray with the proviso, 'Your will be done.'

3 A loving parent might answer a child's request with Yes, No or Wait. Any of these three words might be the answer to a particular prayer. St Paul experienced disappointment when he prayed for the removal of a 'thorn in the flesh.' But with the No, God reassured Paul with a promise: 'My grace is sufficient for you, for my power is made perfect in weakness.' (2 Corinthians 12:7–10)

——— Extemporary prayer ———

Over the centuries, thousands of written prayers have been composed for all the above modes of prayer. Some are very beautiful; some very famous. But many Christians use *extemporary* (or *extempore*) prayer – praying in their own words rather than from a written text. In some traditions (such as Roman Catholic, Orthodox, Anglican) written prayers are usually preferred in public worship. In others (such as Baptist, Pentecostal) extemporary prayer (sometimes very passionate!) is more usual.

Place and posture

Many Christians find it helpful to return to a familiar place which they associate with prayer. This might be a church building; it might be a favourite chair in a particular room. Some people use visual or audio aids – music perhaps, or a cross or a candle.

Again, posture can be important. Some choose to kneel; others prefer to sit in a comfortable chair. Many pray in bed! But prayer can be offered anywhere: while walking or driving or ironing.... Many Christians offer quick 'arrow prayers' throughout the day, and find prayer a comfort if they cannot sleep at night.

Meditation and contemplation

Attention has been given by Christian writers on spirituality to states of mind in prayer and methods of praying. *Meditation* and *contemplation* are defined in various ways and contemplation is often seen as a stage beyond meditation.

In *meditation* we reflect on a text or story or image (often from the Bible or from nature). A famous example comes from the Breton peasant who spent long hours before the crucifix. Asked to describe his experience he replied, 'I look at him; and he looks at me.' Such reflection, in which we try to 'listen' to God, may lead to conclusions which then result in action.

In *contemplation* the reasoning processes are stilled; the person praying gives attention to God through a single act of love and self-offering. This attitude has been described as 'simple attention' and 'one-pointedness'. While some people do move through meditation into contemplation, there are those who experience contemplation at an early stage in their spiritual journey. A parallel may be seen in the wonderment of a child when confronted by something new, lovely and fascinating. The child is completely absorbed, captivated, filled with delight. Since contemplation has something of this character (rooted as it is in adoration), it would be surprising if it were not experienced by some Christians at an early stage, as well as by more mature believers.

Meditation makes use of words and visual images. Contemplation can dispense with both, though it may use a short form of words, or a single word often repeated. Perhaps it is best understood as a "wordless" approach to God, which has no need of the usual thought processes. Christian mystics down the centuries have done their best to write about it, but have freely admitted that it defies adequate description.

Christian worship

Christian worship is from God to God. Worship comes from God in two senses:

- it focuses on who God is and what he has done
- God himself puts into people's hearts and minds the desire for prayer and praise

It is, of course, a human activity; but it is motivated, sustained and inspired by God himself. And so we can say truly that it is 'from God, to God.'

Because worship has this character, it can be seen as a kind of 'conversation' between God and the worshipping community. Through the reading of the Bible, the preaching of a sermon, the singing of psalms, canticles, songs and hymns, and in various other ways, God makes use of human words to speak to his people. He comforts and encourages them, he challenges and inspires them, and he calls them to particular acts of service. The congregation, hearing God's message in this way, responds in creed, prayers and hymns, and with adoration, confession and thanksgiving. The prayers which are offered for the world, and for particular people and causes, are in themselves a response to God. It is our way of declaring interest in, and loving concern for, the world which God 'loved so much that he gave his only Son.' (John 3:16)

It would be mistaken, however, to think that worship is exclusively verbal, though it sometimes seems like that. We need only to think of the *Sacraments* (see Chapter 8) to see how wide of the mark this is. The sacraments have at their centre materials and actions, such as water poured, bread and wine consumed. Silence can be an important feature of worship. Some Christians (notably Quakers: see Chapter 12) make silence central to their Sunday gatherings, as they 'wait upon God.'

Many churches are concerned that the gifts distributed by God's Spirit among the worshippers should be as fully used as possible – gifts of reading and speaking; gifts of music and the visual arts; gifts of leadership and teaching. Word and action belong together.

All worship is rooted in its culture

Worship among Presbyterians in Scotland will be a more sombre experience than worship in a Pentecostal Church in Barbados (Chapter 12). Many people (particularly young people but some adults as well) feel the need to express themselves in a style of worship which may differ markedly from that of more traditional believers. 'Alternative worship' is organised in many places; use is made of music groups, synthesisers, videos, dance and drama. In Britain by the turn of the second millennium there is no 'typical' church service. Variations within the Church of England alone would have astonished earlier Anglicans. But the same criteria apply: wherever worshippers give thanks and praise to God, confess their sins, and seek to serve and follow Jesus Christ in the world, *there* is genuine worship.

Prayer has blossomed and fruited in every conceivable way – from the silence of Trappist monks or the Society of Friends (Quakers) to the formal intonations of the priest; from the succinctness of the Sunday Collect (to 'collect' our thoughts) to the different freedom of the extempore worship-leader. Methodists are better than most at incorporating hymns into their private intercessions. Some Christians pray by the book, as in a 'Daily Office' with its mix of constants and variables; others pray with no book.

As with the prayer of the individual Christian, corporate worship is 'trinitarian' in shape. It is offered:

- *to God the Father* who makes himself known as the Father of the family of believers
- *through God the Son* on whose life and work the Church depends
- *in the power of God the Holy Spirit,* who inspires the worshippers, and bestows gifts on them 'for the common good.' (1 Corinthians 12:7)

Finally, but very importantly, *worship is not confined to services in church; it involves the whole life of members of the congregation,* during the week as well as on Sundays. What happens in a church service is a focus for the worship which believers offer through their everyday activities. *This point is all important.* In the Bible we find a terrible warning: if what happens outside formal worship contradicts what is said within it, then the act of worship is invalidated. (Isaiah 1; Amos 5) Worship, properly understood, is the offering of the *whole* of our lives to God.

'*Therefore, I urge you brothers, in view of God's mercy, to offer your bodies as living sacrifices, holy and pleasing to God – this is your spiritual act of worship. Do not conform any longer to the pattern of this world, but be transformed by the renewing of your mind*'. (Romans 12:1–2)

Send us now into the world in peace,
and grant us strength and courage
to love and serve you
with gladness and singleness of heart;
through Christ our Lord. Amen.
From *The Book of Common Prayer* (USA Episcopal Church)

One of my most vivid memories of praying came from a visit to Namibia during the war there. I was with Bishop James Kauluma driving from Windhoek to visit the main part of his diocese in the north of the country . . . It meant driving without lights to avoid getting caught breaking the curfew by the South African army, on tracks through the bush which had been extensively mined. As we went along the two of us not driving said the office of evening prayer so that the driver could hear and take part. The psalm was one of those imploring God to save us from danger. I found myself praying fervently words that I had been used to re-interpreting in my usual condition of comfort and safety.

The experience showed what I have learned elsewhere in Africa, that . . . what might be called the resources of Christian spirituality – were really designed to sustain people facing difficulty and danger. That has actually been most people's lot all through human history.' (Bishop Humphrey Taylor: from *SeeN*)

Escapism?

Critics might argue that prayer and worship are an escape from 'the real world.' Christians would reply that it is necessary to withdraw from the world from time to time, in order to serve the world. Of course, not all acts of worship are inspiring and challenging. But some visionary writers have seen prayer and worship as nothing less than *a bridge between heaven and earth.*

Thomas Merton was one of the the great spiritual writers of our century. In 1941 he visited an American monastery called Gethsemani, shortly before joining that community. It was a dark and troubled time in world history, especially in Europe where the Nazis were causing havoc. As he watched the monks at prayer, he came to see that activity as a focus of spiritual power. He wrote this in his *Secular Journal*:

'This is the centre of America. I had wondered what was keeping the country together, what has been keeping the universe from cracking in pieces and falling apart. It's places like this monastery – not only this one; there must be others . . . This is the only real city in America – and it is by itself, in the wilderness. It is an axle around which the whole country blindly turns, and knows nothing about it. Gethsemani holds the country together: What right have I to be here?'

In Thomas Merton's view it was prayer – that mysterious and powerful means by which human beings are caught up in the plans and purposes of God – which holds the universe together and checks chaos.

Michael Ramsey (100th Archbishop of Canterbury) made the same point. He asserted that *worship brings healing into a broken world*, because it is a channel through which the love of God flows into our lives. He spoke of some of the great problems facing our world and continued with this 'parable':

'There was once a man who had three nasty big boils, and he went to the doctor and asked for each of them to be treated or removed. And the doctor said "My dear fellow, I can do nothing permanent with these boils unless we get rid of the poison in your system which is causing them." So, too, the human race, very sick and having at least three terrible boils in the social and moral order, wants to be rid of them. But this human race does not grasp that the trouble is a poison in the system and the sickness is that of a deep derangement in the relation of mankind to the Creator. Go to the root. The root is the right relation of man to Creator: and when Christians are concerned about what they call worship they are concerned, not with something remote or escapist, but with the root of the world's predicament.' (*Introducing the Christian Faith*: SCM)*

— High points in the Christian Year —

'Anybody who is found observing, by abstinence from labour, feasting, or any other way, any such days as Christmas Day, shall pay for every such offense five shillings.' (Massachussetts 1659, General Court of New England).

As this statement indicates, some Christians have been suspicious of keeping special 'holy' days. For *every* day is a gift from God. This attitude is held by some Christians even today – in certain Brethren (formerly Plymouth Brethren) churches for example. During the 19th century one such Christian was so appalled at being served with Christmas pudding, that he threw it on to his garden!

But most churches observe the Christian Year, finding its rhythm and changes of mood a helpful aid to devotion, faith and life. Most of these days and seasons relate to events in the life of Jesus Christ. Others recall notable Christians down the centuries – from the first disciples onwards.

Advent

This is the four-week period before Christmas. The title comes from a Latin word meaning 'Coming'. In Advent, Christians prepare themselves for the celebration of Christ's coming at Christmas – and for his 'Second Coming' at the end of this age, when he will judge the world. This season is longer in the Eastern Orthodox Churches (see Chapter 12) than in the West. (One example of a number of variations in the Christian calendar between the Eastern and Western churches.)

Christmas

The anniversary of the birth of Christ, celebrated by most Christians on 25th December, though the actual date of Christ's birth in Bethlehem is unknown. The Armenian Church celebrates Christmas on 6th January. This most popular of all festivals replaced an older, pagan mid-winter festival.

Epiphany

The word is Greek in origin and means 'manifestation'. The date of this festival is 6th January. The Western Church recalls and celebrates the visit of the Magi (the wise men) to the infant Jesus. Matthew's Gospel (2:1–12) tells us that they presented gifts: gold, frankincense and myrrh. This story is taken to represent the coming *to* Christ of the Gentile (non–Jewish) world, and the coming *of* Christ for all humanity. The Eastern Orthodox Churches focus on the baptism of Jesus at this time, and baptismal water is blessed.

Lent

This is the period of 40 days immediately preceding Easter. The name probably has an Anglo-Saxon origin. It comes from a word meaning 'Spring' and marks the lengthening days. Christians reflect on the 40 days which Jesus spent in the wilderness after his baptism. Lent is a solemn time, traditionally marked by fasting, when Christians consider the disciplines of their faith. Lent starts on *Ash Wednesday*, the day after *Shrove Tuesday*. The latter is also known as 'Pancake Day', from the old custom of using up all the items of food which were forbidden in Lent.

Holy Week

At the end of Lent, a week is set aside for focusing on the death of Christ and its meaning for the salvation of the world. In this week occurs *Maundy Thursday*, when the institution of Holy Communion is commemorated. 'Maundy' comes from the Latin phrase *'mandatum novum'* (new commandment) and refers to John 13 when Jesus

washed his disciples' feet and added, 'A new commandment I give you
. . . As I have loved you, so you must love one another.' *Good Friday*
follows *Maudy Thursday*. This is the most solemn day of all, as we
reflect on the cost of our redemption. All the prayers and devotions
concentrate on the crucifixion.

Easter

This is *the* major festival of the Christian year, when Christians celebrate the resurrection of Jesus Christ from the dead, after his crucifixion and burial. *Every* Sunday is a festival occasion because it is a
'little Easter' – the weekly celebration of the resurrection of Jesus
Christ 'on the first day of the week.' On Easter Sunday, many churches include a joyful liturgical response:

> 'Alleluia! Christ is risen.
> He is risen indeed. Alleluia!'

Ascension Day

This celebrates the ascension of Jesus into heaven, where he 'sits at
the right hand of the Father' and prays for the world. We are reminded that Jesus took his, and our, humanity into heaven. This festival
marks the end of Jesus' post-resurrection appearances which lasted
for 40 days. For this reason it is celebrated 40 days after Easter
Sunday, and falls on a Thursday.

Pentecost

The account of the bestowal of the Holy Spirit on the early Church is
given at the beginning of *The Acts of the Apostles*. Each year at Pentecost, 50 days after Easter, the Church recalls this event. Christians
pray that, by his Holy Spirit, God will guide and strengthen the
Church for its work and witness in the world. As with some other
Christian festivals and dates, Pentecost has its roots in the Jewish
tradition. Pentecost is the name given to a Jewish celebration of the
first-fruits of the corn harvest, 50 days after the Passover. An alternative name for the Christian festival is *Whitsun*.

Trinity Sunday

The theme of this day (one week after Pentecost) sums up all the
observances in the Church's calendar from Advent to Pentecost. On

Trinity Sunday the Church is reminded of God's eternal nature – that he is Father, Son and Holy Spirit; three Persons in one God.

Trinity Sunday to Advent

During this period, many aspects of Christian life and witness are brought to the Church's attention. All these are based, in one way or another, on the life, death and resurrection of Jesus Christ and his continuing presence with us.

8

THE SACRAMENTS

In times of conflict, a nation's flag assumes great significance. Indeed, people are sometimes willing to die rather than deny their national emblem. Viewed in one way, this is absurd. Who in their right mind would exchange life for a little bit of coloured cloth? But to those on the inside of that experience it is completely understandable. They *see* a 'little bit of coloured cloth', but they also see, represented in their flag, the past history of their nation and all that it stands for at its best. This notion of ordinary objects taking on deep significance, is a helpful picture to hold in mind as we consider the sacraments of the Church.

When we call Christianity a 'sacramental religion', we refer to the fact that certain actions (eating, drinking) and physical objects (wine, bread, water) 'speak' powerfully of spiritual truths. This insight is found throughout the Hebrew Scriptures and in the Gospels. Later, the Church attempted various definitions. One of the most famous can be traced back to Augustine of Hippo: 'a sacrament is an outward and visible sign of an inward and spiritual grace.'

Christianity has two central sacraments: *Baptism* and *Holy Communion*. Both of these are representations of events in the life of Jesus Christ, but with a specific and personal significance for Christian worshippers today.

In the New Testament, the Greek word 'mysterion' (*mystery*) refers to a truth which was hidden but is now revealed in Jesus Christ – and especially through his death. In the ancient

Latin Bible (Jerome's *Vulgate*: 4th century) this term was translated as *sacramentum*; it is from this that we get the English
word 'sacrament'.

Baptism

The baptism of Jesus

The Gospels tell us that John the Baptist 'preached a baptism of
repentance for the forgiveness of sins.' (Mark 1:4) Crowds went to be
baptised in the River Jordan; among them was Jesus. John expressed
reluctance to baptise the One who was so much greater than he. But
Jesus insisted and John agreed. When Jesus came up out of the water
*'he saw the Spirit of God descending like a dove and lighting on him.
And a voice from heaven said, "This is my Son, whom I love; with him
I am well pleased." '* (Matthew 3:16,17)

John's was a baptism of repentance for sin and this raises a question
for Christians, for the New Testament teaches the sinlessness of
Jesus (1 Peter 2:22). He was the one human being who had no need to
repent. But in submitting to baptism, Jesus was not declaring his
own sinfulness; he was endorsing John's ministry. He was also identi-
fying himself with the people.

Jesus could have stood with John, calling the people to repentance.
Instead, he associated himself with the people; a fitting start to the
ministry of the One who would be called 'friend of sinners' and who
would die on a cross between two criminals.

Baptism in the Church

Baptism features strongly in the New Testament, and in subsequent
Christian history, as a vital aspect of Christian initiation. *But
Christian baptism is a much richer concept than John's baptism. For,
as John declared, Jesus would 'baptise with the Holy Spirit.'*

The Acts of the Apostles gives several examples of people being baptised, among them an Ethiopian official (Acts 8:38) and a Philippian jailor, together with his family (Acts 16:31–34). These show that a lengthy period of preparation was not required. Following confession of faith in Christ, baptism was the immediate next step. In the years following the New Testament period, a lengthy preparation and 'apprenticeship' became common, with most baptisms taking place at Easter or Pentecost. Those being prepared for Christian initiation were called *catechumens* or *the catechumenate*, terms still in use today.

Water

A key passage for understanding Christian baptism is found in St Paul's letter to the church in Rome. He describes baptism as a burial! (Romans 6:4). Baptism links the believer with the crucified Saviour – it illustrates the call of Jesus to 'take up the cross.' This call to 'die to self' is a central aspect of Christian discipleship and it is signified in baptism when candidates go under the water. But baptism is also a symbol of resurrection; the candidates come up out of the water, signifying that they have received new life in Christ.

Water has many other rich associations in the Christian tradition. It signifies that a person has been washed clean from sin. And it points to a promise of Jesus – that he will give the water of life. (John 7:38) Baptism also reminds those present of God's great saving act in bringing the people of Israel safely through the divided sea, pursued by their Egyptian captors (*The Exodus*). They remember too, that Jesus referred to his impending death as 'a baptism'. The sacrament or ordinance of baptism evokes all these associations.

Differences

Different customs have grown up around baptism. These differences, the subject of some controversy between the churches, focus on:

● the candidates for baptism
● the mode of baptism

▶ **Who may be baptised?** Nobody is too old for baptism and all churches baptise adults who come to faith in Christ. But most churches baptise babies too, usually on the understanding that they will be given a Christian upbringing. These churches assert that infant baptism speaks clearly of the grace of God – indicating that his love is for all, even those who cannot consciously respond to it.

> *The sheer gratuitousness of the grace of salvation is particularly manifest in infant Baptism. The Church and the parents would deny a child the priceless grace of becoming a child of God were they not to confer Baptism shortly after birth . . . For all the baptized, children or adults, faith must grow after Baptism.*
> (Catechism of the Catholic Church: 1994)

Some Protestant Christians, notably Baptists and Pentecostalists, believe that baptism should be reserved for believers. Parents take newborn babies to church for a special act of dedication to God. But baptism by water, in the name of the Father, the Son and the Holy Spirit, is delayed until the child grows up and requests it. The Baptism Service then becomes a powerful act of personal witness to faith in Jesus Christ.

This approach does have attractions even for some churches which traditionally baptise infants. One problem for many churches is 'nominal' Christianity. Parents who have little contact with the Church and no real intention of raising their children in the Christian faith, nevertheless desire a 'christening' (a popular term for baptism) to celebrate the birth.

Churches are torn between a desire to welcome everyone into the life of the Church, however fleetingly, and a concern to assert that the Christian faith has content and 'bite'. For in choosing the Christian way, we become disciples of Jesus Christ – with a commitment to serve and witness to our world, through his strength and in his name. To use a phrase made famous by Dietrich Bonhoeffer who was martyred under the Nazis, there is no 'cheap grace.'

The importance of personal choice and radical discipleship as inescapable features of Christianity, are emphasised by those who practise *believers' baptism*. Many Christians who hold that there are good reasons for infant baptism, nevertheless welcome the fact that the centrality of personal commitment to Christ is focused so clearly by their Baptist and Pentecostal brothers and sisters. But they point out that those baptised in infancy also have to make a personal choice as they grow up. They should be encouraged to view their baptism as a call to follow Christ.

▶ **Different modes of baptism** Many churches baptise by *affusion*. This means that the minister pours water on the head of the candidate (child or adult) and administers baptism 'in the name of the Father, and of the Son and of the Holy Spirit.' Other churches baptise by *immersion*. Immersion is almost always the mode of baptism employed by churches which restrict baptism to believers. Their church buildings often contain a 'baptistry' – a sunken area which contains enough water for candidates to be fully immersed. Some churches offer both modes of baptism. Baptisms are sometimes held in the sea, or in a river or swimming-pool. Eastern Orthodox Churches baptise *infants* by immersion – often to the sounds of loud protests from the candidates!

To settle these differences, baptismal practice in the New Testament has been closely studied. But it is not spelt out in enough detail to settle the issues beyond doubt, and some would argue that this gives validity to a range of practices. The Bible certainly records the baptism of entire households. While it seems likely that such households would have included babies and children, this is not explicitly stated. But there is clear evidence that infant baptism was practised from the second century onwards. As for the *mode* of baptism: early Christian paintings depict Jesus standing in the River Jordan, while John the Baptist pours water over his head – a neat way of solving the *either/or* problem!

In practice, there is widespread mutual acceptance among Christians of the baptism administered by other churches. Even when individuals change allegiance and move from one denomination to another, most churches do not insist on 're-baptism'. Indeed, *Ephesians* makes it clear that there is only 'one baptism', just as there is only 'one Lord' (Ephesians 4:5) So most Christians would argue that 're-baptism' is a theological nonsense.

However, some individuals, on experiencing a profound conversion experience, feel the need to express their new-found faith in baptism, despite having been baptised as infants. Many Baptist and Pentecostal churches encourage this. And as these churches believe that infant baptism is not real baptism, many *insist* on believers' baptism for would-be members, even if they were baptised or christened as infants. However, this is not universal. Paul Beasley-Murray (a Baptist) comments: 'Unlike the vast majority of other Baptist groups, most British Baptists have been prepared to make one concession towards other Christians: their practice of "open membership". In many English Baptist churches, it is not necessary to have been baptised as a believer to become a member.' This practice of 'open membership' goes back to the times of John Bunyan (1628–88).

Holy Communion

Jesus spent the week leading up to his crucifixion in Jerusalem. The Jewish Passover festival fell during that week – when Jews ate (as they still do today) a special meal to celebrate their escape from Egypt. They view this event as a great saving act of God. The appropriate Scriptures are read (from the book of *Exodus*) and various dishes are eaten in a specified order.

On the night before his crucifixion Jesus ate this meal with his disciples (see page 20). When he broke the bread, he also broke with tradition, for he added the mysterious words, *'This is my body.'* He then took wine and added, *'This is my blood.'* As he gave the bread and wine to his disciples, he went on to say, *'Do this in remembrance of me.'* That instruction has been joyfully obeyed throughout the centuries. The Last Supper was to become the first of many, many more.

From the beginning, a fellowship meal in remembrance of Jesus Christ, and especially his death, resurrection and promised return in glory, was a central feature of the Christian Church (Acts 2:42). It soon became less of a meal and more of an act of worship, in which the eating and drinking became nominal and symbolic. Regulations gradually developed as to who might preside at the meal, who might participate in it and in what circumstances. The main celebration was held on Sundays, for the Christian community kept that day special (rather than the Jewish Sabbath or Saturday) to honour the Lord's resurrection.

Descriptions of the Last Supper are found in five places in the New Testament. An account is found in each of the Synoptic Gospels (Matthew 26, Mark 14 and Luke 22), in John 13 and in Paul's first letter to Corinth (1 Corinthians 11:23–32). Paul includes a note of warning. Members of the church were abusing the Lord's Supper. He made it clear that to eat the bread and drink the wine 'in an unworthy manner' was a very serious matter. From then on, Christians were encouraged to prepare themselves by prayer – and sometimes by fasting too.

Paul also links the Lord's Supper with the return of Christ in glory, *'For whenever you eat this bread and drink this cup, you proclaim the Lord's death until he comes.'* (1 Corinthians 11:26) This connects with the Gospel accounts, where Jesus tells his disciples that he will not drink wine with them again until *'I drink it anew with you in my Father's kingdom.'* (Matthew 26:29) This theme is picked up in some modern liturgies with the affirmation:

Christ has died:
Christ is risen:
Christ will come again.

The fourth Gospel includes the Last Supper (see Chapter 3) but does not describe the breaking of bread and sharing of wine. Instead, it describes how Jesus took a towel and washed his disciples' feet as an example of humble service. But John does use sacramental language. Following the miraculous feeding of the 5000, he records a discourse in which Jesus says, *'I am the bread of life . . . This is the bread that came down from heaven. Your forefathers ate manna and died, but he who feeds on this bread will live for ever.'* (John 6:48–51)

One meal, several names

Jesus' words about remembrance were frequently repeated when believers met to 'break bread' together. Other words, spelling out the significance of Jesus' death, also became part of the **liturgy** of Holy Communion. Gradually, full liturgical texts for these gatherings around the Lord's Table developed. Various names for this sacrament or ordinance have come into common usage over the centuries.

Holy Communion

This title stresses the *fellowship* aspect of the service or meal.

Sharing the bread and wine fosters communion between the worshippers and God, and between those present. Holy Communion is a *corporate* experience. Believers are encouraged to think not only of 'making my communion' but of sharing one loaf at the Lord's Table, with their sisters and brothers in Christ.

Eucharist

This comes from the Greek word for 'thanksgiving'. It reminds us that when Jesus took bread at the Last Supper, he 'gave thanks'. It also focuses upon the fact that this is a *sacrament of the gospel.* Christians who gather at the Lord's Table wish to express their gratitude to God for his saving love. The focus of the service is upon Jesus, the crucified Saviour and risen Lord. But believers are required to express their gratitude, not only with their lips but with their lives. At the end of the Eucharist, worshippers commit themselves afresh to serve God in the world. Worship is only a temporary withdrawal from the pressures of life and the duty (sometimes joyful; sometimes difficult) of loving service.

The Lord's Supper

This title reminds us of the origins of the sacrament; it was a meal shared between Jesus and the original 12.

The Mass

Holy Communion in Roman Catholic churches is in the language of the people. But this is a recent development, an initiative taken at the Second Vatican Council (1962–65). Before that this Service was in Latin, as it had been for centuries. At the end of the Latin Rite, the priest dismissed the people with the words: *Ite, missa est* ('Go, you are dismissed'). The word 'Mass' – the commonest word for Holy Communion among Roman Catholics and some Anglicans and Lutherans – derives from this phrase. The term contains a challenge. As the Catholic Catechism puts it, *'the liturgy in which the mystery of salvation is accomplished concludes with the sending forth* (missio) *of the faithful, so that they may fulfil God's will in their daily lives.'*

The Breaking of Bread

This term comes directly from the New Testament and speaks for itself. A famous verse (Acts 2:42) makes clear that breaking bread together was one of the key features of the early Church.

> '**T**he spirituality of the Catholic and Orthodox Churches is dominated by the eucharist, though in very different forms. The Orthodox emphasis is much more on the assembled people being brought within sight and sound of the heavenly altar, while in the West sacramental devotion is more personal.' (Gordon Rupp).

Transubstantiation

Over the centuries, differences in emphasis and in understanding of what happens in Holy Communion emerged – especially as theologians wrestled with the meaning of the phrase, 'This is my body.' Strong differences over possible interpretations have been expressed. On the one hand are those who see the breaking of bread and sharing of wine as a powerful means of recalling the focus of our salvation. A highly significant change takes place. It occurs within the hearts and lives of the worshippers, as they consider afresh God's love revealed in the life and death of his Son.

On the other hand are those who believe that something vital happens, not only in the hearts of the worshippers, but to the bread and wine too. This is sometimes referred to as *transubstantiation*. This is the belief that when the priest says the prayer of consecration over the bread and wine, these actually *become* the body and blood of Christ. In 1551, the *Council of Trent* put it like this: 'After the consecration of the bread and wine, our Lord Jesus Christ is truly, really and substantially contained in the venerable sacrament of the holy eucharist under the appearance of those physical things.' This spells out a belief in the Real Presence – Jesus present in the elements of the sacrament in a *real*, not merely symbolic, way.

The following points should be noted:

● Those who take this view do not deny that the communicants eat actual bread and drink real wine. They employ the Greek philosopher Aristotle's distinction between 'substance' and 'accident.' *Substance* refers to the essential nature of a material; *accident* to its outward appearance (colour, shape, taste). On this view, the *accidents* of the bread and wine remain – they still look and taste like bread and wine. But the *substance* changes to that of the body and blood of Jesus Christ.

- The 16th-century Reformers (see Chapter 17) criticised this view, although they did not agree among themselves on every detail. Martin Luther held to *Consubstantiation* – the view that the substance of both bread *and* the body of Christ are present together. When placed in a fire, iron glows because iron and heat are *both* present. A simple analogy like this helps as we consider the eucharist, said Luther, who emphasised that the *fact* of Christ's presence is more important than any explanation or theory. Others pointed to the nature of the language used by Jesus. They argued that he was using the vivid language of metaphor. 'This is my body' means, 'Pay close attention. This bread represents my body which is broken for you.' Bread it remains; but it is set apart for a holy and special purpose.

- This was a very sharp debate. What people believed about the Real Presence in Holy Communion could determine whether they lived or died in 16th-century Europe. Mercifully, much of the heat has now gone out of the argument. Many Catholics and Protestants believe that it does not matter whether all Christians believe in precisely the same way. Some modern Catholic theologians have reworked old ideas and coined new words: Edward Schillebeeckx for example, speaks of *trans-signification* which is the idea that consecration of the bread and the wine is primarily concerned with a change of meaning.

- Church leaders have made efforts to understand each other better and to draw closer together. The World Council of Churches convened an inter-church conference in Lima in 1982 to consider *Baptism, Eucharist and Ministry*. ARCIC (Anglican-Roman Catholic International Commission) – continuing discussions between Roman Catholics and Anglicans – began in 1970.

But Holy Communion, together with related questions of ministry and priesthood, continues to be one of the main issues dividing the churches. Most denominations welcome members of other churches to the Lord's Table. But the Roman Catholic Church officially forbids its members to receive holy communion in other churches, and will not offer communion to non-Catholics.

Perhaps Mother Teresa's simple words, with which all Christians can agree, show that the underlying agreement is more important than the obvious divisions.

> 'When Jesus came into the world, he loved it so much that he gave his life for it. And what did he do? He made himself the Bread of Life. He became small, fragile, and defenceless for us.'

> '. . . the discipline of the Church of England is to welcome to the Lord's Table all who are full members of Christian Churches . . . Because we believe there is only one Church, it is fitting that we should welcome members of different branches of the Church to receive Holy Communion together . . . The Roman Catholic discipline – not to allow members of other churches to receive – stems from their belief that the one Church has been altogether broken apart by the sin of disunity. To receive Holy Communion is a sign of unity already achieved, of the full communion which we still seek. Therefore they believe that Eucharistic hospitality is "papering over the cracks".' (David Sheppard, Anglican Bishop of Liverpool, in With Hope in Our Hearts, Hodder and Stoughton)

Two or seven?

Almost all churches observe the two great sacraments of Baptism and Holy Communion. These are called Dominical Sacraments because they originate directly from commands of Jesus ('Dominical' means 'of the Lord'). All Christians agree that these two are supreme. But the Roman Catholic and Orthodox churches (and some Anglicans) use the word 'sacrament' to refer to five other ceremonies, in addition to baptism and holy communion. The recent Catechism of the Catholic Church (CCC: 1994) explains these very clearly.

Confirmation

In Western churches this is a service of commissioning and full church membership, involving laying on of hands by a bishop. This marks a conscious decision by candidates to follow the Christian way. An important feature is prayer for the strength of the Holy Spirit in the candidates' lives.

'*Confirmation brings an increase and deepening of baptismal grace:*
- *it unites us more firmly to Christ;*
- *it increases the gifts of the Holy Spirit in us;*
- *it renders our bond with the Church more perfect;*
- *it gives us a special strength of the Holy Spirit to spread and defend the faith by word and action as true witnesses of Christ, to confess the name of Christ boldly, and never to be ashamed of the Cross.*' (CCC)

Many Anglicans would agree with this exposition. In the Eastern Orthodox Churches, confirmation is usually administered by a priest, not a bishop, immediately after baptism. This means that even infants are confirmed as well as baptised. They are also given their first holy communion on the same occasion. The service which includes these three sacraments is called *Chrismation*.

Marriage

Christians view marriage (or matrimony) as more than a contract or exchange of promises. It is a vocation and calling, requiring God's grace.

'*The consent by which the spouses mutually give and receive one another is sealed by God himself . . . Authentic married love is caught up into divine love. Thus the marriage bond has been established by God himself. By its very nature it is ordered to the good of the couple, as well as to the generation and education of children . . . The sacrament of Matrimony signifies the union of Christ and the Church. It gives spouses the grace to love each other with the love with which Christ has loved his Church.*'
(CCC)

Ordination

All Christians are called to serve – to exercise 'a ministry.'

'*Christ, high priest and unique mediator, has made of the Church a kingdom, priests for his God and Father'. The whole community of believers is, as such, priestly . . .*' (CCC)

But many churches 'set aside' some men (and sometimes women too) to exercise leadership, to teach the faith and to administer the sacraments.

In Catholic theology, an ordained priesthood has a vital place, especially in relation to the sacraments.

'Through the ordained ministry, especially that of bishops and priests, the presence of Christ as head of the Church is made visible in the midst of the community of believers . . . This priesthood is ministerial. That office . . . which the Lord committed to the pastors of his people, is in the strict sense of the term a service.' (CCC)

Absolution or reconciliation

Absolution involves receiving assurance that God will forgive all who come to him in simple prayer, with penitence and faith. No sin is too bad for God's mercy and forgiveness. Reconciliation involves confession, and this sacrament is sometimes called *penance, conversion, confession* or *forgiveness*. Lutherans have a tradition of absolution as a third Dominical Sacrament (based on John 20:23), though this is sometimes seen as an extension of baptism.

'The movement of return to God, called conversion and repentance, entails sorrow for and abhorrence of sins committed and the firm purpose of sinning no more in the future. Conversion touches the past and the future, and is nourished by hope in God's mercy.' (CCC)

Anointing of the sick

Anointing the sick with oil in the context of prayer and thanksgiving, conveys assurance of God's love and ability to heal. This is based on the New Testament letter of James. (5:14–15) Over the centuries the practice came to be associated with dying and it is sometimes called *extreme unction* or the *last rites*. But health, wholeness and healing have been emphasised since the Second Vatican Council (see page 166). The Anointing of the Sick

'is not a sacrament for those only who are at the point of death. Hence, as soon as any one of the faithful begins to be in danger of death from sickness or old age, the fitting time for him to receive this sacrament has certainly already arrived.' (CCC)

Other traditions

In contrast to the tendency to multiply sacraments, the Salvation Army and Quakers (Society of Friends) have no specific sacraments at all. Rather, Quakers see *all* life as sacramental. On this view, *all* good things – the natural world, laughter, food, love, life itself – speak to us of the love of God. Salvationists view every meal as a sacrament, an opportunity to remember the crucified and risen Lord. This is summed up in the challenging hymn of Albert Orsborn, a member of the Salvation Army:

> My life must be Christ's broken bread,
> My love his outpoured wine,
> A cup o'er filled, a table spread
> Beneath his name and sign . . .

OTHER SIGNS AND SYMBOLS

In addition to the sacraments, Christianity is rich in signs and symbols. Each Gospel has its own symbol: Matthew an angel; Mark a lion; Luke an ox; John an eagle.

Three common visual symbols are:
- Chi-Rho, based on the first two letters of the Greek word for 'Christ' (Christos)

- IHS, a monogram for the name Jesus in Greek

- INRI, taken from the initial letters (in Latin) of 'Jesus of Nazareth, the King of the Jews.' It reminds us that Pontius Pilate ordered this title to be placed on the cross, written in Aramaic, Latin and Greek.

Most famous of all is the ancient fish symbol. As some of the first disciples were fishermen, this is clearly an appropriate sign. But its early, widespread use runs deeper than this. The Greek word for fish is 'Ichthus' and each letter points to a name or title for Jesus.

I	Iesous	*Jesus*	
Ch	Christos	*Christ*	The Chi-Rho
Th	Theou	*Of God*	
U	(H)uios	*Son*	The IHS
S	Soter	*Saviour*	

There are about 50 titles for Jesus in the New Testament and artists have delighted in this rich quarry. Early Christian paintings in the catacombs focus on the Fish and upon Jesus as the Good Shepherd. They were reticent to depict the Cross, which portrayed their Lord and Saviour as a common criminal. Later, of course, the cross became *the* Christian symbol above all others. Nor did the earliest paintings depict Christ in triumph (which later became a popular theme). Rather 'they conceive salvation in the gentle laws of friendship with Christ.' (John McManners)

Moved to tears

Examining the nature of the sacraments by reading about them in a book cannot lead you to the centre of their significance and power. For essentially the sacraments are a *shared experience*. In an attempt to convey this, I will end this chapter on a personal note.

Baptism   One Saturday evening I was invited by a 20-year-old to a Pentecostal Church where he was to be baptised. There were 17 candidates – mainly teenagers, but also one entire family. The Minister stood up to his thighs in water, in the baptistry at the front of the simple church building. Before plunging the candidates under the water, he invited them to say what had led up to that moment of public witness to faith in Christ.

The church was full. We sang and prayed; many smiled and hugged; a few wept. It was a powerful occasion and I was moved by the deep sincerity and contagious faith of the candidates.

I have attended somewhat similar occasions within the Church of England – student baptisms conducted by the chaplain in a college swimming-pool. But more often I have attended baptisms, of adults and babies, in Anglican and other churches, where water has been poured upon heads. Less dramatic, but equally profound.

Eucharist   I confess that I am not always deeply moved at Holy Communion. Sometimes I struggle to maintain concentration; sometimes I am too aware of a cold building, or aching knees! This does not worry me unduly, for I believe that receiving the elements of bread and wine out of simple obedience to the Lord's command, has spiritual value. But I have experienced some wonderfully moving Services.

- I was invited to take part in a Sunday Service of Holy Communion in a prison chapel. It was a high-security prison; almost all the prisoners had committed terrible crimes of violence. As I knelt with those prisoners to receive the bread and the wine, I was keenly aware that I, too, came as a penitent sinner, in need of God's grace and forgiveness.

- I recall another occasion, when I stood with a hundred young people around an altar, with a hundred flickering candles, as we shared deep silence and wonderful singing. And I remember gathering with a group of 40 around a communion table under an oak tree to shade us from the hot sun. During the passing of the peace – an ancient custom, now re-introduced into the eucharist by many churches – people broke ranks and informally hugged and shook hands. I also recall gathering with two others around the bed of a dying woman, and breaking bread and drinking wine in remembrance that Christ had died for each one of us.

- I remember attending Mass in a Roman Catholic monastery, where I was warmly welcomed but not invited to receive the sacrament. I think too, of a Sunday 'Breaking of Bread' Service with the Christian Brethren. About 60 of us sat around a central table on which was placed a huge loaf and unfermented grape juice. There was no appointed leader and different members (men only, unlike the Quakers) read a Bible passage, spoke, or chose a hymn, before the bread was broken and shared.

- I think back to a service with the Russian Orthodox congregation in London. Marvellous singing, no chairs, people coming and going. Some lit a candle, others prostrated themselves, many just stood and watched and listened and prayed. I think back, too, to countless more ordinary services of Holy Communion, where in some indefinable way I have been sustained by receiving bread and wine, by fellowship with other believers, and by the reading and preaching of the Scriptures.

- And I remember too, reading a moving passage about Holy
  Communion in the 19th century, in which Bishop F J Chavasse
  recollected the 'Communion Sundays' of his boyhood: *'My father
  would be extra quiet all day, and shut himself up in his room both
  before and after the service. I have seen him come down from the
  rail with tears in his eyes.'*

Tears are an appropriate response to Holy Communion. Tears of *sadness* – as we recall the coolness of our commitment to Christ, to his Church and to his world; tears of *gratitude* as we reflect upon the cost of our salvation; tears of *joy* as, in fellowship with other believers, we ponder the wonder of God's great love for us, revealed supremely in the death and resurrection of Jesus Christ.

9

FACING DEATH: THE FOUR LAST THINGS

Every religion is concerned with life; every religion is concerned with death. Each religion makes its own distinctive emphasis as its adherents grapple with deep and profound questions raised by our mortality. Traditional Christian theology speaks of *The Four Last Things*: death, judgement, heaven and hell.

Death

The Christian faith sets its face against escapism. Even in the joy of a wedding service, the couple are reminded that the promises they make are 'till death us do part.' This note contrasts sharply with Western culture in general, in which many people are shielded from the harsh reality and supreme mystery of death. Mark Twain, the American humorist, caught the Christian emphasis on realism when he said, 'No-one gets out alive'!

Thomas Hobbes (1588–1679) could say that life is 'solitary, poor, nasty, brutish and short.' In his world, most families knew the sorrow of death, including the death of a child. Relatives would observe the dying process, for most people died at home – and many, including children, would have seen a dead body. Today, most people are not exposed to such experiences, and many do not attend a funeral until their adult years. Further, our life expectancy is much longer. The biblical 'three score years and ten' (itself rather generous in those days) would seem a meagre ration to today's many octogenarians!

Almost all these changes are for the better. But they do push into the background the necessity to consider our own death. This point has been made by many people, not just Christians. The existentialist philosopher Martin Heidegger insisted that we are not authentically human unless and until we have considered our own mortality. This can be seen as morbid, but it need not be so.

In the modern world, many people would prefer a quick death, because it is the *process* of dying which is widely feared. Significantly, Dame Cicely Saunders, a Christian doctor with vast experience of care for the dying (see Chapter 14), speaks of the value of time and space in which to contemplate eternity, and to take practical steps to 'close the book' on this life. This will include saying 'thankyou' and 'sorry' as well as ensuring that a valid and up-to-date Will has been made.

Judgement

In the New Testament we find this terse statement: we are 'destined to die once, and after that to face judgement.' (Hebrews 9:27) The fourth-century Apostles' Creed picks up this theme when it says that Jesus Christ 'will come again to judge the living and the dead.' Alongside its joyful stress on resurrection, the Bible teaches that we are accountable to God. One day we shall be called to account for the way we have used our gifts, our opportunities and our energies. Above all, we shall be required to account for the way we have behaved in relation to the poor, the needy and the marginalised. (Matthew 25:31–46)

But despite the fact of judgement and the call to consider our own mortality, every Christian funeral service includes a strong note of hope – even joy. This does not mean that tears and grief are out of place. Far from it; the bereaved are encouraged to mourn. There is a moving example of this in the New Testament. Following the death of Stephen, the first Christian martyr, we read that 'Godly men buried Stephen and mourned deeply for him.' (Acts 8:2) Their tears were not for Stephen who died with a radiant faith and who was 'on another shore and in a greater light.' (Eric Milner-White) They wept for them-selves. Their spokesman and close friend had been taken from them. They would miss him deeply, and so they grieved.

For Christians, hope and peace in the face of death are not based upon faith in human goodness; they are rooted in the grace of God. The

Bible has a rich doctrine of humanity. It gladly acknowledges our great dignity as creatures fashioned in the image of God – from which we get our ability to reason, reflect, communicate and create. It also focuses on the darker side of human nature: 'all have sinned and fall short of the glory of God.' (Romans 3:23) A popular misconception sees God adding up the good deeds in our lives in one column and the bad deeds and omissions in another. He then subtracts one from the other and our eternal salvation depends upon being 'in credit'. This is a crude description of a not uncommon view.

But the Christian God is not a 'score-card' God. According to the Bible, none of us could achieve heaven if this were the basis of our salvation. But it isn't. What counts is real faith and true repentance for our sins, and the grace and forgiveness of a loving God. The thief who died on the cross next to Jesus gives encouragement to us all. 'Lord, remember me when you come into your kingdom', was his request. Jesus responded with a gracious promise: 'Today you will be with me in paradise.'

Hell

When Jesus taught about hell, he had in mind an actual place – the Valley of Hinnom (Jesus would have used the Aramaic word 'gehinnam' – Greek *Gehenna*; Hebrew *ge Hinnom*), south-west of Jerusalem, where pagan worshippers once sacrificed children to Molech. (Leviticus 18:21) This practice was hated by the prophets, and Jeremiah spoke of it as a place of shame and punishment by God. By the first century BC, Jews were using this valley of shame as a metaphor for the place of everlasting punishment for the wicked.

By the Middle Ages, this notion had become very literal, very picturesque, and very frightening! This can be seen by looking at depictions of hell on stained glass, watching the medieval mystery plays or reading Dante's *Divine Comedy*. Dante's classic text (c1300) portrays hell as nine circles at the centre of the earth. On the gate is the inscription, 'Abandon hope, all ye who enter here.'

Teaching about hell continued down the years. On 8th July, 1741 Jonathan Edwards preached a sermon entitled *Sinners in the hands of an Angry God*, which contains the following passage:

'It would be dreadful to suffer the fierceness and wrath of Almighty God for one moment; but you must suffer it for all eternity. There

will be no end to this exquisite horrible misery . . . You will know that you must wear out long ages, millions of millions of ages, in wrestling and conflicting with this almighty merciless vengeance.'

Jonathan Edwards was not a bloodthirsty monster; he was equally eloquent on the great themes of mercy, forgiveness and divine love. Indeed, his preaching on hell was motivated by love; he had an overwhelming desire to warn, and save, those whom he feared would be lost, without a clear warning. His words would not be unusual in the 18th century, and there are modern preachers who would say much the same thing in much the same way. In general, however, the 20th century has seen a move away from such harsh ideas, which do not square easily with the notion of the love of God, so clearly and frequently spelt out in the New Testament. Various views have been put forward.

- 'Universalists' argue that the love and grace of God must ultimately conquer every human heart. In the end, *all* will be saved.

- Others disagree. Yes, it is clear from the Bible that *'God desires everyone to be saved.'* (1 Timothy 2:4) But God's will can be frustrated by human choice. They point out that of the 12 occurrences of the word 'Gehenna' in the New Testament, 11 are on the lips of Jesus. Jesus was particularly harsh on those who led 'little ones' astray. (Luke 17:2)

- Today's theologians wish to dispense with medieval literalism. They remind us that Jesus was using picture language based upon an actual rubbish dump in the Valley of Hinnom. Hell does not literally involve fire and darkness (which are mutually exclusive!). Those who believe that we cannot reject the concept of hell simply because we do not like it, often speak in terms of 'separation from God', freely chosen.

- The above point has been put with dramatic force. On the Day of Judgement, four words will be spoken: *'Your will be done.'* Addressed by us to God, they assure us of heaven. Spoken by God to us, they have an awful finality. If we insist on enthroning ourselves at the centre of our personal universe, he will allow this to happen. To change the picture: the prison door is open but we must decide to walk out if we are to be free.

- Some theologians speak of 'conditional immortality.' In their view, hell does not involve eternal punishment; it means ceasing to exist.

- Some wish to stress the outrage that we feel in the face of naked evil. Hitler, Stalin and Saddam Hussein caused untold suffering; should they 'get away with it'? And what about less well-known people who spread misery throughout their lives? At the very least, would not extinction be a just outcome – if not actual punishment? Others ask *why* these people behaved as they did. Cruel or indifferent adults may have lacked love in childhood; many child abusers have themselves been abused. Perhaps 'to know all is to forgive all'?

- Taking this line of argument further we might ask, 'Would Hitler be happy in heaven?' Without a massive change of heart, would he not find it intolerable to spend eternity worshipping *Jesus the Jew*? And might not bitter, self-centred people dislike the love and openness which characterise life in heaven? A change of heart is precisely what the gospel requires. Christians call this *repentance*. In giving human beings a measure of real choice, God knowingly places limits on his own power. To over-rule our fundamental freedom of choice is something which God will not do.

- There is no evidence that Hitler repented before he died. Might it be possible for him to repent after his death? The notion of a further opportunity to respond to God's love after death was developed by some Protestant theologians in the 19th century – but resisted by others.

'All sin tends to be addictive, and the terminal point of addiction is damnation. Since God has given us the freedom either to accept his love and obey the laws of our created nature, or to reject it and defy them, he cannot prevent us from going to hell and staying there if that is what we insist upon.' (W H Auden)

Purgatory?

Purgatory is seen as a 'staging post' between this world and heaven, providing further opportunity for sanctification. The idea is found early in the history of the Church. The stress on *torment* in Purgatory was developed in the Middle Ages. With this came the notion of multiple 'masses for the dead' and 'indulgences', from which many were glad to be released at the Reformation (see Chapter 17).

Most Protestants believe that we shall be changed 'in a flash, in the twinkling of an eye.' (1 Corinthians 15:52) At death we pass from time to eternity where everything is *now*. The life of heaven lies just beyond death. Catholics continue to believe in a period of preparation and purification before we enter heaven; but purgatory 'is entirely different from the punishment of the damned.' (*Catholic Catechism* 1994) In traditional Catholic theology, purgatory does not afford a 'second chance' for initial repentance.

In general, Catholics believe in purgatory and Protestants do not. But the lines are not distinct. The Anglican apologist, C S Lewis, wrote an imaginative defence of purgatory in *The Great Divorce*. In this book, Lewis argued that the possibility of hell (seen as separation from God) does not fly in the face of the love of God. Indeed, he argued that our freedom to choose whether to respond to, or reject, God's love, is in itself an indication of that love. The grey world which Lewis represented as hell, relates to the thinking of the Belgian Roman Catholic Scholar Edward Schillebeeckx. He rejects the notion that heaven and hell can in some sense be 'balanced'. Heaven has glorious substance; hell is the terrible absence of all that gives zest to life. Heaven is radiant with glory; hell is dismal and joyless.

C S Lewis reminded us that a consideration of heaven and hell can be a severely practical matter:

> 'It may be possible for each to think too much of his own potential glory hereafter; it is hardly possible for him to think too often or too deeply about that of his neighbour. The load, or weight, or burden of my neighbour's glory should be laid daily on my back, a load so heavy that only humility can carry it, and the backs of the proud will be broken. It is a serious thing to live in a society of possible gods and goddesses, to remember that the dullest and most uninteresting person you can talk to may one day be a creature which, if you saw it now, you would be strongly tempted to worship, or else a horror and a corruption such as you now meet, if at all, only in a nightmare. All day long we are, in some degree, helping each other to one or other of these destinations. It is in the light of these overwhelming possibilities . . . that we should conduct all our dealings with one another, all friendships, all loves, all play, all politics. There are no ordinary people.'
> (From: *The Weight of Glory* in *Screwtape Proposes a Toast* (Collins))

Heaven

The distinctive feature of Christian thought as it faces the brevity of life and the reality and meaning of death, is *resurrection*. Because of his firm belief in this, St Paul claimed to look forward to the world to come, asserting that to die is 'to be with Christ, which is better by far.' (Philippians 1:23) The 20th-century journalist, Malcolm Muggeridge, picked up this theme. He suggested that dying is rather like checking out of a seedy boarding house and being welcomed into a glorious palace, with all expenses paid! In his *Journal*, Pope John XXIII wrote that his bags were packed and he was ready to go.

Christians deny that this is wishful thinking, for the Christian hope is grounded in the love and forgiveness of God, and it is based upon the resurrection of Jesus Christ. Easter celebrates the great fact that Jesus was too good and too great to be held by death. God raised him from the grave.

Some ancient 'nature religions' are alleged to have been centred upon belief in a dying and rising god, for example Osiris (Egypt) and Baal (Canaan). By enacting and reciting their great myths, they sought to ensure that a season of barrenness would once again give way to harvest and fertility. But there is a striking contrast between those religions and the Christian faith. In fertility religions, resurrection operated at a *mythological* level: it was *story* not *history*. Christians believe that in Jesus Christ, the **'myth** became fact'. What 'happened' annually in those nature religions, *actually happened* once for all in Jesus Christ, according to the Bible. The idea became an event – erupting into history and transforming the future. This is the Christian claim and it is for this reason that Easter is the supreme Christian festival.

If true (see Chapter 3), the resurrection of Jesus Christ is clearly a *wonderful* event. From a Christian viewpoint it is also a highly *significant* event. For it was not a question of one man overcoming death for himself. Rather, by raising Jesus from the dead, God defeated death itself. Things would never be the same again. It was a decisive moment for the whole human race.

In the New Testament, Jesus' resurrection is described as the 'first fruits' of a great harvest: *we* are that harvest. To change the image: Jesus threw wide open the gates of glory. John Donne (1571/2–1631), Dean of St Paul's, catches this in his sonnet *Death be not proud*:

> Death be not proud, though some have called thee
> Mighty and dreadful, for, thou art not so . . .
> One short sleep past, we wake eternally,
> And death shall be no more. Death, thou shalt die.

This does not mean that facing death is necessarily easy for Christians. Derek Worlock, Roman Catholic Archbishop of Liverpool, died of lung cancer in 1996. He spoke honestly and movingly about his pain and his faith. *'I remained cold as a stone spiritually and desperately troubled by nightmares.'* He added: *'Our own sufferings and difficulties can seem cruel and pointless unless they are related to the work of salvation. In our hearts we know that properly directed, they can be a way in which we are drawn into the life and purpose of our Saviour. That is never easy for us but it is part of our faith.'* (*With Hope in Our Hearts,* Hodder and Stoughton)

'What a wretched man I am! Who will rescue me from this body of death? Thanks be to God – through Jesus Christ our Lord!' (St Paul: Romans 7:24–25)

'For the first time I examined myself with a seriously practical purpose. And there I found what appalled me; a zoo of lusts, a bedlam of ambitions, a nursery of fears, a harem of fondled hatreds. My name was legion.' (C S Lewis: *Surprised by Joy*)

When the 'book of life' is opened, we may expect to find all those nasty, spiteful and selfish things which we did, said and thought, recorded there in black and white. Even worse perhaps, we might expect to find there all the good things which we failed to do, through indifference or pride or hostility.

To our amazement and joy, the book will contain page after page of blank, white paper. Not because we did nothing wrong, but because our sins have been forgiven. God really does 'forgive and forget.' Because of his love for us, and all that Jesus did for us, our sins will be blotted out.

This great truth can be illustrated by a homely story. A man lost his temper, 'Please forgive me Lord,' he prayed. The following day he lost his temper again. 'Oh Lord, I've done it again,' he wailed in anguish when he cooled down. At that point a voice from heaven asked, 'Done what again?'

'Though your sins are like scarlet, they shall be as white as snow; though they are red as crimson, they shall be like wool'. (Isaiah 1:18 – see also 1 John 1:8–9)

The life of the world to come

What will heaven be like? The Bible speaks of this ultimate mystery in hints, pictures and parables. It *is* a mystery. St Paul reminds us that in this life 'we see but a poor reflection' (1 Corinthians 13:12) and St John admits that 'what we will be has not yet been made known.' (1 John 3:2) But from time to time the Bible pulls back the curtain and we glimpse the glory of heaven.

Heaven will be a place of light, beauty and joy. 'There will be no more death or mourning or crying or pain, for the old order of things has passed away.' (Revelation 21:4) Jesus spoke about a great banquet. Heaven will be a place of friendship and conviviality where Jesus will drink wine with his disciples – his promise given at the Last Supper. All present will be bathed in the light of the presence of God and there will be glorious music sung in worship of 'the Lamb upon the throne.' Alister McGrath points out that *'the New Testament parables of heaven are strongly communal in nature; for example, heaven is portrayed as a banquet, as a wedding feast, or as a city – the new Jerusalem.'*

> *'In heaven we shall know as we are known, perfectly ourselves and perfectly related one to another. It is because heaven is such a participation in the communion of God's love that it is right to believe that we shall see and know those whom we have loved, but we shall see and know them in God . . . (In heaven) human destiny will not be attainment of an eternal and static perfection, but rather an everlasting participation in the exploration of the inexhaustible riches of the divine nature.'* From *The Mystery of Salvation* (A report commissioned by the Church of England: 1995).

The notion of 'reincarnation' is not taught in the Bible. This is the Hindu and Buddhist belief that, after death, some aspect of the self or soul can be reborn in a new body (human or animal). Nor is the popular notion of heaven as a place of 'disembodied spirits' to be found in the New Testament. The Bible is much more *earthy*.

The Old Testament does talk of the human spirit surviving death, but when it does so it usually speaks with dismay. 'Sheol', the shadowy place of departed spirits sometimes referred to in the Psalms, was to be feared, for it was viewed as a twilight world without zest or vitality. The New Testament paints a much richer picture of life beyond death, with its stress on resurrection and glory.

The Christian faith strongly discourages mourners from attempting to 'get in touch' with deceased loved ones. It is understandable that we should wish to attempt to do so, but Christians believe that the Spiritualist route of mediums and séances is a road of heartache. There are strong condemnations of such practices in the Bible. (Leviticus 19; 31; Deuteronmy 18:10–13) Christianity encourages us to commit our loved ones to God and to trust in his faithfulness and enduring love.

As scientist Arthur Peacocke reflects on the puzzle of how we might be resurrected, he draws an analogy from computers. He suggests that 'the pattern in our brains which constitutes the essential you and me' is rather like software. 'We know that software programmes can be embodied in many different kinds of hardware – and yet the software is real enough.'

Historian Gillian Evans considers the modern concern that heaven will be 'beautiful but dull.' She affirms that 'we should be envisaging a freedom from the confinement of time and space which will make it possible for us to be with all our friends at once and individually, to be enjoying an infinite variety of things as we choose, without delay or hurry, crowding or isolation. It is something new, a new quality of life.'

Resurrection of the body

When it talks of the glories of heaven, the Bible does so in terms of *bodily resurrection*, rather than spiritual survival or the 'immortality of the soul.' The Apostles' Creed emphasises this: '*I believe in the resurrection of the body and the life everlasting*.' By 'resurrection', the New Testament writers do not mean mere 'resuscitation.' What is raised will be far more glorious than what is *sown* – just as the butterfly is much freer and more interesting than the chrysalis, and the tulip more beautiful than the bulb. Personal resurrection is to be set within the context of cosmic renewal. 'Behold I make all things new.' There will be 'a new heaven and a new earth.' (Revelation 21:1)

Modern minds addressing this difficult, but fascinating and important subject, find it helpful to focus on the word 'personality'. The teaching of the Bible is that we shall retain our personalities – refined and purified – for all eternity. You will still be recognisably you. We shall be much more interesting and glorious than we are now, but there will be a definite link between you-as-you-are-now and you-as-you-will-be-then.

Every aspect of life and personality which we offered to God during our earthly lives, will be gloriously raised – and handed back to us. Life in the glory of heaven will be full of substance and colour. We shall not lose our identity in an ocean of consciousness. Indeed, it is only *then* that we shall really find and possess our true identity. For the gifts which make us what we are, are *on loan* now. They will be *given* to us then and they will be ours for ever – to be shared in the rich fellowship of heaven.

I implore you, good Jesus, that as in your mercy you have given me to drink in with delight the words of your knowledge, so of your loving kindness you will also grant me one day to come to you, the fountain of all wisdom, and to stand forever before your face. Amen. (*A prayer of the Venerable Bede*)

'Pray for me, and I shall pray for you and all your friends, that we may merrily meet in heaven.' Words from Sir Thomas More's last letter to his daughter, as he awaited execution under Henry VIII.

O Lord, support us all the day long of this troublous life, until the shades lengthen and the evening comes, and the busy world is hushed, the fever of life is over and our work done. Then, Lord, in thy mercy, grant us safe lodging, a holy rest and peace at last; through Jesus Christ, our Lord. Amen. (*A prayer of Cardinal Newman*)

Funeral rites

Because the Christian faith has taken root in so many cultures, each with its own rich traditions, funeral services vary in outward detail, as do weddings and baptisms. In some countries the coffin is left open until the time for burial and the bereaved are encouraged to view the body. In other cultures the body is not seen except sometimes by the close family. In some places the coffin remains in the home until burial; in others it is taken to a church or chapel between death and the funeral service.

For centuries, burial (usually in the ground; sometimes at sea) was the Christian custom, unless there were exceptional circumstances such as the plague – and even then burial was often practised. But the industrial revolution gave rise to large towns and cities, with pressure on space. So the practice of cremation began around 1875 – amid suspicion and criticism. Indeed it was condemned by the Roman Catholic Church until 1963. In its early days, 'free-thinkers' promoted cremation in the hope that the practice would destroy belief in the resurrection of the body. '*It appeared to have no such consequence. In some cases reverence for the human body was more evident in burning than in burial.*' (Owen Chadwick)

Burial and cremation are equally appropriate ways of marking the end of a person's life as the solemn words are pronounced: '*earth to earth, dust to dust, ashes to ashes, in sure and certain hope of resurrection to eternal life through our Lord Jesus Christ.*'

Some funeral services are very simple; others are lengthy and may include a Requiem Mass. Every funeral reminds us of our own mortality – and of the wisdom of fashioning our lives in the light of this awesome fact. Despite differences, the really essential features should be common to all Christian funerals. The dignity which is afforded to the body; the atmosphere of mourning and loss; the sense of Easter joy bursting through; the note of confidence in the love of God and the fact of eternal life.

J G Ballard's autobiographical novel *Empire of the Sun* (Gollancz) was made into an award-winning film. It tells the story of Jim – a boy who survived life in a Japanese prison camp. At one point, he describes how he and two Christian missionaries were burying a dead comrade.

'The women pulled Mr Radik from the cart. Although wearied by the effort, they handled him with the same care they had shown when he was alive. Was he still alive for these two Christian widows? Jim had always been impressed by strong religious beliefs. His mother and father were agnostics, and he respected devout Christians in the same way that he respected people who were members of the Graf Zeppelin Club or shopped at the Chinese department stores, for their mastery of an exotic foreign ritual. Besides, those who worked hardest for others, like Mrs Philips and Mrs Gilmour and Dr Ransome, often held beliefs that turned out to be correct.'

10

CHRISTIAN FAITH IN A SCIENTIFIC AGE

As science has grown in stature, so religion in Europe (the cradle of modern science) has become less central to many people's lives. There is a likely connection between the two facts. Christianity gives an explanation for the existence of the world which focuses on *purpose*: it affirms that the universe was created and is sustained by the will of a loving God. Science also gives an explanation: a different kind of explanation which excludes purpose and focuses on *cause and effect*. It is sometimes supposed that these explanations are mutually exclusive. If so, if they really *are* in competition, there is no real contest. It's Game, Set and Match to science!

A recent survey taken among British teenagers revealed that a large number believe that science has disproved religion. Clearly, if they are correct, then Christian believers have no credibility in the modern world. A book entitled *Teach Yourself Christianity* will be read only by those interested in lost causes! Before conceding this however, we need to examine some significant facts.

— The origins of modern science —

In a remarkable statement, the philosopher John MacMurray asserted that 'science is the legitimate child of a great religious movement, and its genealogy goes back to Jesus.' This is not to deny other important influences: Greek, Chinese, Egyptian, Arabian mathematics, the Old Testament (with its Wisdom literature and Creation narratives) . . .

But it is to affirm the importance for the rise of science, of a wide-spread and particular way of looking at the universe, which Christianity gave to the Western world. Others have made the same point. For example, the philosopher A N Whitehead and the historian Herbert Butterfield both affirmed that science is a child of Christian thought.

As already indicated, some ancient civilisations were deeply interested in mathematical and scientific questions. There were important advances. But in the event it was *Christian* civilisation which, following the Renaissance in Europe (see Chapters 17 and 18), brought scientific thought to birth. Dr Peter Hodgson, Lecturer in Nuclear Physics at Oxford University, put it this way: *'Christianity provided just those beliefs that are essential for science, and the whole moral climate that encourages its growth.'*

On this view, modern science could only 'take off' when certain factors were present. An eagerness to ask questions and a willingness to doubt received wisdom, were crucial. So was a wide range of accepted beliefs about the nature of the universe. Central among these were the belief that:

- the material world is good, because it is created by God
- the same physical laws apply throughout the universe
- time moves forward rather than round in circles (Einstein gave us the concept of the curvature of space-time, but this does not undermine the biblical view that history is shot through with purpose.)
- there is order in the world because God is One and God is rational and loving

These views are expounded in the Bible. In contrast, some religions teach that matter is evil: or that we should be detached from the world; or that different gods rule different aspects of life; or that time goes round in endless cycles; or (in ancient Greek thought) that there is a given pattern to which the 'demi-urge' creator had to conform.

So it comes as no surprise to learn that the prestigious *Royal Society* (founded by a gathering of leading British scientists in the 17th century) is dedicated 'to the Glory of God the Creator, and the benefit of the human race.' Two centuries later the British Association for the Advancement of Science held its first meeting in York. Those who gathered at that meeting in 1831 paid tribute to the Church, 'without whose aid the Association would never have been founded.' They went on to declare that 'true religion and true science ever lead to the same great end.' The Association's first two presidents were clergymen.

Several famous early scientists were devout Christians, some of whom wrote theological books as well as scientific works. Among many others we note: Isaac Newton (1642–1727), who has been called the greatest scientist of all time, Robert Boyle (of Boyle's Law: 1627–91), Michael Faraday (1791–1867) who harnessed electro-magnetism, and Gregor Mendel (1822–84) who laid the groundwork for modern genetics while Abbot of a monastery. James Young Simpson (1811–70) was the first surgeon to employ the anaesthetic properties of chloroform. When asked to name his greatest discovery, his reported reply was, 'It is not chloroform. My greatest discovery has been to know that I am a sinner and that I could be saved by the grace of God.'

The present day

Professor Arnold Wolfendale, when appointed Astronomer Royal in 1991, declared, *'I think the hand of God can be seen everywhere.'* This is not an isolated viewpoint, for many professional scientists believe in God and a number are convinced Christians. The Research Scientists' Christian Fellowship in Britain has some 700 members; its American counterpart has about 2000.

In Britain there is a flourishing Society for Ordained Scientists and Cambridge University has recently established a lectureship to explore the interface between science and religion. Somewhat similar initiatives have been taken in the USA – at Berkeley, California and in Chicago. Many believing scientists – for example, Ian Barbour, Arthur Peacocke, John Polkinghorne and Russell Stannard – have written about the relationship between Christianity and science. (Paul Davies writes from a less orthodox viewpoint.)

Of course, none of this proves that Christianity is true. What it does show is that Christianity and science are not opposed; that they can be held together with integrity. If two teams really are in competition, no key player can be on both sides at the same time. And because scientists are intelligent people, this significant number of scientific Christians also suggests that Christianity is not just a fairy story, suitable only for those who are unable to think for themselves.

The seeds of conflict

If all this is true, why has the view that science has disproved religion become so widespread? We shall consider five reasons.

1 The notion of *purpose* lies outside scientific endeavour, by definition and choice (ie it is a deliberately 'self-limiting' activity). So science as an enterprise excludes the concept of God. Early on, the notion that God was necessary to fill the gaps in scientific knowledge was rightly seen to be false. In principle (much harder in practice), it was claimed that everything could be explained in terms of cause and effect. It was a short step from this to the conclusion that, because concepts like 'God' and 'purpose' are outside the scope of science, they are unimportant or non-existent or anti-science. While many of the *founders* of modern science were convinced believers, some of the later *popularisers* of science were militant atheists or agnostics. They spread their views with missionary zeal.

2 A second factor was *the Galileo debate*. **Galilei Galileo** (1564–1642) remained a Catholic throughout his life, but his bad treatment at the hands of church officials is well known. Galileo built on the work of Copernicus (who was a canon in the church) in suggesting that the earth is not at the centre of the universe – an idea which was resisted by the Church leadership of his day.

At stake was scientific method itself. Observation, followed by hypothesis and experimentation, could not be contained within limits already laid down by religious authority. Although it is over 300 years old, memories of the Galileo dispute live on. It reinforces the popular view that religion is anti-science and that science is a threat to religion.

3 A third factor was the controversy over **Charles Darwin**'s research. His *Origin of Species by Means of Natural Selection* (1859) gave a very different account of the origins of life from that given in the Bible. At a famous debate in 1861 (not with Darwin himself but with T H Huxley), the Bishop of Oxford suggested that it was 'either–or' (*either* Darwin was right *or* the Genesis account of Creation in the Bible was right). Battle lines were drawn up.

Some Christians were unhappy with the Bishop of Oxford's debating stance (although it should be noted that careful research has shown that the Bishop was, and still is, inaccurately reported. He was more subtle than is commonly supposed). They looked again at the Bible and came to the conclusion that the beautiful poetic language of Genesis is just that: *beautiful poetic language, written in a pre-scientific age*. This does not mean that it is unimportant; it *does* mean that it is not a scientific treatise.

Genesis describes and explains the human situation in a most profound way. The glory and the tragedy are both there. It raises deep questions about our relationship with God, with nature, and with one another. The rest of the Bible shows the solution to these vital questions being worked out in the lives of individuals and nations. Such literature is quite different from a scientific treatise on the origins of the universe – but no less important.

Charles Darwin himself was not an opponent of Christianity. It is true that he gradually lost his faith (partly through the death of his young daughter). But in 1872 (13 years after the *Origin of Species*) he gladly accepted honorary membership of the Anglican *South American Missionary Society*, because he was so impressed with their work. In reply to their invitation, he wrote, '*I shall feel proud if your committee think fit to elect me an honorary member of your society.*'

4 A fourth factor relates to the above. Some modern fundamentalist Christians are keen to keep the Darwinian controversy alive. They assert that evolution is a discredited theory and that the chapters on Creation in *Genesis* should be read literally (see page 183).

5 A fifth factor arises from the work of **Sigmund Freud** (1856–1939), who has made an immense impact upon the way we view the world. Freud has given us a new vocabulary (unconscious, ego, id, superego, Oedipus complex, Freudian slip) and a new understanding of ourselves. Freud maintained that he was making a *scientific* analysis of human behaviour – a view contested by some.

He wrote about religion and asserted that a key Christian insight should be inverted. God has not made us in his image; rather, we have made God in our image – according to our deepest needs (see **wish-fulfilment** in Glossary).

Carl Gustav Jung, another of the founders of modern psychology, was much more sympathetic to religion. He made the following remarkable statement: *'During the past 30 years people from all the civilised countries of the earth have consulted me . . . Among my patients in the second half of life – that is to say over 35 – there has not been one whose problem in the last resort was not that of finding a religious outlook on life.'*

But Freud's views are firmly established in popular thought. His insights have been modified and criticised by psychologists and philosophers, but he raises enormous challenges for religious believers. Together with Darwin and Marx (in their very different ways), he gave considerable impetus to a secular way of viewing the world, in which religion is marginalised.

6 Finally we note the hostility or indifference towards religion of some articulate present-day exponents of science. As we have seen, many scientists are practising Christians. But some non-Christian scientists have captured the popular imagination – Richard Dawkins of *The Selfish Gene* and Steve Jones who gave the prestigious BBC *Reith Lectures* in 1991, for example. To some they appear to be speaking 'on behalf of' science, rather than as private individuals whose views on religion are opposed by many of their fellow scientists. Most famous of all modern scientists is cosmologist Stephen Hawking, whose *A Brief History of Time* leaves the door firmly open to the *possibility* of God, in a teasing conclusion.

Resolving the tension: 'complementarity'

'Reductionism' refers to the process of 'reducing' complex areas of life to a simple one-level explanation. Notable among such explanations is Professor C E M Joad's description of human beings.

'Man is nothing but:
- FAT enough for seven bars of soap
- LIME enough to whitewash one chicken coop
- PHOSPHORUS enough to tip 2200 matches
- IRON enough for one medium-sized nail
- MAGNESIUM enough for one dose of salts
- POTASH enough to explode one toy crane
- SUGAR enough for seven cups of tea
- SULPHUR enough to rid one dog of fleas'

In this tongue-in-cheek description, Professor Joad (who came to embrace the Christian faith in later life), provides a classic example of *reductionism.* The flaw is in the phrase 'nothing but.' His description gives a perfectly legitimate description of a human being. But it is not complete; other levels of description are required.

We need to add *psychological* categories, for human beings have emotions and ideas. We might wish to add *sociological* categories: human beings function in communities. And these descriptions do not rule out the possibility of *spiritual* categories: human beings experience love and have an instinct for worship. These various levels of description are 'complementary': each adds to the others and together they give a fuller and more accurate account.

This approach applies to everything. Music *is* vibrations in the air and ink dots on paper (even cat-gut or steel on horse hair, if we are listening to a cello). But it is not *just* these things. Ask the audience! And we are bound to ask how it is that music and art have the power to inspire and disturb us. The same approach is true when we consider the universe itself. We might describe it in terms of its origins in 'the big bang' some 15,000 million years ago. But this explanation, which uses the categories of modern physics, does not rule out the possibility of explaining the universe as the creation of a God of love.

Why does the earth support life? An answer in *scientific terms* will discuss factors like the importance of carbon, the immensity of space, the size of the earth (just right to support an atmosphere) and the theory of evolution. But it is equally possible to give an explanation in *theological terms* – by maintaining that God designed the earth so that these factors apply. If this is the case, then scientists are discovering the way in which God has designed the world – 'thinking God's thoughts after him' as the early astronomer Johannes Kepler put it. Science itself can help us to see the grandeur of God.

Of course, this theological explanation may be untrue. But not *because of* the fact that we can also give a scientific explanation. And it remains true that the lack of an explanation in terms of God might be seriously misleading.

> *'It is the contention of the Christian that, in order to do full justice to the totality of his experience, he finds it necessary to see and interpret the over-all pattern of his experience not only in bio-chemical, physiological or psychological terms, but also in religious terms.'* (Malcolm Jeeves, former Professor of Psychology at St Andrew's and Adelaide Universities.)

Resolving the tension: facts and faith

In a recent radio discussion, a member of the panel asserted that science is about facts, and religion is about faith. Now of course all religions involve faith. But they include facts too. This is certainly true of Christianity which, like science, is based on *interpreted facts*. One fact is the Bible's account of Jesus of Nazareth which, as C S Lewis put it, is very difficult to explain in other than Christian terms. Another fact is the rise of the Christian movement in apparently impossible circumstances (with a shrinking number of demoralised disciples and an executed leader). And so we could go on. There are plenty of facts; and faith arises from these.

Conversely, there is plenty of *faith* in science. Scientific method can be described as observation, hypothesis and experimentation, leading to inference and theory. But it can equally well be described in terms of hunch, intuition, gamble, accident, teamwork, flashes of insight, patient slog, with plenty of faith mixed in; and numerous conversations over coffee and beer! Both sets of factors are present all the time. The great Albert Einstein asserted that *'God does not play dice.'* And his statement of faith, that there is a constancy and reality about nature, is fundamental to the scientific enterprise.

'Science and religion both seek to understand ourselves and our place in the cosmos, albeit by rather different means. I suspect that very frequently the apparent differences between science and religious faith are of scale, rather than of kind. So, for example, although it is sometimes said that religion is a matter of faith, whilst science deals with facts, I would urge that there is generally some experience, some matter of fact, that undergirds religious faith and that some element of belief must underlie scientific statements too.' (Dr Michael Fuller, writing in *The Church of England Newspaper*)

—————————— Humility ——————————

Strictly speaking, there is no such thing as Science. Rather, there are lots of human beings tackling a whole series of interesting puzzles and important questions. Despite their enormously impressive achievement, most modern scientists have a greater humility than many of their predecessors. They do not believe that nature is a book simply waiting to be read. They acknowledge mystery and they stand in awe at the inexhaustible riches within nature which they have only begun to glimpse. The awe-inspiring universe in which we live is both beautiful and terrifying – and full of surprises.

Despite astonishing progress, modern scientists realise their own practical limitations. 'Chaos theory' (an exciting but misleading name for a vital insight) suggests that science will never be able to deliver an accurate long-term weather forecast!

Humility is linked with *wonder*. Science may exclude widespread human experiences of goodness, beauty and obligation – *'But the experience of wonder at the structure of the world is an authentic part of the scientist's experience quite as important and fundamental as anything that can be measured in a laboratory or seen through a telescope.'* (John Polkinghorne) The distinguished theoretical physicist Vicky Weisskopf wrote a book entitled *Knowledge and Wonder* on this great theme.

This journey into humility has already been made by Christians. The days when theology was 'Queen of the Sciences' and every facet of life came within an overarching system of Christian belief and explanation, have long gone. But Christians claim to have some insights into the nature and ways of God – who is both Creator and Redeemer – not because we are clever but because God is gracious. He has revealed himself in Jesus Christ; we glimpse his glory and recognise that he is 'full of grace and truth'. (John 1:14) But many questions remain: 'Now we see but a poor reflection'. (1 Corinthians 13:12)

Faith involves living with questions which we cannot answer. But this is not 'blind faith.' We live with these questions in the light of some great answers which we *do* possess. To the questions, 'Does life have meaning?' and 'Is it all heading somewhere?' Jesus is God's resounding 'Yes!'.

Design?

Many people are impressed by the beauty and order in our universe, observing that many factors are 'just right' to sustain life on earth. Some of these are built into the fabric of the universe; others are 'local happy accidents.'

- Our sun has been burning steadily for billions of years, thus providing energy for the evolution of the earth.

- The unique properties of water as it nears its freezing point – it expands as it cools – means that lakes freeze top down, not bottom up. This is vital to marine life, but bad for water pipes on freezing nights!

- If our moon were bigger, we would suffer massive tidal waves caused by its gravitational pull.

- Without the massive planet Jupiter in our solar system, we might well be bombarded by large meteors. (Jupiter's gravitational pull acts as a kind of life-saving 'magnet'.)

Factors like these, together with the beauty and rich variety in our world, convince many people that our universe has a Designer. Also significant is the fact that mathematics 'matches' reality. Equations on paper (human constructs) enable us to produce sophisticated technology in the 'real world.'

One enduring test of a scientific theory has proved to be whether it is 'elegant' or 'beautiful'. To some scientists all this is highly significant. A rational world suggests a rational God. A world with beautiful mathematics suggests a caring God. Others are less sure. They point to the chaos and destruction which also mark our universe.

Recently, discussion has been focused on the *anthropic principle*. This comes from the Greek word *anthropos* (= *man*) and draws attention to the fact that our world is a good 'home' for life in general and especially for human beings. The odds against this are very high. Three writers spell this out for us:

> 'The anthropic principle is the most intriguing new scientific idea of the last decade . . . It is a massive piece of circumstantial evidence pointing to meaning and purpose in the universe . . . The precise values of the speed of light, Planck's Constant, the mass of protons compared with neutrons, the total quantity of hydrogen and helium – all apparently unconnected conditions which have controlled every detail of the universe's development – seem to have been exactly programmed at or just after the first moment of time, and all to one end: humanity. Any deviation (and the odds on such deviations were tremendous) would have made the development of the universe as you know it, life included, impos-

sible. . . . If in the course of an experiment a scientist produced a result against odds this large, he certainly would not dismiss it as an accident. He would look for a cause.' (Clifford Longley in *The Times*)

'Scientists have discovered that the laws of nature have to be 'finely-tuned' to allow the possibility for life to develop. If the power of gravity, or the charge on the electron, or the nature of nuclear forces, were even a little different from what they actually are, no life could have come into being . . . Life is not possible is 'any old world'; it requires a universe in a trillion.' (John Polkinghorne: Former Cambridge Professor of Mathematical Physics)

'The more I examine the universe and the details of its architecture, the more evidence I find that the universe in some sense must have known that we were coming.' (The distinguished theoretical physicist Freeman Dyson)

Ethical dilemmas

Science has given the world many blessings. Most of us would not wish to live in a world without anaesthetics, without television and without toothpaste. But science has presented us with enormous problems too. The possible destruction of our planet, whether by nuclear explosion or global warming, is not just the stuff of science fiction. Some commentators are very pessimistic. David Bosch wrote:

'It is becoming increasingly evident that the modern gods of the West – science, technology and industrialisation – have lost their magic. Events of world history have shaken Western civilisation to the core . . . we are heading for an ecological disaster on a cosmic scale . . . progress was, in effect, a false god.'

Medical science too, presents us with great problems as well as numerous blessings. To take just one example: we now have the ability to discern early in pregnancy whether a baby is likely to have certain grave health problems and whether it will be male or female. This means that we also have the ability to decide which babies will actually be born. With such knowledge comes a threat to the gender balance.

Numerous new ethical and practical decisions press in upon us at the dawn of the 21st century. Scientists themselves do not wish to carry the burden of decision-making. This is a task for us all. It is a task which Christians, together with many others, take very seriously (see Chapter 14). We believe that prayer and a study of the wisdom to be found in previous generations – especially in the ancient Scriptures – have a practical part to play in seeking to ensure that science enriches, and does not destroy, life on planet earth. In particular, the biblical teaching that we have been given stewardship of our world by God, is a vital insight. The universe is not a treasure-trove to be ransacked; it is a delicate network to be respected, cherished and left in good order for future generations.

> 'It is indeed a sobering thought that the early writings of the Jewish people (ie our Old Testament) encompass all the basic recommendations of world conservation strategy.' (Professor David Bellamy)

Natural allies?

The above quotation from David Bellemy suggests that some scientists view religious faith and scientific endeavour as natural allies, perhaps essential allies. Some of the following statements reveal that this attitude has been, and is, held by some extremely important scientists.

> 'Science without religion is lame, religion without science is blind.' (Albert Einstein, who revolutionised modern physics with his Theory of Relativity)

> 'Religion and natural science are fighting a joint battle in an incessant never relaxing crusade against scepticism and against dogmatism, against disbelief and against superstition, and the rallying cry in this crusade has always been, and always will be: "On to God".' (Max Planck, awarded the Nobel Prize for his work on Quantum Theory)

> 'Science brings man nearer to God.' (Louis Pasteur, who revolutionised microbiology and gave his name to pasteurised milk)

> 'Historically, religion came first and science grew out of religion. Science has never superseded religion, and it is my expectation that it never will supersede it.' (Arnold Toynbee, historian)

'There is evolution, and indeterminacy, and generosity, and chance. There is risk and beauty and joy. Gambling on the God who has so gambled on us does not seem so risky in the end.' (Sara Maitland, novelist)

11

SAINTS, MARTYRS, SINS AND VIRTUES

Before his terrible death by crucifixion, Jesus warned his followers that some of them would die in his service. His grim prophecy has been grimly fulfilled. Throughout the centuries many men, women and children have given their lives because of their allegiance to Christ. This is not confined to the past (see BOX). And, of course, adherents of other faiths have shared in this carnage.

---

40 MILLION MARTYRS

Dr David Barrett has undertaken detailed research into the extent of martyrdom in Christian history up the present day. He calculates that 40 million Christians have been killed for their faith in 220 countries across 20 centuries. He adds, 'the effect of Christian martyrdom on evangelisation over the centuries has been profound.' The 19th and 20th centuries have seen more mass martyrdoms of 100,000 or more than all previous centuries put together. 'Martyrs are not just a handful of special saints and heroes, they are 500 ordinary Christians being murdered *every day* for their witness.' (David Barrett)

The first Christian martyr

The Greek word for martyr simply means 'witness'; it soon came to be associated with 'witness unto death.' The first Christian martyr was

Stephen, a deacon of the church in Jerusalem. A Jew who was well versed in the Scriptures, Stephen reflected on the significance of Jesus. He came to realise that by fulfilling the old prophecies, Jesus had made redundant some of the key institutions of the Jewish nation. His outspoken views were seen as an attack upon *the law* and *the temple* and he was stoned to death.

As Stephen died he saw a vision of Jesus, 'the Son of Man', standing to receive him into heaven. (Acts 7:56) Like his Master, he prayed that God would forgive his executioners. Shortly after this, James, the brother of the apostle John and an important leader in the Jerusalem church, was beheaded by King Herod. The blood had started to flow. It was that blood which became, as Tertullian (c 160–220) put it, 'the seed of the Church.'

Enter Nero

The Roman Emperor Nero (AD 37–68) accused Christians of putting Rome to the torch in AD 64. Many wild rumours circulated about this new sect. For example, the Christians were accused of cannibalism, because they ate the body of Christ! All this was very convenient for a leader looking for a scapegoat. Paul and Peter were almost certainly martyred under Nero. Many other believers died too, some as human torches.

After that, many Roman Emperors persecuted Christians, who – with captives, slaves and other despised minorities – provided sport for the masses in arenas in various cities throughout the Roman empire. There are several passages in the New Testament which illustrate how the early Church leaders encouraged Christians to cope with persecution. They were exhorted to live humble, simple lives – for love and integrity were their only weapons. In the long term such weapons proved to be extremely powerful and many came to embrace Christianity, including the Roman Emperor Constantine (d337).

A problem arose concerning the desire for martyrdom. Some members of the Church coveted 'the martyr's crown' and felt that an early death was a small price to pay. This attitude was always opposed by the Church at large. Martyrdom might be 'given'; it was not to be sought.

'Dear friends, do not be surprised at the painful trial you are suffering, as though something strange were happening to you.

But rejoice that you participate in the sufferings of Christ, so that you may be overjoyed when his glory is revealed.' (1 Peter 4:12, 13)

In AD 156, old Bishop Polycarp of Smyrna was placed in a Roman arena. He was challenged to deny Jesus Christ and embrace the pagan gods. He declared, 'For 86 years I have been his servant and he has never done me any wrong. How then can I blaspheme my King who saved me?' He was burnt to death.

Relics and shrines

The public veneration of martyrs has been practised since the second century; Bishop Polycarp is the first clear example of such veneration. The practice developed in local communities, usually around the martyr's tomb. It was based on:

- The long-standing Jewish practice of venerating the memory of patriarchs, prophets and martyrs by building monuments over the places where their bones lay.

- The belief that Christian martyrs were in heaven, and therefore able to pray for those who invoked their help.

The veneration of saints soon involved 'holy relics'. Tombs contained bones; and bones were visible, and moveable. The bones of Polycarp were considered 'more precious than jewels of great price.' Thus the cult of any individual saint could be moved from one place to another. This practice 'opened European routes to sacred travel, sacred commerce, and eventually, sacred theft' (Robert Markus). And, we might add, sacred fraud.

The relics of a saint were regarded as a source of healing and an agent which gave protection to the church which possessed them. Bones, commerce, superstition and local prestige made a powerful, and corrupting, combination. This is not to say that expressing reverence for saints and martyrs was wholly bad. No doubt many believers were encouraged in their discipleship of Christ, by pondering the deeds of those who had gone before. But concern about malpractice emerged early. In the fourth century, Augustine of Hippo stressed the immense difference between devotion directed to martyrs and worship offered to God. He wrote, *'We build temples to our martyrs, not like temples for the gods, but as tombs of mortal men, whose spirits live with God.'*

————— # The early saints —————

It was natural that stories of heroic deeds, courageous deaths and godly lives should be treasured and passed on. Indeed, this process had already begun in the New Testament (Hebrews 11, 12). From this grew a desire to honour such men and women with official recognition – rather as we award medals today. In this wish we find the seeds of *canonisation*, by which certain individuals are honoured with the official title *Saint*.

The choice of that particular word was confusing, for it already had a different, though related, meaning. Several of the New Testament letters are addressed to 'the saints', a term which means 'dedicated to God for holiness.' It is a common New Testament term for *all* believers, much as we use the word 'Christian' today. To pick out a few particularly distinguished believers as 'saints' led to ambiguity.

The popular gospel song, 'O when the saints go marching in', gives the word its biblical meaning. 'I want to be in that number' runs the lyric. This is not a desire to be a special 'super Christian'; rather it expresses a devout wish to be included in the festival of heaven with *all* of God's people. As one writer put it: 'the Church canonises a few believers; the Bible canonises all'!

The New Testament understanding is caught in the Christian Festival entitled *All Saints' Day* (1st November). In the modern Church this is often taken as a celebration of *all* Christian lives – well-known and unknown, ancient and modern. This great festival enshrines another important emphasis – the *Communion of Saints*. This belief unites *all* believers – past, present and future – in the family of God.

Praying through the saints

The Christian centuries have seen many faithful lives and heroic deaths; it is challenging and inspiring for modern Christians to reflect upon these. For this reason, the Christian calendar commemorates individual saints on particular days. The first disciples of Jesus are given special honour, but many others are included too.

Some ancient saints have a dubious background. St Olave was not a godly woman but a fierce Norse king! St George, patron saint of England (also of Istanbul and the Italian cavalry!), fares slightly better. George, probably a soldier, certainly died as a martyr around 303. But little else is known of him and the story of the dragon is a late arrival on the scene. Alas, St Valentine's route to fame is also shrouded in uncertainty.

One controversial question is whether Christians should pray through – and even *to* – the saints. Some Christians do, feeling their near presence.

They point out that it is natural to ask living Christians to pray for us; so why not ask saints of old, who lived holy lives, who died in the faith of Christ, and who are in heaven? Others believe that there is a danger in praying through, or to, the saints, who were sinners like us. In their view this obscures the uniqueness of Jesus, who prays for us (Romans 8:34; Hebrews 7:25) and through whom – and to whom – we pray.

Mary, the Mother of Jesus

A special place is accorded to Mary, the Mother of Jesus, by all Christians but especially by Roman Catholics. Great devotion has been offered to her, countless statues made in her honour and thousands of paintings perpetuate her memory. *The Annunciation*, the occasion when the angel Gabriel announced to Mary that she would bear a son (Luke 1:26–38), is a scene depicted on countless canvasses, some of them very famous (and priceless!).

At some periods of history (and in some places today) her prayers have been thought to be so effective that she has been called the 'lawyer of sinners.' Other titles given to Mary over the centuries are Mother of God ('Theotokos'), Queen of Heaven, Mother of Humanity, Mother of Angels, even Co-redeemer with Christ. It should be added that popular titles and devotion sometimes go further than official teaching, requiring this correction: *'This very special devotion* (to

Mary) . . .*differs essentially from the adoration which is given to the incarnate Word and equally to the Father and the Holy Spirit.'* (*Catechism of the Catholic Church*)

Other beliefs which have developed over the centuries are the *Immaculate Conception* of Mary (not to be confused with the virginal conception of Jesus – more commonly known as the **Virgin Birth**), her *perpetual virginity* and her *Assumption (body and soul) into Heaven*. The latter was not officially promulgated until 1950, by Pope Pius XII. A Bull (official statement) from the Vatican in 1854 defined Immaculate Conception as the belief that, 'From the first moment of her conception the Blessed Virgin Mary was . . . kept free from all stain of original sin.' (see 1994 *Catechism* for fuller details)

These are official doctrines within the Roman Catholic Church, but many Protestants object on three grounds. First, there is no historical evidence for these views. Second, they do a disservice to Mary who is special enough without these false elaborations (as they regard them). Third, they draw attention away from Jesus who is the only and unique Saviour. Protestants argue that what is truly inspiring about Mary is:

- her humility and reticence to believe that she could be honoured by the visit of an angel and the birth of such a special child
- her obedience and willingness to serve God (Luke 1:38)
- her grasp of God's priorities – his 'bias to the poor'. In the *Magnificat* (Luke 1:46) Mary declares, '. . . he has scattered those who are proud . . . but has lifted up the humble'
- her loyalty to Jesus, seen not only at the wedding in Cana (John 2:5) but by her attendance at his death. We learn that to be chosen by God carries sorrow and pain, as well as joy and privilege.

The Oxford Dictionary of Saints gives a balanced assessment when it says:

> 'In both East and West Mary is accounted pre-eminent among all the saints. The unique privilege of being the mother of one who was, according to Christian belief, both God and Man is at the heart of the special honour paid to Mary, described by Aquinas as "hyperdulia", ie a veneration which exceeds that paid to other saints, but is at the same time infinitely below the adoration (latria) due to God alone, which it would be blasphemous to attribute to any creature.'

Thomas Becket, Archbishop of Canterbury from 1162–1170, opposed King Henry II. He was exiled to France but returned to Canterbury in 1170. Thomas was murdered in Canterbury Cathedral by knights from the Royal Court, although the King protested his innocence. The episode caused a sensation throughout Europe, and churches from Iceland to Sicily were dedicated to *Saint Thomas*. (He was canonised in 1173.) 703 miracles were reported at his tomb within ten years.

Reformation martyrs

The 16th century saw an enormous upheaval in Europe (see Chapter 17). Medieval unity, already creaking, was cracked apart and the Church was divided. Controversy was often bitter and it produced martyrs on both sides. Among Protestants who died were Thomas Cranmer (1489–1556) and William Tyndale (1494–1536) – both of whom helped to shape the English language.

Thomas Cranmer was a quiet, scholarly man and a liturgical genius who wrote *The Book of Common Prayer* (slightly amended in its final version in 1662). He was elevated to Archbishop by Henry VIII and lived during three turbulent reigns. He piloted the Reformation throughout the reign of the young Edward VI but was denounced as a heretic under the Catholic Queen Mary. Cranmer hesitated but eventually signed a recantation – an action which did not save him. As he was burning at the stake, he thrust the hand that had signed the recantation into the flames.

William Tyndale was appalled at the ignorance of many clergy and set himself the task of making the Bible available to ordinary people. The English Bible had been banned since 1408 but Tyndale translated Hebrew and Greek texts into English. Though banned, his translation had enormous influence upon the King James or 'Authorised' Version (1611), which became *the* standard English Bible for more than 300 years.

He completed the New Testament and substantial sections of the Old Testament before he was betrayed and arrested near Brussels in 1535.

English Church leaders feared his Protestant ideas and a year later he was strangled and burnt at the stake. Tyndale died with a prayer on his lips 'Lord, open the King of England's eyes.' His prayer was answered. In 1538, Henry VIII – for reasons rather different from Tyndale's – ordered that an English Bible should be placed in every parish church.

Many devout Catholics were equally courageous during those turbulent years. Two such were Edmund Campion and Margaret Clitherow.

Edmund Campion (1540–81) was a Roman Catholic priest (a Jesuit: see Chapter 17) who worked hard in Protestant Britain to sustain the faith of his fellow Catholics. He was betrayed, tortured and condemned to death. When sentence was declared he sang the *Te Deum* ('We praise thee, O God . . .'). Edmund was visited in his cell by the man who betrayed him. His own life was in danger and he needed Father Edmund's help. Campion wrote a letter of introduction to a nobleman in Germany. His betrayer escaped; Edmund Campion was dragged through the streets to Tyburn where he was hanged and quartered.

Margaret Clitherow (1556–86), a butcher's wife, was described by her contemporaries as good-looking, witty, merry and caring. She was a devout Roman Catholic who lived in the ancient city of York. Accused of harbouring priests, she was brought to trial. Margaret refused to defend herself in court because in this way she could save her children from being forced to testify against her. She was crushed to death under immense weights. Her hand – a holy relic – is held in the Bar Convent just outside the city walls of York. Edmund Campion and Margaret Clitherow were canonised by the Roman Catholic Church in 1960.

Modern saints

The practice of *canonisation* – the declaration by the Pope that the Church shall recognise an individual as an official saint – continues within the Roman Catholic Church. A more informal procedure for declaring 'saints' operates within the Eastern Orthodox Churches. In modern times strict criteria are applied by the Vatican – no Norse king need apply!

One of the most recent saints to be canonised was a Polish Roman Catholic Franciscan Priest called Maximilian Kolbe. Maximilian was arrested by the Nazis during the Second World War. In the infamous concentration camp of Auschwitz, his dignity and faith sustained many of his fellow sufferers. Because of an attempted escape, several prisoners were condemned to death by starvation. One victim, a sergeant called Francis Gajowniczek, was very distressed. He had a wife and children, so Maximilian volunteered to change places.

The guard agreed to this grisly act of barter. The married man was spared; the rest were locked away in Cell 18 without food. Two weeks later all were dead except four men. Only Maximilian was fully conscious, and on 14th August 1941 he was given phenol poison. He was 47. On 14th August 1982 Maximilian was declared an official saint by the Polish Pope John Paul II. This was a moving occasion attended by Francis Gajowinczek, the person whom Father Kolbe had saved.

Heroes but not always 'Saints'

Maximilian Kolbe's story reminds us of the tens of thousands of men and women who, in the 20th century, have given – and are giving – their lives for their faith. Comment has been made elsewhere on the Church in the USSR and Nazi Germany (page 195) and in China (page 164). Relatively few of the martyrs under those regimes, or the other 40 million (page 144), have been formally canonised.

One notable recent death from another continent was that of the Roman Catholic Archbishop Oscar Romero of El Salvador. He sided with the poor and denounced the abuses of an established order which was locked in a struggle against Marxist guerrillas. As he celebrated mass in March 1980, he was shot through the heart. A few years before this, in Uganda, the Anglican Archbishop Janani Luwum was assassinated for speaking out against the atrocities perpetrated by Idi Amin in the 1960s.

Uganda has a particularly distinguished place in the history of martyrdom. In 1885 a tribal leader named Mwanga waged war against Christianity. One day, 19 men (all under 25 years old) were asked if they wished to remain Christians. Following their reply, 'Until death', they were wrapped in reed mats and burnt alive. Their courage and remarkable cheerfulness remind us of many early martyrs, including Stephen. More Ugandan deaths were to follow – both Roman Catholic and Protestant. In this century, Stephen Neill, a well-travelled

Anglican scholar-bishop, found their memorial site outside Kampala to be the most moving place on earth. The bishop of Uganda commented to him, 'I think the Baganda (the local people) would be ready to die for Christ today; it is living for him that they find difficult.' The Ugandan martyrs were formally canonised in 1964.

Whatever their views on the formal canonisation of saints, in all churches the memory of martyrs and other distinguished believers is kept alive, as a challenge and inspiration. Indeed, some Christians are 'canonised' unofficially by the world at large; for example Dr Martin Luther King (a Baptist pastor) and Mother Teresa (a Roman Catholic nun). Some churches occasionally authorise new liturgical calendars, with new names to be remembered on particular days.

The writer of the New Testament letter to the Hebrews gives a long list of heroes of the faith. (Hebrews 11) He has a particular purpose in mind. '*Since we are surrounded by such a great cloud of witnesses*', he writes, '. . . *let us run with perseverance the race marked out for us. Let us fix our eyes on Jesus, the author and perfecter of our faith.*' (Hebrews 12:1–2) Look at them, he says. Draw inspiration from their example, and keep on keeping on in your discipleship.

Sins and virtues

'Holiness' is what makes a saint. So when we use the word 'saint' in its biblical sense we see that holiness should characterise *every* Christian. Holiness means 'set apart for God.' It involves avoidance of sin, victory over temptation and the cultivation of Christian virtues.

Seven deadly sins?

The centuries have seen the development of the popular notion of *seven deadly sins*: pride, covetousness, lust, envy, gluttony, anger and sloth. The Bible does not limit the number of sins to seven, but it certainly speaks of sin's 'deadliness'. '*For the wages of sin is death, but the gift of God is eternal life.*' (Romans 6:23) Sin is serious. At root it is hostility or indifference towards God, his truth and his standards, which results in alienation. It is so serious that, according to Jesus, we can be enslaved by sin: locked into it and unable to break free from it. (John 8:34) But by the death of Christ we may be forgiven. And by the Spirit of Christ we may be sanctified – given strength to struggle and overcome.

The Cathedral of Notre Dame in Paris displayed the following pithy sentence: '*Sin is a refusal to grow bigger.*' This captures another important truth. We sin when we lower our horizons and our moral and spiritual ambitions. We sin when we ration our love and act out of self-interest. We sin when we settle for second best and become small-minded. From such an approach to life come those many manifestations of sin – irritability, greed, laziness, selfishness – which damage our relationship with those with whom we live and work. Ultimately these things seriously diminish us as human beings.

Salvation means being set free to be fully human. Jesus Christ bids us to take the risk of following him. He points us to a world in need; and he calls us to love and serve it in his name and by his strength.

Three glorious virtues

All this can be put positively. Christian discipleship involves opening ourselves to God's Spirit, that we might grow in *faith*, *hope* and *love*. These virtues, above all, are the marks of holiness – of sanctity or 'sainthood'.

Faith In one sense, faith is universal because all human beings base their lives on assumptions which cannot be proved with mathematical certainty. *Every* human being lives by probability; so nobody can opt out of believing. This applies to the 'big' questions: questions about God and whether life has purpose and ultimate meaning. Christians *believe* that God exists. Atheists *believe* that God does not exist. Agnostics *believe* that we don't have enough evidence to decide either way. The indifferent person *believes* that it doesn't matter anyway. Total certainty – mathematical proof – is out of the question, though most people can give some reasons for their beliefs.

Faith is important in other areas of life too. It applies to our commitments, for example, 'I *believe* that everyone should have equal access to medical care, whether they can pay or not.' And it applies to our relationships: '*I trust her*' is the highest form of praise.

Christians are called 'believers', not because they alone live by faith, but because they live by *faith in Jesus Christ*. Faith is not a substitute for reason; indeed it can be firmly based on reason. Christians argue that they have good reasons for believing in Jesus (see Chapters 1 and 3). Arising from those reasons and that belief come active faith, commitment and obedient action.

Of course, some Christians have doubts. Many would argue that these can have a positive outcome: Archbishop George Carey testified that 'doubt has stirred me to deeper faith.' A helpful parallel can be drawn from personal relationships. If we doubt a friend's loyalty, we put our reasons for doubting our friend alongside our experience of his faithfulness. Christians do the same in their relationship with God. They consider afresh God's love and faithfulness; they reflect again on the significance of Jesus. Then they put their doubts within this framework.

Faith has a passive element: 'Let go and let God.' This is caught in a famous prayer of Reinhold Niebuhr: '*God grant me the serenity to accept the things I cannot change, the courage to change the things that I can, and the wisdom to know the difference.*' But as that prayer shows, faith has an active side too: it involves obedient action. Dr John Vincent captures this: '*Our word believe does not get the force of the Greek word. It really means give yourself over to, risk your life on.*'

Hope Christian hope is captured by Mother Julian's great statement, '. . . all shall be well and all shall be well and all manner of thing shall be well.' We shall not consider this at length here, for 'the hope of heaven' is spelt out in Chapter 9. At this point we simply note two points:

- **Christian hope means facing the future with confidence**. In ordinary speech, the word 'hope' can be a weak concept. 'I hope I will win a fortune on the national lottery' is a sentence running through many minds. But they are fairly sure that they will not do so! Christian hope has a much more confident quality. It should enable believers to face the unknown future in quiet confidence that 'in all things God works for the good of those who love him.' (Romans 8:28) Christian hope is rooted in history, and focused in Jesus Christ. It is as strong as the evidence for Jesus and his resurrection: readers must evaluate this for themselves (see Chapters 1–3).

- **Christian hope is joyful**. Christians are not often optimistic about this world, where realism sometimes makes us feel gloomy and sad – even desperate. There are good reasons for tears (James 4:9) as we ponder the state of our world, the poverty of our spiritual lives, and the cost of our redemption. Saints are often thought of as other-worldly, solemn figures, associated with pain and death. But, overall, the New Testament is a joyful book and people who live close to God are often joyful and serene, with wide concerns. God's saints can be good fun to be with! (*Note*: From recent research, social psychologist Michael Argyle found that church-goers tend to be more than usually happy. Not the best reason for attending church perhaps,but interesting none-the-less!).

Love The most frequent word for love in the Greek New Testament is 'agape'; this refers to self-giving, sacrificial love. Jesus himself showed deep compassion to those in need and especially to people who experienced rejection. He demonstrated that love must sometimes be heroic; he died on the cross. He showed that love must sometimes be small-scale and domestic; he washed the disciples' feet. The New Testament insists that love is practical and creative, and that it includes forgiveness.

'Love is patient, love is kind. It does not envy, it does not boast, it is not proud. It is not rude, it is not self-seeking, it is not easily angered, it keeps no record of wrongs. Love does not delight in evil but rejoices with the truth. It always protects, always trusts, always hopes, always perseveres.' (1 Corinthians 13:4–7)

'Therefore, as God's chosen people, holy and dearly loved, clothe yourselves with compassion, kindness, humility, gentleness and patience. Bear with each other and forgive whatever grievances you may have against one another. Forgive as the Lord forgave you. And over all these virtues put on love, which binds them all together in perfect unity.' (Colossians 3:12–14)

Christian Love (*agape*) is Christianity's greatest gift to the world. Tony Bridge, when Dean of Guildford Cathedral, posed the question, 'why value love at all?' He went on to say that after 2000 years of Christianity, this question sounds idiotic. It is taken for granted that love is a wonderful quality, even if we do not often live up to its high demands. But he then made an important contrast. *'Other civilisations have assumed no such thing. Courage, stoic endurance, the search for wisdom, intellectual integrity, strength, detachment – these are the virtues normally worshipped by mankind and preached by his many religions. And love is a contradiction of many of them.'*

Ultimately, and rightly, outsiders judge Christianity by its fruit. Does it 'deliver the goods'? How many bitter people have been softened by its influence? How many nervous people have been given courage? How many selfish people have been so touched by the love of Christ, that they too have been inspired to loving service? How evident in the life of Christian believers are 'the fruit of the Spirit – love, joy, peace, patience, kindness, goodness, faithfulness, gentleness and self-control.' (Galatians 5:22) This is the key test which faces Christians in every generation.

There have been many failures in the Church. But the chapters in this book on history and society reveal some triumphs too. Thousands of unloved children have been rescued from death by exposure, tens of thousands of desperate people have been given a listening ear, millions have been helped to die with peace and hope.

Perhaps the clearest testimony comes from those who do not belong to the Church. In Chapter 14 we shall consider the witness of the Roman Emperor Julian. He complained that his attempts to reintroduce pagan gods failed because of the love of the Christians who 'care not only for their own poor but for ours as well.'

A somewhat similar testimony comes from modern Russia. Staff from a hospital were invited to a service of worship in a Baptist church. Chief Physician Valentin Kozyrev, an atheist, was invited to speak. He said that the formula for curing sick people is 'chemistry with love.' He went on, 'We can provide the first part, but are incapable of fulfilling the second. Only you can provide that and we have very much appreciated your contribution.' (From: *Gorbachev, Glasnost and the Gospel* by Michael Bourdeaux)

Love is the supreme test and the supreme mark of the saint, whether formally canonised or living in obscurity in your street. It is the most important quality of all. The apostle Paul ends his great hymn about love with this summary: *'And now these three remain: faith, hope and love. But the greatest of these is love.'* (1 Corinthians 13:13)

'If the world is to be saved, it will be saved by the spirit. Politicians, or bankers, or soldiers, or businessmen, or even authors and artists are not the essential people. We need saints. The most relevant figures are not those who understand the world but those who can bring to the world something from outside itself, who can act as the transmitters of grace . . .God does not force humanity to survive, but at least we are sent enough saints in each generation to show us the possibility. A world guided by saints and the spirit would not only be a better world but also far, far safer into a much longer future.' (Lord Rees-Mogg, *The Independent*)

12

ONE CHURCH, MANY CHURCHES

The Christian Church is like a great mountain. If we stand looking at it, and even if we are on it, we cannot see all sides at the same time. The view from another vantage point may be very different from ours. The aim of this chapter is to walk round and up the mountain to gain a fuller impression of the whole; an institution, a community of peoples and a vital factor in any view of world history.

If it is One Church, one mountain, why are there so many different churches? All Christians, whatever their race or status, are united 'in Christ' – in his love, grace and forgiveness. So there can only be One Church, one body of Christians, spread through all generations and throughout the world (for which the Greek word is 'Katholikos'.) Hence the phrase in the Nicene Creed – an important ancient summary of belief – 'We believe in one holy, *catholic* and apostolic church.'

But this Church consists, and always has consisted, of people with different histories and cultures, living in different places. When local believers gather together they are the church there; not the same body as a group meeting in another place half-way across the world. So the language about 'One Church but many churches' makes sense; it already occurs in the New Testament, for example, the churches of Asia, the churches of Galatia, the churches of the Gentiles.

The differences are not only of place. Differences in modes of worship, beliefs and ethical requirements are found between different denominations. Such differences were apparent even in the first few decades covered by the New Testament writings, for example, between the

Jewish Christians and Gentile Christians (Acts 6:1) and between the apostles Peter and Paul. (Galatians 2:11)

As the centuries wore on, Christianity spread through all the nations of the known world and its detailed beliefs and practices were hammered out. Different opinions and claims about authenticity and authority caused some groups of Christians to separate from others. At times they even fought and persecuted each other. One encouraging feature of the 20th century is that Christians are recognising each other again, coming together in discussion, in mutual agreement and, in some cases, in visible reunion (see Chapter 13).

But great Christian 'blocs' remain and in this chapter we shall outline the main distinctive features of:

- The Eastern Orthodox Churches with 213 million members
- The Roman Catholic Church with 980 million members
- Catholic Christians who do not owe allegiance to Rome (six million members)
- Protestant Churches with approximately 350 million members
- Anglican Churches with 58 million members
- Pentecostal/Charismatic Churches with 460 million members
- Indigenous Churches – non-white churches which began without reference to foreign Christianity - with 192 million members

In addition there are about 33 million members of groups that claim to be Christian but which are outside mainstream Christianity (such as Jehovah's Witnesses, Mormons, Christian Scientists, Unitarians, Spiritualists and British Israelites). All the above together make up 34 per cent of the world's total population (Muslims make up about 18 per cent, Hindus 13½ per cent, Buddhists 6 per cent, Jews 0.3 per cent).

Church statistics

More statistical accounting of a precise nature takes place each year among the Christian world of denominations and agencies than for any other global movement. However, it is important to note the exact definitions of all categories thus enumerated. Almost every church has more members than regular worshippers and a few have more attenders than members!

- Many, who do not *formally* belong, profess publicly to believe in Jesus Christ, and many of these regard themselves as 'belonging' to the Church in a loose sense. Britain illustrates this. Regular church attendance (about 10 per cent) is lower than in many other countries, but repeated surveys reveal that about 70 per cent claim to believe in God and to pray regularly. Many of these people regard themselves as 'belonging' to a church or denomination, even though they seldom attend.

- Statisticians distinguish 'cultural Christians' from 'committed Christians'. The former are defined in the preceding paragraph; the latter are defined by varying degrees of attendance, profession, giving of money and so on. The scene is by no means static. As the world population increases rapidly, so does the number of church members.

- The Church world-wide is currently growing by 106,000 members every day. This is made up as follows: 178,000 new Christians are added each day, being 130,000 births into Christian families, plus 48,000 converts from other religions or 'irreligion'. At the same time 53,000 Christians die each day and 19,000 defect to other religions or 'irreligion'.

- The number of churches is increasing all the time. Recent research has revealed more than 200 different denominations in Britain; there are far more than this in the USA (some 2,000). Out of the world total of around 25,000 distinct denominations (many of them relatively small), the World Council of Churches now has 330 member denominations. This 330 includes most mainline 'historic' churches (but not Roman Catholic), so it represents a sizeable proportion of the world's Christians.

  - Note: Most statistical information in this chapter was provided personally by Dr David Barrett, a leading Church statistician based in the USA. I am extremely grateful to him for all his help. A new edition of his monumental *World Christian Encyclopaedia* (OUP: 1982) is in preparation. Another authoritative source was published in 1997: *The World Churches Handbook*, edited by Peter Brierley (Christian Research).

The Orthodox churches

We start with those churches which have preserved ancient structures and forms most tenaciously throughout the centuries. These are the churches of Eastern Europe: the Greek, Balkan and Russian 'Orthodox churches'. 'Orthodox' means right teaching. These churches maintain they have kept the apostolic faith most faithfully, while alleging that Catholics and Protestants have diverged from it – by adding what is new or ungenuine, or subtracting what is original and authentic.

To go into an Eastern Orthodox church is like stepping back a thousand years or more; neither the furnishings nor the ritual seem to have changed at all. Often the building itself is centuries old and crumbling, with clouds of incense surrounding the worshippers. Religious paintings (icons) are placed around the church. They are surrounded by candles, with people bowing in reverence in front of them. Behind an elaborate screen (the *Iconostasis*) priests and deacons move about in glorious vestments, engaged in ancient ceremony.

And a small choir at the western end raises you to heaven with the rise and fall of persistent chanting, in Greek or Old Church Slavonic, with the deepest of bass voices you have ever heard coming through to shiver your timbers in ecstasy. Often there are no pews; just seats around the edge for the infirm (as in medieval churches; hence the phrase 'the weakest to the wall').

To be a faithful Orthodox Christian you have to attend the liturgy, pray to God, Jesus, Mary and the saints, and obey your parish priest. The parish priest is usually a married man of local origin. He is likely to remain in his village all his life; in this too he is like his flock. In general, learning belongs not to the parish clergy but to the monasteries, where celibacy, poverty and total obedience to superiors are required. All bishops come from the monasteries, although there is a long tradition of lay theologians – highly educated lay people who are teachers and writers. Orthodox congregations – often small – have established themselves in Britain and the USA.

Similar to the above churches are the ancient groups of Christians known as *Oriental Orthodox*, found in Egypt, Ethiopia, Syria, Iraq, Iran, South India and Armenia. These churches felt obliged to leave

The Russian Orthodox Church experienced great hostility with the Revolution in 1917 and 70 years of Communist (officially atheistic) rule – as did most churches throughout Eastern Europe. Religion was strictly controlled – many active believers were persecuted and imprisoned; large numbers were martyred (David Barrett calculates a staggering 16 million).

The Orthodox churches survived by making an uneasy truce with the ruling powers. If they were willing to keep out of politics, to concentrate on the devotional life and curtail evangelism, they were allowed to function. Of course, this policy was controversial and some members (such as Alexander Solzhenitsyn, the Nobel Prize winner) encouraged the church leadership to be more courageous.

With the demise of the totalitarian state, doors are now open to travellers, and the Orthodox Church faces what it sees as a new 'threat'. Missionaries from some Protestant churches, as well as Western sects and cults, are gaining a following, especially among younger people.

the mainstream in the fourth and fifth centuries. They did so because they could not agree with various definitions of the faith hammered out by the majority at great Councils of the Church, such as Nicaea (325), Constantinople (381) and Chalcedon (451). The Eastern and Western churches alike tended to regard these other groups as 'heretical', and for this reason they have lived in isolation from other Christians. The term 'heretical' originally meant separate, different, cut-off, but came to mean, 'having wrong beliefs.' To be an Oriental Orthodox Christian is to be like the Eastern Orthodox in many ways, but to be even more tenacious in holding to inherited traditions. This tenacity comes from the fact that they feel under attack from other Christians, or by Muslims who form the majority in most of these countries.

Further East

The churches of India, China and Japan tend not to be Orthodox but more closely aligned with the Western churches. India and Japan have minority churches (about 4 per cent of the population in India; 3 per cent in Japan, of whom the majority are Catholics in communion with Rome). These churches reflect the divisions of Western Christendom since they were founded largely through missions from the West during the last few centuries. The Philippines is the only Asian country which is predominantly Christian (Roman Catholic), though the situation throughout Asia is fluid and many churches are growing. South Korea has the largest single church in the world: the Yoido Full Gospel Church in Seoul with a membership of 900,000. China has one of the most remarkable of all stories to tell.

CHINA'S REMARKABLE STORY

Perhaps the biggest surprise is to be found in modern China, where the Church has faced great hostility. Only now can the amazing tenacity and courage of Chinese Christians be seen.

Edmond Tang, an expert on the Church in China, wrote this remarkable paragraph in the *Church Times* (December 10th, 1993): 'Since 1987 the Chinese government has been openly showing its concern about the Christianity fever. Protestant Churches together were estimated to have 700,000 members in 1949 at the time of the establishment of the People's Republic. During the period of the Cultural Revolution 1966–1976, all places of worship were closed and Christian leaders were sent to work in factories or in the countryside. Today Protestant Christianity boasts of a membership exceeding 6.5 million, according to official sources. Unofficial estimates put the number anywhere between 20 and 50 million. And the Roman Catholic Church has grown from three million in 1949 to today's 10–12 million.'

In 1996 Dr Barrett could write: 'Today, a post denominational Christianity has a huge membership, carefully calculated as 80 million.' He speaks of 'the mushrooming expansion of Christianity.'

At the same time observers express concern at the human rights record of modern China. *'Human rights defenders are ruthlessly persecuted. Torture is endemic – causing many deaths in custody each year.'* (*Amnesty International Report* 1996). No doubt many Christians fall victim to this.

—— The Roman Catholic Church ——

When Christianity started, the known world was under the control of the Roman Empire. The two greatest Christian leaders, Peter and Paul, were executed in Rome under the Emperor Nero, probably in AD 64 and 67. There is a strong tradition that Peter asked to be crucified upside down, because he felt unworthy to die exactly like his Lord. A church (believers, not a building!) was founded early in Rome, through the evangelism by believers whose names are not recorded. Before long the bishop of Rome was asserting his position as supreme leader in the whole church. Other patriarchs, such as those of the great Christian centres of Jerusalem, Alexandria, Antioch and Constantinople, disagreed. They could not accept that the teachings and practices of Rome should be definitive for the whole of Christendom, nor that Rome had authority over them.

This was one of the main causes of *the Great Schism of 1054*, when the Eastern and Western churches finally divided, each declaring the other not to be the one true catholic and apostolic Church. As we have just seen, we call the Eastern Church 'Orthodox'. The Western Church took to itself the name 'Catholic' and remained broadly unified for five more centuries. But the Western Church was not always united even before the Reformation (see Chapter 17), because there were substantial groups which remained separate from Rome. These included the Celtic churches (responsible for christianising Ireland, Scotland, Wales and much of northern and south-west England, together with Flanders and north Germany). These churches remained distinct until the seventh century when they were absorbed by the greater power of Rome (see Chapter 16).

The bishop of Rome came to be called *Pope* (from Latin *Papa* or *Father*). The Church which remained faithful to his supremacy through all the changes of the Reformation period, is now known as the Roman Catholic Church. It has spread from Europe to most parts of the globe and is the largest of the Christian churches. If the main characteristic of the Eastern Churches is conservatism, that of the Roman Catholic Church is central authority. The papal system keeps a strong hand over new ideas and threatened changes but when it approves of them, it imposes them vigorously and quickly. Some modern Catholics, especially those in the USA and Europe, are prepared to question papal authority and even to ignore it (for example, in matters of contraception: see Chapter 14).

Roman Catholics today live under the heritage of the *Second Vatican Council* (1962–65), which instituted considerable changes in the hitherto rigid structures and practices of that church. Most obvious was the shift from Latin to national languages for the mass. To be a Roman Catholic is to be conscious of belonging to a church of immense size and global spread, which claims to be the nearest to the sort of Church that Christ wants. It is also to be part of a long tradition of colourful worship and deep spirituality. Worship styles vary despite the rigid outward structures.

The Roman Catholic Church has often been able to tolerate and live with local customs, religions and beliefs to such a degree that some other Christians accuse it of compromise – even of encouraging pagan practice and superstition. But Pope John Paul II has spoken out against astrology and horoscopes as being incompatible with Christian faith. Even so, they remain popular throughout the Western world, including Italy.

The Second Vatican Council led to a greater openness within the Catholic Church. As a result, the Pope and the Orthodox Patriarch of Constantinople mutually lifted the dual excommunications which had divided the Eastern Orthodox and Catholic Churches since 1054.

The monastic movement has always played a significant role in Roman Catholicism. At their best, monasteries have been power houses of prayer, worship and evangelism, and centres for experimental change. There are some married Roman Catholic priests but they are the exception. Most parish priests are required to be celibate, so the distinction between parish priests and monks is not so obvious as in the Eastern Churches. Whether clergy should be celibate is keenly debated within the Roman Catholic Church. Some of its members believe that papal insistence on this is one cause of an alarming fall in vocations to the priesthood. A remarkable 20 per cent of the world's Roman Catholic priests (100,000 out of a world-wide total of 500,000) are forbidden to function as priests, because they have chosen to marry after ordination.

The teaching of the Roman Catholic Church since the Reformation has been largely focused in three Councils: Trent (1545–63), the First Vatican Council (1869–70) and the Second Vatican Council (1962–65).

From time to time various decrees ('Bulls') are issued by the Pope on specific matters – most famously in recent years on sexual morality. Decrees of the 1870 Council were the cause of a breakaway church by those Roman Catholics who could not accept what they saw as the novelty of *papal infallibility*: a doctrine which was declared at the First Vatican Council. Today they constitute small groups known as Old Catholics; they are found mainly in Holland, Germany and Austria, and are in communion with Anglican churches.

Protestant Churches

In the 16th century there was turmoil in Europe. The Reformation – a movement for reform within the Medieval Church – was the inspiration and ultimate cause of most churches other than Orthodox or Catholic. The Reformation resulted partly from the rediscovery of the ancient languages of Hebrew and Greek, which meant that the Scriptures could be read in their original form. For the previous 12 centuries, the Latin tradition had totally dominated the West. A second cause of the Reformation was the growing nationalism in various countries of Europe; an unrest which led them to want freedom from the influence and power of Rome. An additional cause was reaction to the abuses which grew up in the Western Church, during the later decades of the Middle Ages (see Chapter 17).

The Reformation could have resulted in reforms in teaching and practice *within* the Western Catholic church, had it not met total resistance from the central authority in Rome. All attempts at reconciliation failed and new church groupings emerged. Each of these protested at the claims and power of Rome, hence 'Protestant' churches. (The term was first used at the *Diet of Speyer* in 1529.) These churches emphasised different elements in the practice and beliefs of the Church before it was corrupted (as they saw it) by Rome. Because of this, and since they emerged in different countries at a time when nationalism was so strong, they fell into four main groups:

- Lutheran
- Reformed (or Presbyterian)
- Baptist
- Anglican

In later centuries they were joined by two other 'breakaway' churches: Methodist (18th century) and Pentecostal (20th century). All these churches placed great emphasis on the Bible as the controlling authority for belief and practice. They wished to make the Scriptures readily available and easy to read. And they wanted to simplify worship, so that important elements would stand out and not be overwhelmed by trivial or misleading ceremonies, or by ornate music. They emphasised the importance of preaching alongside, or above, the administration of the sacraments. Many churches in the 16th century substituted the authority of the local monarch for that of the Pope in Rome.

Lutheran Churches

The Lutheran churches (now estimated at about 56 million members) were at first dominant in northern Germany and Scandinavia. They are now found in Africa, America, Asia and many countries in Europe. Martin Luther (1483–1546), in northern Germany, was the principal protagonist of the Reformation. Many of the features listed in the previous paragraph owe their force to his preaching and writing. The Lutheran tradition allows old customs to stay, as long as they are not deemed to be contrary to New Testament teaching. So in many Lutheran churches, customs, vestments and furnishings are still maintained – as well as an episcopal ministry (bishops) – from the old days of the united Western Catholic Church.

The teachings of the Lutheran churches are historically summed up in the *Augsburg Confession* (1530). This is a moderate statement of the universal Christian faith with an emphasis on the grace of God, which is to be responded to by faith. It is *faith* which is seen as the 'justifying' or saving factor, not good works: these must follow as a thanksgiving for God's grace. Lutherans share a faith which has strong roots in the home, with family prayers.

In church, Lutherans worship with quiet dignity: hymns, Bible reading, preaching and the sacraments are the most important elements. The clergy are well trained in theology and there is a comprehensiveness which allows quite varied practices to exist. In this century, monasticism has been revived within the Lutheran Church, but the numbers involved remain small. Lutherans have made a distinguished contribution to the *Ecumenical Movement*: the moving together of churches to talk, to co-operate, and even to unite (see Chapter 13).

——— Presbyterian Churches ———

As Lutheran churches were banding together against Rome, John Calvin (1509–64) was teaching similar doctrines in Geneva. But he was more radical in breaking with past customs in organisation and liturgy. With great rigour, he regarded the Bible as the sole authority in all matters of faith and practice. This led him to reject the ministry of bishops and all forms of decoration in the churches, as well as most music and ceremony.

These churches, founded by Calvin and his followers (called Calvinist, Reformed or Presbyterian), have a membership of some 51 million and are the dominant form of Christianity in Scotland, Holland, and Switzerland. They are well represented in most countries in Europe, America and Africa. Calvinism is usually an austere form of Christianity with dignified, simple worship and deep spirituality. Its members have made strong contributions to Christian missions world-wide and to honesty, fairness and hard work in public life.

The ecumenical movement of recent decades has led to some churches in these two major Protestant traditions coming together locally. This has resulted in United Lutheran and Reformed churches in many parts of the world. So, to the 56 million Lutherans and the 51 million Reformed Christians, we must add another 83 million in these united churches.

——— Baptist Churches ———

The above two church groupings were not the only ones to emerge from the Reformation. Some felt that true Christian discipleship had been largely displaced by nominal Christianity. Virtually everyone was baptised in infancy and these new churches rebelled against this (see Chapter 8). They came to be called Baptists because they insisted on the practice of immersing believers totally under the water; not just pouring water over the forehead of infants. Baptists now number about 60 million and are particularly strong in the southern states of the USA.

William Carey is often credited with starting the modern Protestant missionary movement when he sailed from England to India in 1793. He was a Baptist cobbler with little formal education. Carey had a brilliant mind and during his life-time he translated the Bible (whole or part) into 25 languages and dialects. These emphases – love for the Bible and enthusiasm for evangelism – characterise modern Baptists. So does William Carey's motto: *'Expect great things from God; attempt great things for God.'*

Anglicanism

In England, the old Western Catholic Church went its own way at the Reformation. It was greatly influenced by both Luther and Calvin but did not join either of those two church groupings. So the Church of England maintained a position, Luther-like in its conservative attitude to tradition and Calvin-like in its doctrine. Many Anglicans dislike being called Protestant, arguing that they are both Catholic and Reformed. Its basis was defined in the *Thirty Nine Articles* (1563 Latin; 1571 English) and the English *Book of Common Prayer* (finalised in 1662 but based on the work of Archbishop Thomas Cranmer a century earlier).

The British (and other European) churches expanded widely to other parts of the globe during the 17th, 18th and 19th centuries. This expansion arose from:

- the colonising process which resulted in the British Empire (although some missionaries found it necessary to oppose policies of the colonisers)
- missionary zeal which wanted to take the gospel to new areas

One result was a great world-wide network of churches called the Anglican Communion, which numbers some 58 million today. Anglican churches are sometimes called Episcopal or Episcopalian (from the

Greek word for 'bishop'). Anglicans are distinguished by having created a fellowship which allows for considerable doctrinal and liturgical differences, within a recognisable organisational unity. Anglican provinces are autonomous, but still look to the Church of England as the founding church and to the Archbishop of Canterbury as 'first bishop among equals.'

Every ten years, Anglican bishops from around the globe gather for the Lambeth Conference (the first was held in 1867). The ordination of women to the priesthood has been accepted in many Anglican churches in the final few decades of the 20th century. This initiative, welcomed by many, has caused controversy and division.

Catholic, Liberal and Evangelical

There are three broad, sometimes overlapping, streams within Anglicanism: Catholic, Liberal and Evangelical.

- Anglo-Catholics (or 'Catholic Anglicans') are 'high church' in worship. They stress the mystery and awesomeness of God, using colourful vestments and incense (hence the affectionate nickname 'smells and bells' for high church worship!).
- Liberal theology lays stress upon questioning the tradition and requiring the Faith to respond (sometimes radically; hence *'radical theology'*) to changes in culture and outlook in the world outside the Church.
- Evangelicals (not to be confused with fundamentalists – see Chapter 13) stress the importance of the Bible and the need for conversion and commitment. In recent years, evangelicals have become strong within the Church of England. Their worship tends to be 'low church' in style with minimal ceremony, in an attempt to make Church services accessible to outsiders. Evangelicals have been relatively effective in recent years in attracting young people, a task with which most European churches struggle.

The Charismatic Renewal Movement has influenced all three streams, especially the evangelical. But it is important to stress that the boundaries between these three groups are not hard and fast; some Anglicans would claim allegiance to more than one, or perhaps none.

The Oxford Movement (see Chapter 18) resulted in the foundation of

Anglican monasteries and convents. Today there are about 2000 monks and nuns within the world-wide Anglican Communion. Other types of Christian community have also been established (such as Lee Abbey in Devon; Scargill House in Yorkshire).

BRITAIN

Research shows that about 10 per cent of the population attend church on Sundays. Of these:

- about 3 per cent attend a Church of England Service
- about 4 per cent attend a Roman Catholic Church
- most of the rest attend a range of Protestant Churches: Baptist, Methodist, Presbyterian or United Reformed, Pentecostal, Salvation Army, Independent

There are strong regional variations in church attendance: less than one per cent in some parts of some cities; about 14 per cent in Scotland and 35 per cent in Northern Ireland.

About six new congregations are founded each week because 'church planting' is a policy adopted by most mainstream and independent churches. These new congregations often meet in schools and community halls, even pubs.

Britain has not become a nation of atheists. About 65 per cent claim some church allegiance, around 72 per cent claim to believe in God and surveys suggest that around 70–80 per cent pray. About eight million regularly watch and listen to religious programmes on television and radio.

Other world faiths are found in Britain, mainly as a result of immigration in the 1950s, 60s and 70s. But numbers are not huge: adherents of all other faiths taken together amount to no more than about 4–5 per cent of the British population.

OTHER COUNTRIES

- In the USA, church attendance represents about 42 per cent of the population.
- In Italy about 33 per cent attend mass regularly, out of 85 per cent who claim to be Roman Catholics.
- In France the rate of churchgoing is about 13 per cent.
- In Southern Ireland well over 50 per cent attend mass in the Roman Catholic Church.

Methodist Churches

The Church of England was not always comprehensive and open. When a reform movement began in the 18th century, led by two Anglican priests, the official Church resisted it. John and Charles Wesley and their followers were nicknamed 'Methodists' because of their orderly (methodical) approach to life and faith. So a new church grouping was created which took that name with pride.

Today there are Methodist Churches around the world with 34 million members. Methodists have developed strong lay leadership and a travelling ministry. They are distinguished by the prominent place given in worship to hymn singing. Many of the fine hymns written by Charles Wesley are sung wherever English is used in worship, regardless of denomination (see Chapter 20).

Salvation Army and Quakers

Some smaller groups have made an impact beyond their size. For example, the Salvation Army is renowned for a combination of outdoor evangelism, brass bands and social action among the homeless and others in desperate need. It has a highly effective (and confidential) ministry in tracing missing persons and offering the possibility of reunion with their families.

'The Army' was started by William Booth, a Methodist living in Victorian London. He did this in an attempt to bring the gospel to the thousands living in poverty, following the Industrial Revolution. The Salvation Army, with its musical, practical and evangelistic concerns, has spread to other countries and is especially strong in the USA. Salvationists (together with some other Christians) have taken a clear stand against what they perceive as the damaging effects of alcohol.

The Quakers (more correctly, the *Religious Society of Friends*) have no ordained ministers. Silence is central to their tradition, as they 'wait upon God' in their Sunday meetings. Anyone may speak, under the prompting of the Spirit. Quakers have a distinguished record of pacifism and heroic war service in non-combatant roles – usually para-medical. In this they are like the Christian Brethren (formerly 'Plymouth Brethren'), a group of autonomous churches with no ordained ministers.

——— Pentecostal Churches ———

Pentecostalists are named after the Church's festival which celebrates the gift of the Holy Spirit to the first disciples. God's Spirit enabled the disciples to go out with zeal to spread the gospel, and gave them miraculous powers to speak in languages which they did not know (see Chapter 15). Pentecostal Christians believe that such powers are still available today, through the Holy Spirit. Pentecostal Churches were established early in the 20th century and are growing fast throughout the world. Because of their independent character they are difficult to enumerate, but detailed surveys put membership of Pentecostal/Independent/Charismatic churches at around 460 million. Their worship is informal, exuberant and partly unplanned, because of their belief in the immediacy of the gifts of the Spirit. The word 'charismatic' is often used for this expression of Christianity, but charismatic worship of an exuberant kind is often found in the mainstream churches too (see Chapter 13).

——— Independent Churches ———

Independent Churches (indigenous or locally founded churches) are springing up in many places in Africa and Asia as well as in Europe and the USA. Some African and Asian churches have arisen partly in adverse reaction to the Western elements which inevitably became associated with the missionary work of previous centuries. They are strong numerically (approximtely 200 million) but diverse in character. Often they are Pentecostal in emphasis but some stress the practices (and sometimes also the teachings and culture) of their countries before the missionaries arrived. Throughout the world, Independent, Pentecostal and Charismatic churches are growing faster than any other tradition.

—— A shifting centre of gravity ——

Christianity started in the Middle East and was found very early in North Africa (see Acts 8:27). But throughout most of its history Europe has taken the lead, dominating both its thinking and its expansion – although the USA has taken over this leadership role during the twentieth century.

The 19th and early 20th centuries saw a remarkable burst of missionary zeal. Britain, the USA and other countries sent missionaries to the four corners of the earth. As a result, the Christian Church has been planted in every continent and in almost every country. Christianity has shown itself capable of adapting to all cultures. In every society there are customs which need to be challenged in the name of Christ. But in every place, aspects of local custom and culture are found to be effective vehicles for Christian teaching and worship. Today, it is the relatively young churches which are flourishing. So the Christian Church world-wide is growing and the Christian faith continues to spread (page 161). Meanwhile, the Church's centre of gravity is shifting rapidly

- *from* Europe and (to a lesser extent) the USA
- *to* Africa, Asia, and Latin America

Population trends in these continents mean that the Church in the 21st century will be increasingly young, energetic, non-white and poor. And it will probably be increasingly Pentecostal/Charismatic. The 21st century is likely to see a culture shift in the Christian Church, as its younger branches take control, shape its future and send missionaries and mission-partners to other nations.

Disharmony

The main-stream historic churches have moved closer together throughout the 20th century. But some of the newer churches are aggressive in their evangelism and ready to 'proselytise' – to win converts from other churches. We have noted the problems caused by this policy for the Russian Orthodox church. The same problem faces the Roman Catholic Church in Latin America. *The Independent* (February 10th, 1996) reported a visit by the Pope to Central America and spoke of 'the fastest-growing problem for the Roman Catholic Church in the region: the surge of Protestantism.'

Many Independent churches, in whichever country they are found, are not interested in working with other Christians. So while there is a strong movement towards unity within many 'historic' churches, there is also a counter-movement towards independence and fragmentation among the newer churches.

Conclusion

At the beginning of this chapter, the image of a mountain was used to illustrate the one Church in its different aspects. Another image is the river which flows from one single spring. The spring is Jesus Christ himself, who gives 'living water' (John 4:10). At first it was concentrated into a small area but gradually it spreads out over a wider bed. Some streams are deep and narrow, others shallow and wide, eventually dividing into separate streams which themselves divide again later. The water is all one, all flows from the same source, but also becomes many streams. Separate as we are, we acknowledge that the water matters more than any particular river!

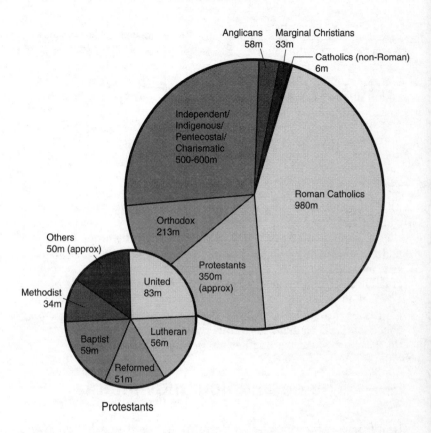

The relative size of the major Christian confessions in 1996. Based on: 'Status of Global Mission, 1996' *International Bulletin of Missionary Research (January 1996, page 25)*

13

MODERN MOVEMENTS

As we have just seen, individual Christians belong to a particular local church, and (very often) through that to a 'denomination' or world-wide Communion of churches (Roman Catholic, Anglican, Lutheran and so on). But it would be a mistake to think that these bodies are self-contained, or sealed off from one another. Some are, but there is a great deal of communication between the various churches. So, in addition to belonging to a local church and a denomination, many Christians are influenced by widespread movements which cross denominational boundaries. In this chapter we shall consider some of the movements which are influential in Church life today.

The ecumenical movement

Unity among the disciples of Jesus is a key theme in the New Testament. Jesus prayed for his followers *'that all of them may be one, Father, just as you are in me and I am in you.'* (John 17:21) The apostle Paul urged the Christians in Ephesus to *'Make every effort to keep the unity of the Spirit through the bond of peace.'* (Ephesians 4:3)

But as the centuries passed and the Christian movement grew, serious divisions occurred (see Chapter 12). Throughout the 20th century, a new spirit of togetherness has developed. This was anticipated by the formation of the *Evangelical Alliance*. In 1846, individuals from more than 50 American and British Protestant denominations agreed to pursue religious liberty and to cooperate in various evangelistic and educational activities. But the intended unity was selective: one aim was to unite Protestants in resistance to Catholicism.

The Evangelical Alliance (EA) continues to flourish and in 1996 the 150th anniversary was marked by celebrations and special events. In Britain the EA has pioneered *Spring Harvest* which mixes holiday activities with services of worship and seminars on different aspects of Christian faith. These annual gatherings, based in holiday camps, are attended by tens of thousands from a wide range of churches, mainly Protestant and Anglican.

In 1987, EA initiated *March For Jesus*. This is now global and on 25th May 1996, 12–15 million Christians from more than 170 nations walked the streets to witness to their faith. The stress was on celebration and song in an atmosphere of carnival.

The 20th-century ecumenical movement attempted to bring together churches with widely differing approaches to the Christian faith. In 1910, at an international missionary conference in Edinburgh led by the American Methodist John R Mott, 1000 delegates shared his desire for Christian unity. Structures were established in an attempt to give shape and substance to their vision. Eventually this initiative gave rise to the formation of the *World Council of Churches* (WCC). 351 delegates from 147 denominations and 44 countries gathered for the first General Assembly in Amsterdam in 1948. The movement was earning the right to call itself 'ecumenical' – a term which comes from a Greek word meaning 'the whole inhabited earth'.

Further General Assemblies were organised every six years or so. At New Delhi in 1961 there were two important developments: the *Russian Orthodox Church* joined the Council and a formal *Confessional Basis* was adopted. This stated that:

'The World Council of Churches is a fellowship of Churches which confess the Lord Jesus Christ as God and Saviour according to the Scriptures and therefore seek to fulfil together their common calling to the glory of one God, Father, Son, and Holy Spirit.'

In the 1960s, the WCC caused controversy by its *involvement in political issues*. The Council made grants to 'freedom fighters' in national struggles, arguing that they were oppressed minorities in a 'just war'. Some member churches expressed strong disagreement with the leadership of the WCC on this matter. Critics pointed out that the

WCC leadership was selective in the causes it championed – appearing to be less critical of Marxist and Maoist regimes. They also argued that the WCC is not a 'super church', but should be a servant of all churches; it has no mandate to take sides in this way.

Conspicuous by its absence from these ecumenical endeavours has been the Roman Catholic Church. Issues such as the primacy of the Pope, the nature of the priesthood and the meaning and practice of the eucharist have made it difficult for that Church to participate. However, from 1961 senior Roman Catholics have attended WCC Assemblies as official observers. Under the leadership of the reforming Pope John XXIII, the Second Vatican Council (1962–5) opened the door to closer ecumenical activity. For the first time the Roman Catholic Council acknowledged that there are authentic Christians ('separated brethren') outside the Roman fold. Reflecting this new spirit, in December 1968 the Patriarch of Constantinople and the Pope mutually lifted the excommunications which had divided the Catholic and Eastern Orthodox Churches since 1054.

Several churches have entered into bi-lateral or multi-lateral talks – sometimes on specific issues (eg Baptism, Eucharist and Ministry), sometimes about the possibility of uniting. Organic unity has been achieved in some cases: for example in 1947 several churches united to form the *Church of South India* (CSI). Some attempts at formal unity between churches (such as Church of England and Methodist) have so far failed. Critics of such schemes argue that variety in worship and church order is a good thing (matching different histories, theologies and personalities), provided there is an underlying unity of spirit and purpose.

In Britain and some other countries, relationships between members of different churches at a local level is often warm, and united endeavours in outreach and social action are common (but see page 176). Some commentators believe that this is where the future lies; co-operation at a local level rather than grand schemes for reunion.

Liberation Theology

Liberation Theology emerged in Latin American in the 1960s. In 1968, at a conference of Roman Catholic Bishops from Latin America held in Columbia, some members insisted that the starting point for theological reflection must be the situation of the poor. Liberation Theology was born. At the forefront of this movement is the belief that *the God of the Bible is on the side of the downtrodden and marginalised*. Liberation theologians remind us that:

- God heard the cry of the children of Israel when they were enslaved in Egypt.
- The Old Testament prophets were passionate in demanding social justice.
- Mary's song (*the Magnificat*) is revolutionary: God 'has filled the hungry with good things but has sent the rich away empty.' (Luke 1:53)
- Jesus showed particular concern for the poor and those on the edge of society.
- Christianity is a 'this-worldly' religion; concerned with the welfare of mind and body, as well as redemption of the soul.

The Bible is seen as a very practical book, concerned with freedom from physical oppression and freedom of the human spirit. Liberation Theology is concerned with reflection, action ('praxis') and raising the awareness of poor people concerning issues of justice. Something of its mood is caught in these statements:

- 'As a sign of the liberation of humankind and history, the Church itself in its concrete existence ought to be a place of liberation . . . The point is not to survive, but to serve. The rest will be given.' (Gustavo Gutierrez)
- The poor man, the other, reveals the totally Other to us. (Guttierrez)
- Theology has to stop explaining the world and start reforming it.' (J Migguez-Bonino)
- The Church in liberation theology is rooted in a faith in God and an option for the poor.' (Marilyn J Legge)
- The God of the Future is the crucified God who submerges himself in a world of misery. God is found on the crosses of the oppressed rather than in beauty, power or wisdom. (D D Webster)

In the 1970s and 80s many priests in repressive Latin American states opposed those regimes. Several paid with their lives. While Rome did not like 'politicised' priests, it disliked the persecution of priests even more. All this affected the Roman Catholic hierarchy. The Pope does not encourage priests to get involved in direct political action, but he frequently emphasises human rights.

Alongside the rise of Liberation Theology came the rise of *Base Communities,* a separate but related phenomenon. This movement arose in part as a way of coping with a chronic shortage of Catholic priests in Latin America. It is essentially *a lay movement* flourishing among largely uneducated Christians, often in shanty towns. Small groups (usually around 10 or 20 strong) gather weekly for worship services, Bible study, discussion, pastoral care and social awareness. They are a force to be reckoned with: in Brazil in 1985 there were over 100,000 base communities.

Similar communities have developed within Protestant churches; in Guatemala there were 200 Protestant or Ecumenical Base Communities in the 1980s. Within these groups, liberation theologians have attempted to raise awareness of the power of ordinary people, working together for change ('conscientisation').

Liberation Theology has spread around the world and in some places (such as South Africa) it has become a powerful force. Always there are those who argue that Christianity should confine itself to matters of the spirit. In reply, Archbishop Desmond Tutu spoke for many when he said; *'I am puzzled about which Bible people are reading when they suggest religion and politics don't mix.'* This approach has spilled over into the life of more affluent churches too, for example in feminist theology, which views women as an oppressed majority within the Church (page 190).

Needless to say, Liberation Theology has its critics inside and outside the Church. It has been viewed by some conservative Christians as a Marxist political movement rather than a spiritual movement. Archbishop Helder Camara answered his critics by saying, *'When I give food to the poor they call me a Saint. When I ask why they are poor, they call me a Communist.'* Liberation theologians argue that to rest content with the status quo in unjust societies is to side with the oppressors against the oppressed.

'Structural sin' (ie unjust systems and structures in society) rather than personal sin is emphasised. Critics argue that Liberation Theology reduces salvation to political liberation and neglects the transcendent and eternal dimensions of Christianity. Others (such as Professor David Martin) argue that intellectual liberation theologians do not serve the real needs of poor local communities. Feminist theologian Professor Rosemary Radford Reuther, while being sympathetic to the movement, asserts (controversially) that early liberation theologians omitted 'women, nature and indigenous peoples' from their concerns. But the influence of Liberation Theology remains strong and many Christians endorse its challenge to the view that the Church should concentrate only on 'spiritual matters'. They argue that Christian faith, and hence the Church, must be concerned with the *whole* of life, because the God of the Bible is concerned with the whole of life.

Fundamentalism

Fundamentalism is often in the news and fundamentalists usually get a bad press, because they are perceived as dangerous. Sadly, this suspicion is sometimes well-placed. Christian fundamentalists have been violent towards doctors who practise abortion; Muslim fundamentalists sometimes practise terrorism, including suicide bombings. Jewish fundamentalists obstruct the peace process in Israel, demanding that land must not be traded for peace. The world was shaken when, in 1995, Israeli Prime Minister Yitzhak Rabin was shot by a Jewish fundamentalist. The assassin Yigal Amir claimed that he was acting on orders from God, and in the best interests of Israel. Thus fundamentalism has become synonymous with bigotry, with unshakeable certainty and with a passionate, and often violent, commitment to a range of dubious causes. Some commentators see fundamentalism within the world's various religions, as a major challenge to international peace and stability.

The term *fundamentalism* originated in a series of tracts written in America between 1909 and 1915. These pamphlets were called *The Fundamentals*. They were written by scholarly conservative Protestant Christians who wished to re-state 'the fundamentals' of the Christian faith. The authors would be amazed at the journey taken by their title.

Christian fundamentalists claim to follow the Bible in all matters of life and belief. Sometimes they oppose modern science, asserting that evolution is a discredited theory and attempting to replace it with a 'young earth' view, known as Creationism. They claim to have, from the Bible, a clear outline of the events leading to the end of the world, and the return of Jesus Christ in glorious majesty.

As noted above, deep suspicion of some fundamentalists is well placed. But relatively few modern Christian fundamentalists espouse violence and many are loyal church members and good citizens. Following the lead of their influential leaders, many fundamentalists have espoused *a political agenda*, especially in the USA. On some issues, such as abortion and euthanasia, they have made common cause with Roman Catholics, even though their understanding of 'Church' is very different in many ways. (However, they do share an emphasis on the authority of Church leaders.)

Evangelicals and fundamentalists The word 'fundamentalist' has become a term of abuse due to its bad press. To label someone as a fundamentalist can be a useful substitute for sound argument, ensuring that opponents are dismissed out of hand. The word is sometimes applied to Christians who hold a 'high' view of the Bible as the Word of God but who do not share the negative characteristics described above. Such Christians rightly protest, and prefer the term 'evangelical'.

Evangelicals, unlike fundamentalists, accept biblical criticism (see Chapter 5), while insisting that it be applied responsibly. They also recognise that not all biblical passages should be read literally. Evangelicals are not committed to particular doctrines concerning the return of Christ and the end of the world. And while being realistic about human nature and sin, evangelicals do not dismiss modern culture as totally in the grip of the devil, as many fundamentalists do.

A number of distinguished scholars, bishops and other leaders within the historic churches are happy to embrace the term 'evangelical', but they object to being called fundamentalist. Notable among them is Anglican Dr John Stott, Rector Emeritus of All Souls' Church in London's Langham Place. Through writing, travelling and organising, he has exercised a remarkable world-wide ministry during the second half of the 20th century.

―― The Decade of Evangelism ――

In the 1980s, Church leaders began to consider appropriate ways of marking the millennium, with its 2000 years of Christian history.

Pope John Paul II suggested that the 1990s should be a Decade of **Evangelisation**. And the 1988 Lambeth Conference of Anglican Bishops world-wide, declared a Decade of **Evangelism**. Almost all mainstream churches have come to support these initiatives, with their vision of *'a renewed and united effort to make Christ known to the peoples of the world.'*

For many people, evangelism is closely associated with famous evangelists such as Dr Billy Graham – a widely respected American preacher who concluded his huge meetings with an invitation to 'get up out of your seat.' In this way 'enquirers' were invited to go forward in order to receive Jesus Christ as Saviour and Lord. The word 'evangelism' also evokes images of American style 'Televangelists', some of whom have an affluent lifestyle and questionable methods and morals.

Neither of these models was uppermost in the minds of most Christian leaders when they called for a Decade of Evangelism/Evangelisation. They were more concerned to make outreach with the gospel a natural feature of local church life. Their concern was to help ordinary Christians to know their faith more deeply, hold it more securely and share it more confidently. The *Catholic Catechism* (1994) states: *'Lay people also fulfil their prophetic mission by evangelisation, that is, the proclamation of Christ by word and the testimony of life.'* The Anglican Bishops made a similar point at the 1988 Lambeth Conference: *'Every Christian as an agent of mission.'* They did not wish to make individual Christians 'pushy' and aggressive. They were concerned that churches should be warm in their welcome, with adventurous and attractive programmes and inspiring worship.

The call for a Decade of Evangelism was an acknowledgement that *all* churches in the modern world are in a missionary situation, including (perhaps *especially*) churches in so-called 'Christian countries.' It was an acknowledgement too, that in the modern world there are many voices seeking to gain people's allegiance. Some of theses are benign; others are pernicious, damaging and exploitative. The call for a Decade of Evangelism was an attempt by Christian leaders to say to all the churches, 'alongside these other voices, let the Christian voice be heard.'

BUT WHY?

Enlarging the church – or, in the West, stemming the decline – is only one reason for a Decade of Evangelism. *The main concern is truly to be the 'Servant Church'*.

Christians believe that they have good news to share: good news which can bring hope, confidence and courage to people who often live lives of quiet desperation. At times of distress and reflection many people ask deep questions:

- Is the universe 'friendly'? Can we *really* find God, meaning, truth and love at the centre of our universe?
- Or do we live in a cold, uncaring world which grinds relentlessly on, reducing us all to rubble and dust in the end? Worse still, do we live in a 'Cosmic madhouse'?
- 'Is that all there is?' runs the lyric of Neil Simon's wistful song. Perhaps the truthful answer is: 'Yes, I'm afraid it is.' Perhaps Bertrand Russell was right when he said: 'When I die, I rot.'

Like everyone else, Christians live with many unanswered questions. The Christian faith does not offer glib answers to these deep problems; but it does claim to shed light on these great issues. *Because of God's revelation of himself in Jesus Christ, we can find meaning, truth and love at the centre of our world. Even more important, we can find these great qualities at the heart and centre of our personal lives.*

All this is to be shared with humility, boldness, love, sensitivity and friendship. D T Niles, an Asian Christian, gave this pithy definition: *'Evangelism is one beggar showing another beggar where he found bread.'* Mother Teresa is credited with an equally beautiful definition: *'Evangelism means to carry Jesus in your heart, and to give the presence of Jesus to someone else.'*

The intention in calling for a Decade of Evangelism is that outreach with the gospel (the good news of Jesus Christ) should once again enter the bloodstream of the churches; thus ensuring that every subsequent decade is a decade of evangelisation, even if it does not carry that label.

The Sea of Faith

A small but articulate group of intellectuals has formed the Sea of Faith movement. Most members of this movement take a very radical approach to Christian theology. Don Cupitt, former Dean of Emmanuel College, Cambridge, is a leading member. He believes that God and heaven have no reality outside human language and imagination. These concepts, and the Bible stories which carry them, are useful (and for some perhaps, essential) symbols and myths enabling us to construct and lead purposeful and moral lives.

Don Cupitt is happy to use traditional Christian terminology like, 'Christ is Lord of my life.' But he means something very different from more orthodox believers; he means 'a commitment to values, that's all.' And when he talks about resurrection, he does not mean that God raised Jesus from the dead but, 'I choose to live the risen life.' By the 'risen life' he means 'solar living.' Like the sun we burn for a while, spreading light and heat. Then we burn out – forever.

An articulate 'Vicar who doesn't believe in God' has news value and his views are given considerable space in the media. Supporters of this approach to Christianity argue that it is bracing: facing bleak reality without offering escapism. There is no God 'out there'; life after death is an illusion. We must face squarely the glory and the tragedy of being a human being.

Critics raise the obvious point that Christian faith without a real God and with no hope of heaven, is very anaemic indeed. Some question whether it can properly be called Christianity. They also argue that for all its bleakness and boldness, this theology lacks a true sense of the depth of human tragedy and helplessness. It 'works' for people who – through upbringing and temperament – are upright, moral and interested in religious ideas. But the gospel is for *everyone*. Malcolm Worsley (page 77) would argue that he could not 'choose to live the risen life.' Without a *real* God, who offers *real* strength, grace and forgiveness, he would still be in the gutter.

The Charismatic Movement

In 1960 Dennis Bennett, an Episcopal (Anglican) rector in California, became national news. Things were happening in his church which were usually associated with the Pentecostal churches founded 50 years earlier. Church members claimed to be 'baptised in the Spirit' and to 'speak in tongues.' Similar phenomena took place elsewhere, and the movement spread around the world with remarkable speed.

At first this movement influenced Anglican and Protestant churches; but by the late 1960s it had made an impact upon the Roman Catholic Church too. In the early 1970s its influence was also felt within the Greek Orthodox Church. This is remarkable, given the stress on tradition and the inbuilt resistance to change and innovation, which mark the Eastern Orthodox churches (see Chapter 12).

Within the Charismatic Movement (sometimes called the *Renewal Movement*), emphasis is placed upon openness to the influence of the Holy Spirit. Charismatic worship is usually informal, with prayer, singing and 'ministry' – one or two people (often lay people) praying for individuals within the congregation. Speaking or singing in *tongues* ('glossolalia') is common: words are uttered, not in a language usually spoken by the person involved, but in a language of transcendent prayer and praise. Worship is often exuberant but fine singing and silence are significant features in some churches.

The importance of a direct experience of God's Holy Spirit is stressed and charismatic worship generates a sense of warm fellowship. All members of the congregation are invited to participate; even to take a lead. They might feel moved by the Spirit to offer a word of prophecy, or to lead the congregation in prayer, perhaps using 'a tongue'. Or they might offer an interpretation of someone else's prayer in tongues. The gifts of the Spirit (1 Corinthians 12–14) are encouraged, including the gift of healing through prayer – and 'power evangelism' through 'signs and wonders' (especially healing).

In 1994 a new phase began with the so-called 'Toronto Blessing'. Some Christians believe that God has begun to prepare his people for a widespread revival of the Church, by a new outpouring of the Holy Spirit. This movement started in the Airport Church in Toronto and spread quickly around the world.

The phenomena associated with Toronto are often bizarre. People who are 'slain in the Spirit' might lie on the ground for several minutes – perhaps laughing or crying. Others bark like dogs or roar like lions. Not unnaturally, some Christians, even those sympathetic to charismatic renewal, are suspicious and hesitant about acknowledging this development as a genuine movement of God's Spirit. Others testify to a new love for Jesus, the Bible and for other people, following such an experience.

The large number of charismatic Christians in every denomination has forced the mainstream 'historic' churches to take the charismatic renewal movement seriously. This is seen by the fact that since 1960, well over 100 official denominational documents on the movement have been produced. Assessments have become increasingly positive and it has been espoused by some leading figures, such as the Roman Catholic Cardinal Suenens from Belgium.

In Britain, one result of the Charismatic Movement has been the formation of House Churches (sometimes called New Churches). Frustrated by what they perceived as the straightjacket of traditional Christianity, but not attracted to the classical Pentecostal churches, some Christians began to meet in homes, schools, community centres or pubs in the 1960s and 70s. Some of these have grown into well-organised networks of churches, such as the Ichthus Fellowship in London. The Charismatic Vineyard Fellowship from California has spread to other countries under the leadership of John Wimber.

The impact of charismatic renewal on the mainstream churches has been considerable. In some places it has been divisive and some church members are suspicious of what they perceive to be an excess of emotion and enthusiasm. But many individual Christians and churches are less formal and more open to spontaneity than hitherto – even if they do not see themselves as 'belonging' to the charismatic movement.

The laity

Most of the above movements are, in one way or another, a move away from a priest or minister centred Church, to a more biblical notion of the Church as 'the body of Christ.'

'Laity' derives from a Greek word (Laos) meaning 'people'. In most churches today, the unity of *all* Christian believers – clergy and laity together – as 'the people of God' is stressed, along with the doctrine of 'the priesthood of all believers' (page 112). The classical Bible passage on the Church as 'the body of Christ' is 1 Corinthians 12–14. This stresses the fact that all members have gifts to be exercised 'for the common good.' Bishop John Robinson put it like this: *'The laity are not the helpers of the clergy, so that they can do their job. The clergy are the helpers of the laity so that they can be the Church of the world.'*

One remarkable lay-led initiative is to be found within universities. Several student-led religious societies are in evidence and an evangelical Christian Union is the largest single student society in some British universities.

—— Issues of gender and sexuality ——

Issues of gender and sexuality are currently being widely discussed in many churches, particularly in the West. Although not focused within a single movement, it will be convenient to consider some of these issues at this point.

—— Gender and language ——

God as Mother?

Throughout this book we have encountered traditional language for God; God is thought of as Father and referred to as 'he' (or, in older usage, *He*). This is offensive to some. They do not deny that this usage is to be found in the Bible and throughout most subsequent Christian history, but they argue that such language is culturally determined. In their view, it does not arise from essential theological considerations.

Strictly speaking, God is not a 'Person'. 'He' is a *supra* personal (not *sub*-personal). But, because personal categories are the highest we can imagine, we rightly use these. For centuries, following the teaching of Jesus, Christians have referred to God as 'Father'. But, runs the argument, it is equally valid to refer to God as 'Mother' or *She*. Indeed, they point out that the Bible describes God's love by using pictures from Motherhood: *'As a mother comforts her child, so will I comfort you.'* (Isaiah 66:13; see also 49:15)

We cannot avoid using images and metaphors when describing God. Motherhood suggests compassion, faithfulness and sacrifice: all highly appropriate to the God revealed in the Scriptures. Some advocates of this view also remind us that the word for Spirit in Hebrew (*RUaCH*) is feminine and in Greek (*pneuma*) it is neuter. Neither word is male! None of this is new. Anselm, Archbishop of Canterbury from 1093–1109, wrote, *'Jesus . . . you are gentle with us as a mother with her children.'* In the 14th century Mother Julian of Norwich spoke of 'Mother Jesus' and wrote, *'As truly as God is our Father, as truly God is our Mother.'*

In response, attention is drawn to the fact that the concept of the Fatherhood of God is persistent and central in the New Testament and throughout Christian history. Opponents of change argue that we are not at liberty to create a new and fashionable 'tradition'. They are concerned too that the notion of God as Mother has overtones of paganism and **New Age** thinking. Some are uncertain and hesitant about these issues. (I recall a conversation with a well-known and controversial bishop who frequently followed the word 'God' with the qualifying phrase, 'He, She or It'!)

The debate is not a 'battle of the sexes.' Men and women are to be found on both sides of the debate (Or, more accurately, *all* sides of the debate. As with most issues in this section, there are more than two viewpoints.)

Sons of God

Some Christians object to 'inclusive' language. For centuries, the word 'men' has been a commonplace for 'all human beings'. This will not do, say the objectors: men are men and women are women. Some modern liturgical texts are taking these concerns into account by reworking such phrases as 'for us men and our salvation' (in the Nicene Creed) and 'against our fellow men' (in the *Confession*).

Some also find difficulty with the biblical term 'Sons of God' when referred to women as well as men, preferring 'children of God', which is also found in the New Testament. Some feminist writers feel the force of all this very keenly. Dorothy McMahon expressed their controversial viewpoint with great clarity: *'There is no doubt in my mind that women sit in the pews of the churches year after year and fail to hear the Gospel. They listen to the Word like observers – they appreciate it, but they never claim it as their own. I believe that sexist language, that which excludes women and offers them only a male image of God, is a salvation issue. To ignore it is to be careless and half-hearted about the communication of the Gospel.'*

Some women strongly disagree with this viewpoint, arguing vigorously for the retention of traditional language.

Sexuality

Jesus and women

Contrary to the norms of his society, Jesus appears to have been unmarried. This is an inference from silence; the Bible says nothing definite either way. It is clear that he enjoyed the company of women and that he was at ease with them. As Hans Küng points out, Jesus' attitude was in striking contrast to the prevailing attitudes of his day.

Jewish men were advised to talk very little with women, including their own wives. Women were to be withdrawn from public view as far as possible and were required to avoid men's company in public. In the Temple they had access only to the women's forecourt. They were regarded (by Josephus, for example; see page 12) as inferior in every respect. Jesus confronted these attitudes. His behaviour on some occasions was regarded as scandalous by many of his contemporaries – for example, when he allowed a prostitute to wash his feet with her tears and wipe them with her hair. (Luke 7:36–50)

Christian history

History shows that the Church has often fallen short of Jesus' example. Women came to be regarded as a source of temptation; much was made of Eve's part in Adam's downfall. Sexual intimacy became suspect; virginity and celibacy were exalted. There has been a proper reaction against these attitudes in the 20th century. Sexual intimacy within marriage is to be welcomed as a gift from God. The *Song of*

Solomon, a celebration of erotic love in the Old Testament, has come into its own again.

Some would argue that the pendulum has swung too far. They assert that traditional Christian values and practices are under attack from the secular world in which the Church is set *and* from some within the Church itself. One thing is clear: issues of gender and sexuality are high on the agenda. The Anglican bishops debated *polygamy* at the 1988 Lambeth Conference because this is a live issue in parts of Africa. *Marriage, co-habitation* and *divorce* are under debate in the Western churches.

The notion of a *celibate priesthood* is often criticised from within the Roman Catholic Church. But the Vatican shows no signs of yielding to this pressure, even though around 20 per cent of priests marry and therefore cannot function as priests (page 166), and many would-be priests choose work where celibacy is not a requirement.

Homosexuality

This is another matter which challenges many churches. Some Christians argue that a homosexual orientation is 'given' by nature and, therefore, by God. All agree that promiscuity is wrong (whether heterosexual or homosexual). But in their view, faithful, loving relationships are blessed by God, whatever the gender of the parties.

Others strongly disagree. From certain Bible passages (few, they would concede, but clear) they argue that same-sex genital acts are sinful. Those with a homosexual orientation are welcome within the church, but their calling is to sexual abstinence.

These issues relating to human sexuality are likely to exercise (and perhaps divide) Christians well into the 21st century.

14
CHURCH AND SOCIETY

From the earliest days the Church has needed to work out its position in relation to Society. At first it was a minority group, often persecuted. The small but growing band of disciples sought to work out a distinctive lifestyle based on love for God and neighbour, and witness to their risen Lord, within a suspicious and hostile society. They recalled the vivid images used by Jesus; they were to be 'salt', 'light' and 'peacemakers' within their communities.

A radical change took place when the Emperor Constantine embraced the Christian faith in 312 AD (see Chapter 15). In a short time their fortunes were transformed. No longer outlawed or marginalised, Christians had to learn how to wield secular power. There were attempts to turn back the clock. The pagan Emperor Julian ('the Apostate': c 331–363) wished his subjects to honour his gods and worked hard to bring this about. He failed, and in a moving testimony he paid tribute to the power of Christian love. It is a clear example of the Christian faith at its best, making an impact on society. Julian referred to Christian believers as 'atheists' and 'godless Galileans', for they worshipped one invisible God and denied his gods.

> *'Atheism* (ie Christian Faith) *has been specially advanced through the loving service rendered to strangers, and through their care for the burial of the dead. It is a scandal that there is not a single Jew who is a beggar, and that the godless Galileans care not only for their own poor but for ours as well; while those who belong to us look in vain for the help that we should render them.'*

Power and persecution

Jesus came, 'not to be served but to serve.' At the Last Supper he washed his disciples' feet as an example of humble service (John 13:15). But the Church has not always stayed close to its Founder's intentions. In its strength the Church has often betrayed its Lord. This is partly due to the fact that Christians share the prejudices and many of the assumptions to be found in every culture and period of history. It also results from the fact that the Church has sometimes been corrupted from within. Men far from the Spirit of Christ, and with little regard for the teaching of Christ, nevertheless found positions of power within the Church of Christ. As a result, the impact of the Church on society has sometimes been harmful.

But the Church itself has been subject to tyranny. Over the centuries Christians have had to work out how to live under a range of repressive regimes. Should they seek to co-exist or to resist? In the 20th century, the Church in Europe found itself in the shadow of two especially hostile ideologies.

Nazism

Like many politicians and ordinary citizens, Church leaders found it difficult to see the shape of things to come, when Hitler took power. Within the Roman Catholic Church, leadership was sometimes weak and uncertain. But some bishops and priests stood firm and several were martyred. The Catholic dean of the cathedral at Berlin, Lichtenberg, protested from his pulpit against the persecution of Jews; he died on the way to a concentration camp. Opposition by Church leaders caused Hitler to drop his 'euthanasia for incurables' plan. And *'Pope Pius XII secretly allowed himself to be used as a channel of communication between the German conspirators against Hitler and the British government.'* (Owen Chadwick)

Among German Protestants, the Confessing Church held firm against the Nazi regime. The Lutheran pastor Martin Niemöller was a leading member who was imprisoned in a concentration camp by Hitler in 1937. He refused offers of conditional release and stayed there until the war ended. Dietrich Bonhoeffer was another important figure (page 18).

'The resistance of the Confessing Church to the policies of Hitler continued into and through the war years. It also survived the bitter attack on all opposition and non-conformity, and raised its voice constantly in 2,000 pulpits and in every possible way.' (E H Robertson).

Marxism

Karl Marx (1813–83) declared religion to be 'the opium of the people' because it could be used by the wealthy to exploit the poor, by promising better things in the world to come. Following the Russian Revolution of 1917 the Church entered turbulent waters as it came under an atheist dictatorship. Some 8000 priests and nuns were assassinated during Lenin's life-time. Under Stalin (1877–1953) it was difficult for Christians in the USSR even to meet for worship.

Subsequent leaders proved little better – especially those with a KGB (Secret Police) background. There was tension in Communist lands between those Christians who felt that they should oppose an atheistic regime, and those who believed that it was possible to make an uneasy alliance with the State (see page 162).

Christians in China, North Korea and elsewhere continue to face the acute problem of following Christ in an officially atheistic and hostile state. But as we have seen (page 164) there is clear evidence that the Church in China is growing rapidly.

Christian initiatives

Today in the West, the Church wields influence rather than power. Individual believers have to take a stance with reference to 'the world'. Some see the secular world as essentially evil; in their view the Church is called to be an active counter-culture. Other believers take a more favourable attitude towards secular power, seeking to work for the Kingdom of God in the midst of the kingdoms of this world. They are willing to consider individual issues on their merits and wish to work with all people of good will, regardless of creed.

The Christian impact on Society has been enormous, as many sections of this book make clear. It was the Church which gave birth to universities and hospitals in medieval Europe. And the Church built glorious cathedrals, and gave patronage to artists and musicians (see

Chapters 19 and 20). On the political front it has been argued that the very notion of the liberal democratic State 'owes its existence very largely to Christianity in its Protestant forms and rests upon certain values of freedom and the worth of persons which are authentically, if not exclusively, Christian.' (Basil Mitchell)

Sadly, the churches have often lacked urgency and vision. But in 19th-century England individual Christians were at the forefront of those who opposed the slave trade (William Wilberforce) and regulated working hours for children (Lord Shaftesbury). A wide range of other issues exercised Christian consciences: the treatment of mental illness (also Lord Shaftesbury), chimney boys (Charles Kingsley), nursing methods (Florence Nightingale), prison reform (Elizabeth Fry), social conditions in the new towns (William Booth).

Individual Christians were deeply involved in the care of children, many of whom were homeless in Victorian England. Most successful was 'Dr' Barnardo, in whose name homes for children have been established around the world. Other distinguished organisations which were started then and continue to serve children now, are the Children's Society (Anglican), the National Children's Homes (Methodist), Spurgeon's Homes (Baptist) and Muller Homes (Christian Brethren).

Modern critics of Victorian reformers can be harsh, and those reformers are certainly not above criticism. It is also true that many other Christians lacked their vision and that some non-Christians made a vital contribution to a range of reforms: Christians do not claim a monopoly on compassion and justice. But many of the initiatives outlined above were visionary and desperately needed. Lord Clark (not himself a Christian) in *Civilisation* described Wilberforce and Shaftesbury as two of the greatest names *'in the history of humanitarianism.'* Of Elizabeth Fry, he wrote that her *'spiritual influence on the prisoners at Newgate was really a miracle.'*

The impact upon society of Christian individuals and groups has continued into the 20th century. Christian Socialists like Archbishop William Temple helped prepare for Britain's Welfare State (page 252) and many modern caring agencies have Christian origins:

Samaritans began as a result of the concern of an Anglican rector in London. Chad Varah became aware that a large number of people were in despair and suicidal. He invited them to ring Mansion House

9000. Within 20 years this telephone ministry of listening and befriending had grown into an international movement.

Shelter is an influential pressure group for good housing in Britain. It began on 1st December 1966 as the result of the united concern of five housing organisations, three of which contained the word Catholic, Christian or Church. Christian leaders were key figures in those early days and Shelter's first chairman, Bruce Kenrick, was a Christian minister.

Habitat for Humanity is an American initiative which builds subsidised homes for needy Americans in the USA. It has also pioneered 'appropriate technology' homes in other continents and countries (Tanzania, for example).

Several Christian Organisations work among refugees and in areas struck by famine, drought and long-term poverty. In addition to bringing emergency aid, many of these organisations seek to influence long-term policy. Christian missionaries have a record of distinction in the fight against leprosy.

The Hospice Movement was started in Britain under the inspiration of Dame Cicely Saunders. She pioneered pain control and saw the need for small, intimate units, where terminally ill patients could be cared for and families and friends welcomed. Dame Cicely gladly acknowledges that without the inspiration and power of Christ, she would have lacked the strength needed to establish the movement. Her idea caught on and hospices are now found around the world.

Amenesty International was started by Peter Benenson, a Christian lawyer. Concerned at the plight of prisoners of conscience, he prayed in the crypt of St Martin-in-the-Fields in London's Trafalgar Square. He developed the idea of a network of people who would write to, and about, prisoners of conscience, and speak on their behalf. At a practical level, the existing network of churches was important. Peter Benenson launched the movement on Trinity Sunday 1961 to emphasise *'that the power of the Holy Spirit works to bring together people of diverse origins by influencing their common conscience.'*

When the first 200 letters came, the guards gave me back my clothes. When the next 200 letters came, the prison Director came to see me. When the next pile of letters arrived, the Director got in touch with his superior. The letters kept arriving, and the President was informed. The letters still kept arriving, and the President called the prison and told them to let me go.' From a letter by a former prisoner of conscience.

The above movements are not limited to Christian believers; in most cases a wide range of views and beliefs are to be found among their activists. But it remains true that these organisations have been built on Christian foundations.

A focus for dissent

The Christian Church has often been a natural focus for dissent against established authority. In the 20th century this has been extremely important in many places and for many issues.

Martin Luther King (1929–1968)

Few individuals are honoured shortly after death by the creation of an annual public holiday in their name. This honour marked the achievements of Martin Luther King – Pastor of Ebenezer Baptist Church in Atlanta. By personal charisma, courage, brilliant organisation and moving rhetoric, he led a massive non-violent movement in an attempt to establish equality for black citizens in the USA. The achievements of the *civil rights movement* were considerable, but related issues, such as positive discrimination, are still high on the political agenda in the USA. Like Gandhi, upon whom he based his campaign of non-violent resistance, Dr King was assassinated.

The Berlin Wall

As Marxism came to a swift end throughout Europe in the late 1980s, the Christian churches were a natural rallying point for dissent from the old order. Large prayer vigils were held, with flickering candles, communal singing and inspiring addresses. The churches in Eastern Europe are finding life in the new order easier (in that they are no longer persecuted) but more complex. Materialism, commercialism and hedonism may yet prove more corrosive than Marxism. Some Eastern Europeans look back to the old order with nostalgia.

South Africa

The old white-dominated order in South Africa claimed to be Christian, and the ruling white party was closely linked with the Dutch Reformed Church. But dissent often found expression in the Christian Churches. Best known among black Christian leaders is Archbishop Desmond Tutu (A Nobel Peace Prize winner), but there are many others.

The new democratic South Africa is, thus far, a 'success' story, but there is a long road to travel and levels of violence – a legacy from the days of apartheid – are still extremely high. In his autobiography (*Long Walk to Freedom*) Nelson Mandela is not uncritical of the churches, especially the Dutch Reformed Church. But as a member of the Methodist Church he speaks affectionately of the church of his childhood: '. . . *the Church was as concerned with this world as the next: I saw that virtually all of the achievements of Africans seemed to have come about through the missionary work of the Church.*' He pays special tribute to his black Methodist housemaster (Reverend Mokitimi) and to Archbishops Trevor Huddleston and Desmond Tutu.

Failure

As with all human endeavours, we find the bad alongside the good. No Christian can feel anything but shame when contemplating 'the troubles' in Northern Ireland, the terrible massacres in Rwanda and the war in the former Yugoslavia. None of these were, or are, religious wars: they are about land, power, tribalism, independence and nationalism. Their causes are complex and embedded in history, but the divisions are sometimes strongly related to religious allegiances. Some Christians in these arenas have been distinguished by their contribution to peace, but others have failed to live up to their high calling to be 'salt' and 'light' in society. Many failed to be peacemakers; some engaged in violence.

Current Issues

The pace of change continues to accelerate and new ethical issues surface frequently. In this section we shall touch upon a few of the most pressing issues facing society and consider the Christian response

– or in most cases, the Christian *responses*. As we shall see, with the possible exception of the Roman Catholic Church, there is a solid Christian 'party line' on very few issues. In the Western churches in particular, lively debate is often regarded as a healthy sign. Christians are encouraged to work things out for themselves on the basis of:

- principles drawn from the Bible and Christian tradition – giving special attention to compassion and justice
- prayerful dependence upon the Holy Spirit
- consultation and discussion
- pragmatic implications

The churches have been energetic in thinking and acting on a wide range of issues. Such consideration takes place at international and national levels, and the churches have specialists upon whom they can call. But concern is also shown at the local level. For example, many Roman Catholic churches have a 'Justice and Peace' group. And in many British cities and towns, Christians have practical schemes to help homeless people.

Consideration of even a few of these issues would require at least a book, if not a series. Here we can do no more than note some of the main issues and briefly consider one or two – to give some idea of the way in which Christians approach these questions. Over the past few decades, the churches have been involved in debate about the following:

- Can there be a 'just war' in a nuclear age?
- Terrorism: is a freedom fighter a criminal or a soldier?
- The expanding world population: food and other resources, world trade and third world debt
- Ecology and the integrity of creation
- The use and abuse of drugs
- Human sexuality, including homosexuality
- Human fertility: the status and protection of the human embryo
- Animal rights
- Marriage, co-habitation, polygamy, divorce and the family
- The welfare of children
- Aids, abortion, euthanasia, gambling
- Life in a multi-cultural and multi-faith society

This list could be extended. We will consider briefly four issues: abortion, contraception, euthanasia and the Christian attitude to other Faiths.

Abortion

As the world at large debates this issue, so do the churches. Some Christians are 'pro-choice'. They see abortion as a question of women's rights. They argue that the main focus must be upon the woman, rather than upon the embryo which is no more than a *potential* human being. But most Christians strongly disagree; they are 'pro-life' rather than pro-choice. The Roman Catholic Church and the 'Christian Right' (ie conservative Christians) in particular, have taken a strong stance – especially in the USA. They argue that life is God-given and that a human being is brought into existence at conception, not at birth.

They apply the Bible's emphasis on care for the vulnerable. In the Old Testament, protection for powerless people (widows, orphans and strangers) is emphasised. Nothing is more vulnerable and less able to defend itself, than a foetus. So the Church must fight on behalf of the unborn child. Those who perform abortions are called 'baby-murderers'. The notion that a woman has the right to choose what she does with her own body (the pro-choice stance) is dismissed on the grounds that the foetus is an independent life, not simply a disposable organ of the mother.

For some, the rights of the foetus are absolute. Others would make exceptions for exceptional cases, such as pregnancies resulting from rape or incest, and those which threaten the mother's life. For some, pragmatic considerations are important. To make abortion illegal would not stop abortions; it would drive the practice on to the back-streets. This would endanger desperate, vulnerable women – especially teenagers. Christians who take this view argue that abortion should be legalised – but more carefully controlled and safe-guarded by law than at present.

Contraception

This sharply divides the churches. The official teaching of the Roman Catholic Church is that all contraception is wrong, apart from abstinence and the use of the 'rhythm method' (tuning into a woman's monthly cycle). Leaders of the Roman Catholic Church argue that it is sinful for mere mortals to interfere with God's sovereign will, by preventing conception in any other way. Sexual intercourse should always carry with it the possibility of procreation. '. . . each and every marriage act must remain open to the transmission of life' (*Catechism of the Catholic Church*). Most other churches sharply disagree on three grounds:

1 The population explosion is a major issue. It is irresponsible to encourage large families – especially in the 'developing world' (a term which is used for the world's poorest countries and which often hides the fact that some nations are growing poorer).

2 Responsible stewardship requires adults to plan their families according to their means, their preferences and their health.

3 Sexual intimacy within marriage is good in itself; the fact that it need no longer be linked with the possibility of conception is to be welcomed with thanksgiving.

It is evident that even within the Roman Catholic Church, private judgement on this matter is widespread. In Italy, 85 per cent of the population claims to be Roman Catholic and about 33 per cent attend Mass regularly. But Italy has the lowest birth-rate in Europe. One strand of Christian ethics has always acknowledged the supremacy of the individual Christian's conscience – even over teaching by Church leaders.

Euthanasia

Advances in medical science have made it possible to prolong the lives of very sick people. Some individuals have lived on in a coma ('persistent vegetative state') for years. Should such people be kept alive artificially for such long periods? Many people are clear that the answer is 'No'. Others point out that some individuals thought to be beyond recovery have resumed an active life. Some Christians urge that a human being remains a human being – even in a PVS. And *every* human being has a right to food, drink and air. To withhold nutrition is wrong, in their view.

Such debates are new. In earlier centuries – indeed for much of the 20th century – this was not an issue. Such victims would have died because of inadequate knowledge and technology. This is a clear illustration of the way in which advances in medical science raise new ethical issues.

Improvements in medical care also mean that, in the developed world, more people live much longer than hitherto. Clearly this is good news; but not for everyone. For it does mean that some people live for long periods in severe ill health, pain and distress. From this springs the desire to legalise *euthanasia* or 'mercy-killing', to make possible an 'easy death' for those who request this. Holland has already passed such legislation.

All Christians have sympathy with this viewpoint and some have felt the force of it within their families. But most Christians are against legalising euthanasia – which does not necessarily mean that they believe that very sick people should be kept alive by all possible means. The Christian response is based on theological principles.

- *The sanctity of life*, which is a gift from God.
- *Concern* that human beings should not 'play God' in matters of life and death.
- *Compassion* On a practical level, the hospice movement (pioneered by Christians) has made enormous advances in pain control. And it has helped countless patients, and their families, to face death.
- *Care for the vulnerable* The practical outcome of euthanasia would be counterproductive, causing widespread distress for sick and elderly people. It is a short step from legalising voluntary euthanasia, to causing elderly people to wonder if they have a *duty* to die, in case they are (perhaps unwittingly) a burden on their families.
- *Human sinfulness* Although most advocates of euthanasia have good motives, society is not to be trusted with such a fundamental change in the law. Those who argue against euthanasia on these grounds (as does Dame Cicely Saunders), sometimes point to abortion. What began as carefully worded legislation for hard cases, has virtually become 'abortion on demand' in some societies. Slopes can be slippery and steep.

One world, many faiths

It is impossible to consider the Church in Society without giving thought to the Christian response to other faiths. We are accustomed to the notion of a 'global village'. Through travel and television, we have insights into other nations and cultures which were impossible before the middle of the 20th century. As a result, many people have some acquaintance with a few of the world's various religions.

For the most part these are situated in clearly identifiable cultural blocs. Saudi Arabia and Pakistan are strongly Muslim; India is predominantly Hindu, with some Muslims, Christians and others; Europe has its roots in Christianity. But some nations have experienced a cultural mix during the 20th century. For example, many immigrants came to Britain in the 1950s, 60s and 70s – and they naturally wished to keep their own culture and religion. Many Christians from the West Indies found traditional British Christianity rather reserved, so they formed Black Churches. Muslims and others came in large numbers and tended to form communities in certain urban areas, such as Bradford, Birmingham, Leicester and Southall.

In relation to Britain's 55 million population, the number of adherents of non-Christian faiths is relatively small. Some towns have many Temples, Synagogues and Mosques to cater for Hindus, Sikhs, Jews, Muslims and others. But the total number following faiths other than Christianity in Britain is no more than 4–5 per cent. Some Christians are keenly aware of the need to understand and communicate across cultural and religious boundaries. Indeed, some commentators see constructive inter-faith dialogue, together with environmental issues, as two of the most pressing issues facing modern civilisation.

Multi-cultural discussion is often in the arena of social concerns – on issues such as racism, policing and education. But sooner or later members of different faith groups must tackle issues of ultimate truth. How much do the different religions have in common? Indeed, are all religions really saying the same thing? If not, can they all be true? As Christians have grappled with the relationship of Christianity to other faiths, three broad responses have emerged.

An exclusive approach

'God has revealed the Way and the Truth and the Life in Jesus Christ and wills this to be known throughout the world.' (Hendrik Kraemer 1888–1965) Jesus Christ is not merely a teacher or a prophet. He is the Son of God, the Word made flesh. He is also *the* Saviour of the world, not one saviour among many.

Some who take this view believe that those who do not turn to Christ will not be saved – whether or not they have heard the gospel of redemption. From this belief they have found great energy for evangelism and missionary endeavour. 'To save the lost' was a driving force for many during the missionary expansion of the 19th century. In the 1830s The Church Missionary Society advertised in London for missionaries for West Africa, warning that life expectancy in the 'white man's grave' was not more than six months. Scores volunteered to go.

Others who hold an exclusive position about Jesus Christ nevertheless take a different view on salvation: the great Swiss theologian Karl Barth (1886–1968) for example. He declared that salvation is only possible through Christ. Christian faith is God's revelation; all other religions are human constructions. However 'at the end of history . . . God's grace will triumph completely, and all will come to faith in Christ.' (Alister McGrath's summary of Barth's view.)

An inclusive approach

The Roman Catholic scholar Karl Rahner believes that Christianity is unique and absolute, for Jesus Christ is the self-revelation of God. But God's will is that *all* should be saved (1 Timothy 2:4). So Rahner argues that despite their shortcomings, non-Christian religions are capable of mediating the saving grace of God to their members. Faithful followers of other faiths are to be regarded as 'anonymous Christians' – they are saved because they are inspired by Christ, without realising it. 'More know him (Jesus) than know him by name', as one summary puts it.

Critics of Rahner's view argue that it is 'triumphalistic' – a Christian takeover bid. Others argue that it is the only approach which does justice *both* to the authentic experience of God to be found in other religions *and* to the Christian conviction that in Jesus, God is revealed in a unique way.

A pluralist approach

John Hick argues for the need to move away from a Christ-centred approach to a God-centred approach. He believes that all religions lead to the same God. Christians have no 'special access'; God is universally available through all religions. John Hick's critics argue that his desertion of Christ as a reference point means that he has abandoned any claim to speak from a *Christian* perspective.

As Christians ponder these important questions, the following practical steps are open to us.

- It is important that in dialogue, the various faiths should be true to themselves. 'Fudging' issues is not helpful. Of course the great world religions have features and teaching in common, especially the three great *monotheistic faiths* (Judaism, Christianity and Islam). Muslims, for example, honour Jesus as a prophet. But there are fundamental differences too. It is for this reason that many adherents of various faiths, including many Christians, are unenthusiastic about *multi-faith worship.* It leaves too many questions hanging in the air, and too many traditional forms of prayer must be excluded in order to save offence. Of course, this does not mean that members of different faiths should not gather to mark great occasions or terrible tragedies. At such times, shared silence can be very powerful.

- No one pretends that dialogue is easy. How can a Muslim progress in conversation with a Christian, when the Muslim believes that Jesus did not die on the Cross, and that the doctrine of the Trinity verges on blasphemy? But conversation is vital, especially as in some parts of the world, relations between different faith communities are bound up with land, property, prestige and political power: an explosive mixture. In some countries, with the rise of fundamentalism, relations between Muslims and Christians have deteriorated in recent years: a cause for concern and prayer.

- It is important, too, that followers of the world's various faiths should allow the best possible representation of religions other than their own. It is too easy to take aberrations as the norm and to allow caricatures of other faiths to form the popular view. Many Muslims are not fundamentalist; not every Hindu is happy with all aspects of the caste system; few Christians endorse the Crusades or intransigence in Ireland.

Perhaps, in the end, only one thing is more important for the safety of our world than inter-faith dialogue. And that is inter-faith friendship.

15

THE FIRST FIVE CENTURIES

Author's note   *Some readers will welcome an outline of the history of the Church. It will, of course, be very sketchy and it will involve some repetition of material contained in previous chapters. But to set ideas and developments within a historical framework will, I hope, be helpful.*

The Church is born

The Jewish religion at the time of Jesus was made up of many groups. They disagreed sharply on some issues but all groups owed allegiance to One God and to the sacred institutions of *Law* and *Sabbath* (and most of them to the Temple, too). In those early days following his death and resurrection, all the disciples of Jesus were Jews; they observed the ways of Judaism and often met in the precincts of the Temple in Jerusalem. Their one distinguishing feature was allegiance to Jesus. The opening of The Acts of the Apostles in the New Testament shows a group of about 120, waiting in Jerusalem. They did this in response to an instruction of the risen Christ, just before his ascension into heaven. (Luke 24:49)

Pentecost

The **Feast of Pentecost** was an important Jewish Festival which brought many visitors – Jews from various countries – to Jerusalem.

The disciples of Jesus were 'all together in one place' when God's Holy Spirit came upon them. The result was a noisy and undignified exhibition! There were 'tongues of fire', a strong wind, and an ability to speak 'in other tongues as the Spirit enabled them.' (Acts 2:4)

A crowd gathered. The confusion was so great that some cynics accused them of being drunk. Peter took the opportunity to preach. He drew on the Hebrew Scriptures, explaining that the words of the prophet Joel had just been fulfilled: *'In the last days, God says, I will pour out my Spirit . . . .'* (Acts 2:17; Joel 2:28) He went on to assert that:

- Jesus, a descendant of King David, had been raised from the dead by God.
- God had made him, 'both Lord and Christ.'
- He was now seated at God's right hand.
- Their own nation had crucified this Jesus.
- They could be forgiven through repentance and baptism.

About 3000 responded.

A famous New Testament verse (Acts 2:42) describes the lifestyle of those early followers of Jesus.

The main features were:

- The Apostles' teaching
- Mutual fellowship
- Breaking bread together
- Prayer
- Sharing possessions
- Joyfulness

Persecution

Throughout this period there were many outstanding leaders such as John the apostle, James the Lord's brother, Barnabas the missionary, Philip the deacon and Stephen the first martyr. But Peter was clearly the main teacher and leader. This comes as no surprise, because Jesus himself had told Peter that he would be the rock on which he would build his Church. (Matthew 16:18)

Future generations of Christians were to draw strength from the fact that Peter was used in this way. For in the Gospel records Peter often failed: in particular, he denied Jesus just before the crucifixion (Mark 14:66–72). In describing Peter's failings with such honesty, the Bible assures us that God has a place for the weak as well as the strong; for the coward as well as the brave.

The rapid growth of this new group caused unrest among the Jewish leaders. They thought that they had stopped a dangerous movement by crucifying Jesus, but now it seemed stronger than ever. They issued threats; they imprisoned Peter; they stoned Stephen; James, the brother of John, was beheaded by King Herod. But the courage and confidence of these leaders only encouraged others. *Persecution resulted in dispersion. And dispersion meant that the gospel spread far and wide* (Acts 8:4). It spread, not only by the energy and commitment of named leaders, but by the enthusiasm, integrity and love of ordinary believers. For example, the Christians who founded the Church in Rome itself at an early date, are unknown to us.

One man, a Roman citizen from Tarsus in Cilicia, took a strong lead in attempting to stop the spread of the movement. Saul was a Jew of 'the dispersion' – the name given to the many Jews who lived outside Israel. He turned his enormous energy and single-minded determination against the followers of 'the Way', until his famous conversion to Jesus Christ while travelling to Damascus (Acts 9:3–6). The seeds of his conversion may have been sown at the stoning of Stephen, the first Christian martyr. Saul hated all that Stephen stood for, but it is likely that Stephen's courage and faith made a deep impression upon him.

Following his conversion, *Saul of Tarsus* became *Paul the apostle to the Gentiles*. His decision to take the gospel to the Gentiles – to all people regardless of race or rank – was of the utmost importance. Indeed, Paul would not have called it a 'decision'. It was, he claimed, a task given to him by God. Paul's dynamic energy, his single-minded vision, his brilliance as a debater, his persistence as a pastor and letter writer, and his courage as a traveller, ensured that the gospel was preached in many countries around the Mediterranean before he died (probably executed in Rome under the Emperor Nero in 67 AD).

Crossing boundaries

At first it was Jews who joined this new movement. But soon Gentiles (a term for all non-Jews) were converted to Christ, in Antioch in Syria where believers were first called 'Christians'. Gentiles presented the young Church with major problems. Should it be preaching to non-Jews at all? In a remarkable vision, God made it abundantly clear to Peter that Gentiles should be incorporated into the Church (Acts 10; page 76). But then came another issue. Was it necessary to become a Jew before following the Jewish Messiah? Should Gentiles who wanted to join the Church be required to convert to Judaism first – by embracing the Jewish Law, including dietary rules and the practice of circumcision?

The answer of Paul, the great missionary strategist and theologian, was 'No'. This was highly contentious for many Jewish Christians. They had simply never imagined that it might be possible to follow the one true God, except by being a devout Jew. The key contention of Paul and Peter was that salvation was a release from 'law'. Being a Christian was a matter of being 'saved', or put right with God, through faith in Jesus Christ and what he had done. This being so, nothing else could contribute to salvation. So it seemed both unnecessary and misleading to expect Gentiles to be circumcised. A great controversy ensued. This led to the Council of Jerusalem in about 49 AD, at which the views of Peter, Paul and Barnabas (endorsed by James), triumphed (Acts 15).

These very early events in the life of the Church were momentous in ensuring that Christianity crossed national, cultural and social boundaries. A different decision would have meant that the 'Jesus movement' remained as one strand within Judaism, with little potential for growth.

This kind of problem was to recur frequently: the need for the Church to distinguish between the core tradition and matters of cultural or religious addition. The latter may be good in themselves but are not essential to the gospel. They can become subtly dangerous, standing in place of the message of salvation through Christ. And they can be used by one group in the Church to impose its authority over another.

Remembering the story

It thus became a matter of the utmost importance to have *a record of the life and teaching of Jesus*, as a touchstone in debate. The four Gospels were completed in the last 40 years of the first century (some scholars would date them rather earlier). The evangelists were interpreters, or 'portrait painters', who wanted the authentic voice of Jesus to be heard.

As the apostles and their successors died, and as the challenge of heretics became more acute, it was necessary to define what was to count as authoritative Scripture (see Chapter 5). The broad outlines of this were quickly established ie which books focusing on Jesus should be regarded as Holy Scripture ('New Testament'), alongside the Hebrew Scriptures ('Old Testament').

— Confronting heresy and division —

Meanwhile, as the first century wore on, the Church continued to expand rapidly because of:

- the relevance of the good news of God's love shown in Jesus Christ
- the power of the Holy Spirit
- the attractive lifestyle of ordinary Christians
- the vision and energy of Christian leaders

Growth sometimes took place in the teeth of fierce persecution. This was sporadic and local; there was no official policy because the Roman Empire regarded the early Christian movement as insignificant. So the Church had a vital breathing space in which to develop policies and structures to deal with its own internal problems – particularly heresy and schism.

Heresy

This is already detectable in the New Testament period. It is evident in the Church in Corinth, where knowledge and spiritual gifts were thought to more important than love; and in Colossae, where angels were worshipped. These are two of the cluster of Greek ideas which characterise *Gnosticism* – a term which comes from the Greek word for knowledge (*Gnosis*). Gnostics believed that there was an esoteric, secret knowledge available to some, which would enable them to pass beyond the present evil world and achieve salvation. 'Christian' Gnostics saw Jesus as the redeemer but argued that he could not possibly have taken our material, human flesh, which they considered to be evil. Gnosticism is a word which covers a wide range of ideas, many of which presented a considerable threat to genuine Christianity. The Church's defence against heresy was threefold:

- heretics were disciplined and sometimes excommunicated
- the spiritual riches of the Christian Faith were explored more deeply
- a renewed emphasis was placed on sound, effective ministry

Church leaders insisted that the gospel was not a secret way available only to some, as the Gnostics believed. It was open to all. Hence the importance of:

- a grasp of the basics (creeds)
- authoritative sources (New Testament Scriptures)
- sound teaching (an authoritative ministry)

In the New Testament there is no prescribed structure for ministry in the Church. But during the second century a pattern of authorised ministry developed, which came to be widely accepted. This had a threefold order: deacon, priest (or presbyter) and bishop.

Schism

Breaking away from other Christians usually resulted from dissatisfaction with the spirituality, order or discipline within the Church. As the Church became more structured, there was a loss of fervour and distinctiveness. As it was 'institutionalised' it became more concerned with consolidation than with advance; more concerned with the definition of office than with the spontaneity of shared gifts. Some Christians resisted this.

In the second half of the second century Montanus began to prophesy, speaking in 'tongues' in Phrygia. His followers included two women, Prisca and Maximilla. Montanists reacted against the perceived intellectualism, formalism, compromise and authority of the official Church. They included at least one outstanding theologian, namely Tertullian (c 160 – c 220). This movement raised an important question: *how far does authority lie with those who hold office within the Church? And how far does it lie with prophets who claim a direct 'word' from the Holy Spirit – a word which sometimes goes beyond anything which the tradition allows?*

Christianity and culture

Other controversies arose. There were those who regarded the State as the abode of satan. They saw martyrdom as the highest honour – a means of fellowship with Christ. But others looked forward to a time when the dominant culture would understand and accept Christ. The former tended to be world-renouncing; the latter world-affirming. The latter presented the Christian message in a way which was sympathetic to the dominant Greek culture. Their most important representative was Justin Martyr (c 100 – c 165).

The growing impact of Christianity is evident from the fact that a leading pagan intellectual called Celsus published a sharp attack upon it (c 178). This, in turn, was countered by a great Christian theologian, Origen (c 185 – c 254). He was the outstanding representative of '*a new tradition, that of the sophisticated Christian scholar who could match any pagan philosopher.*' (David Bosch)

Ordinary life

Then, as now, the real test of Christianity is to be found in ordinary homes, towns and local churches. What was it like to be a Christian in those early days?

There were many distinguishing features. While pagan men slept with their slave girls as of right, Christian husbands were expected to be faithful to their wives. Attitudes to children were markedly different too: Christians opposed the killing of unwanted babies by exposure, actively rescuing foundlings. They deplored abortion, putting it on a level with infanticide.

Sex appears to have caused unease within the Church; as it did in later centuries. The Bible celebrates erotic love in *The Song of Solomon*. But by the mid-second century, the apocryphal *Acts of John* felt it necessary to present St John as a life-long virgin. Around AD 400, 'Jerome was confident that even married apostles lived in mutual continence, after the example of their unmarried Lord and his ever virgin mother.' (Henry Chadwick)

From early days, Christians were reticent to become soldiers. The vivid military imagery in the New Testament is about *spiritual* warfare. One aspect of this battle was against poverty. The Church sought to protect widows and orphans, and provide hospices for the sick. By AD 250 the Roman church was feeding 1500 distressed persons; late in the fourth century the church in Syrian Antioch had feeding programmes for 3000, complete with a register of names.

Perhaps the most remarkable feature of Church life was the way in which, at its best, it *overcame barriers of race, class and gender*. 'There is neither Jew nor Greek, slave nor free, male nor female, for you are all one in Christ Jesus', wrote St Paul (Galatians 3:28). Slaves sang hymns with slave owners; some women, such as Lydia and Priscilla (Acts 16 & 18), played a leading role in church life.

Coming to terms with the Roman Empire

As the Church grew, persecutions were more sustained. Those in the third and early fourth centuries were particularly severe, culminating in the Great Persecution under the Emperor Diocletian in 303–312. This was really a vain attempt to roll back Christianity which was becoming ever stronger. In 312 Constantine became Emperor, having declared his allegiance to Christ before a decisive battle with his main rival. In 313 he issued his famous Milan Edict giving religious toleration.

Very soon the Church was given special privileges. Many of the most accomplished leaders and thinkers were Christians and, though there was still sporadic opposition, its position was very strong. It now had to cope with being popular – a friend of the State rather than a foe. Secular and political considerations entered into Christianity in a new way. Problems in the Church were no longer a matter of indifference to the State. Decisions of the Church in matters of discipline or doctrine might have an enormous impact on the unity of the Empire.

Church, State and Schism

One major issue of discipline was how to treat those Christians who had denied their faith under persecution ('apostasy'). This was no academic debate. In North Africa, Caecilian was made Bishop of Carthage (311) and one of the consecrating bishops present was a 'traditor' (ie he had surrendered the Scriptures under threat). Caecilian was tainted by association and unacceptable to many. So they elected Donatus as bishop. There was a deep schism fuelled by local dislike of the Roman (pro-Caecilian) colonists and by economic unrest.

The question for the State was how to put down a rebellion inflamed by Christian convictions. The question for the Church was ultimately one of authority. When the Church was divided, was its true voice the local majority or the wider majority? This issue rumbled on for hundreds of years. Distinctions between Church and State became blurred. Constantine made a judgement against the Donatists and tried (unsuccessfully) to enforce it by arms. Christian leaders such as St Augustine of Hippo (354-430) urged that the judgement of the *whole Church* had authority over any particular part: schismatics should be suppressed by force. All this greatly weakened the North African Church, which was virtually wiped out by the advances of Islam in the seventh and eighth centuries.

—— Church, State and doctrine ——

Two major theological questions came to divide Christians.

- the doctrine of the Trinity (see page 15 and Glossary)
- the relationship of the human and divine natures within Christ

Arius (c 250 – c 336) was an Alexandrian priest who taught that Christ was inferior to the Father. His views split the Eastern Church and again the State became involved. The Emperor Constantine called the Council of Nicaea (325), the first really international, or 'ecumenical', Council of the Church. It affirmed that Christ was 'of one substance with the Father'. The Council left ambiguities and the conflict continued. The doughty guardian of orthodoxy throughout this debate was St Athanasius (c 296 – 373), Bishop of Alexandria.

He suffered for his stand, being exiled from his *See* (official 'seat') five times. Again, the State, in the shape of Constantine's successors, played a key role, often against orthodoxy. Eventually the Emperor Theodosius convened the Council of Constantinople (381). This Council, in the process of giving us the Nicene Creed, strongly asserted that both the Son and the Holy Spirit were of 'one essence' with God the Father.

These *Christological controversies* (questions about Jesus Christ) centred around two great cities:

Alexandria emphasised the divinity of Christ: sometimes, as with Apollinarius (c 310 – c 390), in a way which denied that Christ was fully human.

Antioch emphasised Christ's humanity, but in a way which sometimes suggested that Christ had a 'split personality': one human nature, one divine nature, always kept distinct. The matter was further complicated because it became part of a bitter conflict for supremacy between the Sees of Constantinople and Alexandria.

A decision was reached at the Council of Chalcedon (451). The Council declared that Christ was *'acknowledged in two natures, without confusion, without change, without division, without separation.'* But he was acknowledged as one Person, not *'parted or divided into two persons.'* Though a definition was worked out which still remains the touchstone of orthodoxy, it was far from satisfactory to a significant group called *Monophysites*. They maintained that Christ had only one nature, which was divine. Despite many efforts, they could not be reconciled. They eventually emerged as the Syrian, Coptic and Abyssinian Churches (see Chapter 12).

However necessary, the definitions of Nicaea, Constantinople and Chalcedon were purchased at a high price. Philosophical abstractions could too easily obscure the sense of a personal relationship with God through Jesus Christ. Politics, whether in the (sometimes unseemly) rivalries of theologians, bishops and great ecclesiastical centres, or in the different agendas of emperors, could too easily become dominant. The Church was discovering that it is perhaps more difficult to be true to its Lord when it is large and influential, than when it is ignored or persecuted – a lesson which was to be repeated throughout the centuries.

— Ministry, eucharist and authority —

The threefold structure of ministry – bishops, priests and deacons – emerged in the second century. (It was stated by Ignatius of Antioch as early as AD 106.) Two further ideas began to dominate:

- the importance of bishops being in line of apostolic succession from the first apostles
- the use of priestly language in relation to the administration of the eucharist

The idea of *apostolic succession* was first applied to *all* leaders and teachers, for they taught the apostles' doctrine. But by the time of Cyprian (Bishop of Carthage d 258), it focused on the claim of a bishop to be standing in a direct line of succession, reaching back to the apostles. This became important in disputes with those who questioned his authority.

The earliest Church did not define ordained ministry in relation to the sacraments. Gradually the term 'priest' began to be applied to *presbyters* ('presbyter' is derived from the Greek New Testament term for minister). With this shift came the notion that the minister's central role was in relation to the eucharist. Bishop Cyprian saw the priest as a *'cultic official, offering sacrifice . . . the sacrifice of Christ himself in the consecrated elements.'* (A T Hanson) This was a far cry from the idea of the whole people of God offering a sacrifice of praise and a life of service. It gave justification to the emergence of a priestly 'caste'.

Rome naturally had a certain supremacy, because of its central place in the Empire. But in the middle of the third century, Bishop Cyprian of Carthage argued vigorously with the Bishop of Rome about the equality of all bishops. The conversion of Emperor Constantine (312 AD) inevitably made Rome even more important. Paradoxically, this increased in the fifth century, as the Empire went into marked decline and fall.

In 410 Rome was sacked by Alaric the Visigoth and the Roman Empire began to crumble. In contrast, the Bishop of Rome represented permanency and authority in the midst of collapse. Leo I (pope from 440 – 61) was very powerful. He advanced papal claims considerably by his assertion that the apostle Peter spoke through him. His claims were, in turn, backed by the Empire, which saw him as a bulwark against the advance of the barbarians. But the Eastern Church did not accept his claims and the seeds of future conflict were sown.

The birth of Monasticism

The idea of giving up everything for Christ ('asceticism') runs deep in the New Testament. By the second century it began to be linked to virginity. Here were the beginnings of monasticism, a movement advanced by the conversion of Constantine and the consequent ending, or so it seemed, of the self-sacrifice of martyrdom (but see page 144). The very popularity of Christianity was a problem for some. They wished to escape from church politics; to find a place for prayer and discipline. Growing numbers had a thirst for God and a determination to do battle with the forces of evil, away from the temptations of everyday life.

Around 285, Antony of Egypt (c 251–356) went into the desert as a hermit. He became a well-known role model whose story was recorded by Athanasius. The next development was from *hermit life* to *community life*. This came through another Egyptian, Pachomius (c 290–346), who laid down rules for communal monasteries. The movement spread rapidly. Through Basil of Caesarea (c 330–79) it developed a *concern for the poor* and deprived, as well as for the development of the *interior spiritual life*. Evagrius (346–99) added a more *contemplative*, mystical and intellectual strand.

The movement which started in the East was encouraged in the West by John Cassian (c 360–435). Monasticism was later given its classic definition by St Benedict (c 480–c 550), who laid down the Benedictine rule. This struck a sensible balance between work and prayer and became definitive for Western monasticism. By the fifth century, the foundations of monasticism had been laid, with all its strengths (self-sacrificial service to the Lord) and with its weaknesses, namely a tendency:

- to regard its expression of Christianity as the only truly legitimate one
- to put a greater emphasis on human 'works' than on divine grace

Conclusion

By the fifth century, Christianity was *the* credible spiritual and intellectual force in an Empire crumbling fast in the West. It was St Augustine in his *City of God* who was able to give a coherent explanation of what was happening. Yes, the barbarians might be about to come through the gates; but the Kingdom of God was not bound to the Roman Empire. Indeed, it lay beyond time. This knowledge would prevent Christians from falling into undue pessimism, in the face of the collapse of existing institutions.

In any event, the barbarians were not the end of everything that was important. Rather, they were a challenge to the Church. Could it find ways of converting them? It had the organisation and motivation to undertake this task. As the Empire collapsed, the Church was the only credible institution remotely able to take its place. This was a tribute to the achievements of the previous 500 years. It was also a heady and dangerous power. The next chapter reveals how imperfectly and patchily it responded to these challenges.

16

ONE THOUSAND TURBULENT YEARS: 500–1500 AD

This period can be seen as the Church's most glorious era. It dominated Europe and witnessed the building of breath-taking cathedrals, the production of superb works of art and much fine music (see Chapters 19 and 20). But the same period also brought shame on the Church – with the Crusades, the Inquisition, anti-Semitism, the degradation of women, and the spiritual poverty of many of its leaders.

The 'Middle Ages' brought immense pressures and temptations to the Church. It was the one remaining institution in a society facing endless *waves of invaders* (Vikings, Arabs, Moguls). The challenge came first from the barbarians who rolled back the Roman Empire, at any rate in the West. But in time, the Church was able to convert the barbarians.

A much more serious and long-lasting threat came from the forces of Islam. Muhammad (570–632) established the Muslim community which, together with economic factors, led to conquests of huge Christian areas (Persia, Syria, Egypt, North Africa, Spain and Palestine – including Jerusalem itself in 638). Muslim forces threatened the whole of Europe. Only the victory of Charles Martel, at Tours in 732, turned them back.

The plundering raids of the Vikings were a further problem. The result of all this was that the West was inferior both to the Christian East ('Byzantium') and to Islamic nations, in organisation and culture. Hence, from a Western perspective, this period is sometimes called the 'dark ages'.

— Evangelism of and from England —

The Christian faith came to Britain shortly after the death of Jesus, as soldiers, traders and other travellers in the Roman Empire 'gossipped the gospel.' The Edict of Milan (313 AD) had encouraged an embryo organisation. Indeed, three British bishops travelled to the Council of Arles in Southern France in 314. Invading Saxons drove the Christian Britons West into Cornwall, Wales and Strathclyde. It is the descendants of these invaders who were evangelised by Augustine and the Celtic missionaries. (*Note*: St Augustine, first Archbishop of Canterbury (d 604 or 605), should not be confused with the great theologian, St Augustine of Hippo in North Africa (354–430: page 76.)

Pope Gregory I (c 540–604) had, as a youngster, seen Rome sacked several times. A man of great ability, born to nobility and wealth, he was an urban prefect at the age of 30. He gave this up to become a monk and he became Pope in 590. He used the vast powers of the papacy (the greatest landowner in Italy) to good effect. He reformed the Church, made peace with those who threatened Rome, engaged in acts of charity and wrote books of pastoral guidance.

Gregory encouraged missionary work, and sent a reluctant Augustine to England. After a false start, Augustine arrived in Kent in 597. He and his 40 monks came into Canterbury carrying a cross and singing an antiphon for God's mercy; they would have preferred to be in Rome! But they were well received. Augustine found a Christian Queen (Bertha from Gaul) and a cautious King (Ethelbert) who was soon converted. Kings were influential and, according to a letter written by Gregory, within a year Augustine had baptised 10,000 Saxons.

Gregory's commission to Augustine represents a break from the very confrontational approach towards paganism of earlier missionaries such as Martin of Tours (d 397). In contrast, Gregory urged that temples and other holy places should not be destroyed but rather *'converted from the worship of devils to the service of the true God.'* The Venerable Bede (c 673–735) records that the first Canterbury Cathedral was a one-time Roman basilica (see Chapter 19).

Celtic missionaries

St Patrick

However, it was Celtic missionaries who achieved most in the conversion of Britain. This began with Patrick who was born, probably in Scotland, around 390. He had a tough apprenticeship as a slave for six years. Then, after studying in France, he was made a bishop, and he travelled to Ireland to spearhead its conversion. A century later, it was Ireland which was sending missionaries to mainland Britain.

St Columba

Columba (c 521–97) sailed to Iona in the Hebrides where he established a monastery. From this centre, missionary monks sallied forth to convert most of Scotland and northern England. Of particular importance was the way in which they adapted their methods to the social and cultural customs of the tribal societies which they encountered. Scholars today point to this as a good example of the process of 'inculturation' – presenting the gospel in ways appropriate to the culture of the people being evangelised and not importing 'cultural baggage'.

St Aidan

One of the most celebrated of the Iona missionaries was Aidan (c 600–651) who established his base at Lindisfarne. This monastery on the Northumbrian coast became the centre of Celtic Christianity in the north. From there, missionary monks evangelised the area. Lindisfarne is famous for the beautifully scripted and illustrated *Lindisfarne Gospels*.

Thus England was evangelised. On the one hand, Celtic missionaries from Ireland and Scotland; on the other, missionaries from Rome based in Canterbury. But the Celtic and Roman understandings of the way in which the Church should be organised were significantly different. The Celts emphasised a loose structure of monastic communities, with a high degree of freedom and mobility. The Romans preferred a more highly organised, settled and hierarchical Church structure.

There were other differences: about the dating of Easter, the organisation of monasteries and the shape of the tonsure (a monk's haircut!).

These matters were debated at the Synod of Whitby in 664. At Whitby the Roman views gained the ascendancy, though the Celtic understanding continued to be influential.

St Boniface

Those who had been converted to Christ wanted to take the gospel message to others. So missionaries soon began travelling *from* England. Here the outstanding figure is St Boniface (680–754) who evangelised Germany. Born in Devon, he was trained under the influence of Canterbury and went to Germany as the representative of the papacy. He was highly successful. Indeed, the new overarching political institutions which began to emerge under the Emperor Charlemagne (c742–814) were, in some measure, built on Boniface's achievements. In 754 he joined 'the noble army of martyrs', protecting himself from his attackers with nothing more than his Gospel book.

'When Boniface wrote to other bishops, he had a way of invariably reminding them that Christian authority meant service. The service of the pastor was exemplified in Christ's washing of his disciples' feet, and so, whatever little present he might have received from another bishop, back went a towel from a seemingly inexhaustible linen cupboard.' (Henry Mayr-Harting)

Expansion

The coronation of Charlemagne as *Holy Roman Emperor* by Pope Leo III in 800 represented something of a triumph for the Church – and particularly for the papacy. But it brought problems. For many centuries, the question of the relationship of Emperor and Pope was to be a matter of contention. Further, Charlemagne was a soldier who was willing to use forceful methods to expand the Church; a policy which was openly criticised by the scholarly Alcuin of York (c735–804). Charlemagne regarded himself as another King David and his military methods help to explain why the expansion of this period was often superficial.

This was made worse by the fact that Church leaders were not concerned to translate the Bible or the Liturgy into local languages. For example, none of Augustine's party spoke English; nor did they think it important to learn it, or to produce an Anglo-Saxon Bible or Service Book. This Roman mind-set is evident in the unbending commitment to the Latin liturgy on the part of the Western church.

Missionary expansion in the East took a different character. On the one hand, it was even more an arm of the government. On the other hand, those missionaries were concerned to understand the language and culture of the people. The two great evangelists to the Slavs, the brothers St Cyril (826–69) and St Methodius (c815–85), translated the Bible and the liturgy into the vernacular. Because of this, they became key figures in the development of Slav culture.

The papacy

By 800 AD the Church had immense and dangerous powers. Within the boundaries of the Holy Roman Empire, it reigned supreme. Great figures in the Church were often great figures of State too. They grew increasingly remote from their own clergy and people. This corrupting effect can be seen most clearly in the papacy itself.

In the middle of the ninth century a forged document called *The Donation of Constantine* began to circulate. It claimed to be a grant by Constantine (the first Christian Emperor) to the Pope, not only of power over all the churches but of imperial power in Rome, Italy and all the provinces of the West. In effect, this 'historical' document made the Pope a powerful temporal, as well as spiritual, lord. Nobody realised that it was a forgery and it was used until its falsity was demonstrated in the 15th century.

The late 9th century until the mid-11th century was a low period for Western Christendom. It was a time of general breakdown within political institutions, particularly in the face of threats from the expansionist Vikings. Famine was an additional problem. As the year 1000 approached, some people expected the end of the world. Popes were often just one more warring force, sometimes noted for their lack of moral scruple. What was true of popes was also true of archbishops and bishops. Inevitably their poor example had an adverse effect on ordinary clergy. In addition, many monasteries had become lax. The Church was in desperate need of reform.

Reform

The first sign of reform was the founding of a new monastery in the Benedictine tradition at Cluny in France in 910. It freed itself from lay control and returned to the old ideals. Cluny had a succession of outstanding abbots and was influential in spreading its ideals to other houses. Most importantly, it influenced the papacy. The key figure in this regard was a monk called Hildebrand (c 1020–85) who became Pope Gregory VII in 1073. He set reform in motion and was against both 'kings who oppose divine justice and bishops who set a bad example.' In the pursuit of the first aim he became involved in a violent dispute over whether the Emperor, Henry IV, had the right to appoint bishops – a practice called lay investiture.

There were moments of high drama, with the Emperor pleading for absolution, standing barefoot for three days in the January snow at Canossa in 1077. It remains a matter of debate whether Pope Gregory gained anything lasting from this conflict. But he certainly bolstered papal claims to domination over the State and he pressed forward with his reform of the Church. Gregory opposed simony (the purchase of benefices) and clerical deviations from celibacy.

Mutual Excommunication

Tensions between *Greek-speaking Christians* (East) and *Latin-speaking Christians* (West) had always been present. In the early Middle Ages these strains were considerably reduced, as old Rome and new 'Rome' (Constantinople) found common cause against the new threat from Islam. Between 654 and 752 the majority of popes came from the East or from areas with Greek influence such as Sicily. But the accord was fragile.

In 668 St Theodore (602–90), a Greek-speaking monk from Tarsus, was sent to be Archbishop of Canterbury – this showed that a measure of harmony had been achieved. But Theodore was accompanied by Hadrian (d 709) from Africa, to ensure that Theodore would introduce *'no Greek customs contrary to the true Faith.'* The old suspicions and rivalries were still alive. These grew, particularly as the axis of the Western Church began to move northwards when France, Germany and England became influential. The coronation of Charlemagne by Pope Leo III (800 AD) as the first Emperor of the 'Holy Roman Empire' constituted a challenge to the Eastern Empire. His coronation was a symbol that the political unity of the old Empire was finally broken. It was only a matter of time before this would be expressed institutionally.

When the separation of East and West eventually took place, almost nobody noticed. The trigger was the Western Church's addition of the *'filioque clause'* in the Nicene Creed – a clause which states that the Holy Spirit proceeds from the Father *'and the Son'*. This became a major difference between the Eastern and Western Churches. It reached a climax in 1054 when each side excommunicated the other. Ironically, disunity came at a time when reviving trade in the Mediterranean was bringing East and West back into contact. But contact did not bring understanding and the pressure from the West was for total uniformity (on its terms!). Any such notion was unacceptable to the urbane, sophisticated, Greek-speaking Christians.

——— Everyday Christian life ———

Writing under this heading in *Christianity* (SCM), Hans Küng points out that the Middle Ages were complex ('they were by no means a unitary Christian culture!'). But life for all was dominated by the Church. Church bells told the time and marked festivals. Church buildings were highly visible. Sundays and feast days broke the routine of hard work. The people were united in collective joy (*festivals*) and collective anxiety.

Life was hard and life-expectancy short, especially when pestilence or famine struck. But the Church was there. *'It did not let people die alone; they died in the midst of the community, surrounded by members of their family and strengthened by prayer and the church's rites for the dying.'* (Hans Küng) Perhaps surprisingly in such a tough world, atheism and suicide were extremely rare.

Care for the sick and the poor was organised, and a leading role in this was played by *women*. Education, political influence and leadership in the Church were closed to most women. However, noble women would exercise power and were sometimes more educated than their husbands, who were often illiterate. Nunneries were numerous (and in the early Middle Ages, virtually closed to all but the aristocracy). There were several female mystics; the Cistercian convent of Helfta in Germany became an important centre for mysticism – and there were others. Sexual intimacy was discouraged even within marriage, apart from the purpose of procreation. Contraception was regarded as sinful, on a level with abortion and the abandonment of unwanted children.

While acknowledging the distortions of New Testament faith which developed (such as the flagellant movements) Hans Küng can strike a positive note: *'And yet there were countless medieval people who wanted to live out an* authentic discipleship of Jesus *unpretentiously in everyday life.'*

——— Crusades and corruption ———

The Turks were pressing in the East. Pope Gregory VII had contemplated a *Crusade* and the idea was taken up by his disciple and successor, Pope Urban II (c 1042–99). The first Crusade set out in 1096, aiming at the conquest of Jerusalem. In 1099 it succeeded *'and by 1153 the whole Syrian coastline from Ascalon to Antioch was in Latin hands'* (Colin Morris). This first Crusade roused fanatical enthusiasm, fed by Urban's declaration that Crusaders who died in a state of repentance and confession would gain immediate entry to heaven. But Islam was united under Nureddin and his successor Saladin, and Muslims ruled Jerusalem again in 1187. The idea that the Church could conquer by the sword was bound to corrupt; thus began another slide downwards. This Crusade and its successors (they continued until the 15th century), brought little glory and much shame on the Church.

A whole succession of popes made claims to vast power. They had no desire to be 'the servant of the servants of God.' By the middle of the 12th century it was common to take the title 'Vicar of Christ' rather than 'Vicar of St Peter'. But the higher the claim, the more it required political methods to promote it. By the 13th century the political ambitions of the papacy were undisguised. The need to raise money was consequently acute and its commitment to reform was slight.

In 1296, Boniface VIII (Pope: 1294–1303) issued a 'bull' declaring that secular powers could not impose taxation without the permission of the papacy. Such claims debased the power of the papacy and triggered strong opposition by powerful rulers. The so-called *Babylonian Captivity* of the papacy (1309–77), when it was 'imprisoned' in Avignon, is a good example of this. During this period successive popes lived in France rather than Rome. When the papacy moved back to Rome, a rival claimed to be the one true Pope – hence 'the Great Schism'. At one point there were three rival claimants.

There were attempts within the Church to curtail the power of the papacy. *The Conciliar Movement* of the late 14th and early 15th centuries tried unsuccessfully to assert the authority of Councils over the Pope. The papacy won, but the damage to the spiritual integrity of the Church was considerable.

'The Renaissance prince-popes left a glorious artistic legacy. Sixtus IV (1414–84) built the Sistine chapel and supported charities. The warrior Pope Julius II (1443–1513) engaged Raphael to decorate the Vatican and Michelangelo as architect for the rebuilding of St Peter's. But their lifestyle was notorious. The most notorious of these Renaissance prince-popes was the Spaniard Roderigo Borgia, who as Alexander VI presided at his daughter's wedding and flaunted a young mistress within the Vatican itself. His son, Cesare, the model for Machiavelli's *Prince*, gave a party in the Vatican in 1502 at which 50 prostitutes danced naked, picked chestnuts off the floor with their teeth and were competed for by the men present.' (Eamon Duffy)

Monasticism

As we have seen, the driving force for reform in the tenth century came from monasticism. This was true for much of this period. In 1097, a group went to a most inaccessible place (Citeaux), where they determined to follow the Benedictine rule as literally as possible. *The Cistercians* (as these monks were called) had some outstanding early members. Stephen Harding (d 1134), one of the earliest abbots, expressed their ideals in enduring form in the *Carta Caritatis* (the Charter of Charity). He even found ways of bringing the laity (albeit in an inferior role) back into monasticism. Bernard of Clairvaux (1090–1153) was another leader of immense and magnetic spiritual influence. By 1300 there were 694 Cistercian abbeys. *The Carthusians* were founded in 1084; they placed great emphasis on silence. In general they avoided the decline which the Cistercians and most other monastic orders experienced in the late Middle Ages.

It is difficult to exaggerate the importance of monasticism. Monasteries were 'the symbol of stability and immutability in a world of flux' (R W Southern). They provided the inspiration for reform as well as intellectual and spiritual leadership. They cared for the deprived and marginalised. They included craftsmen and architects of distinction.

A visit to the great Cistercian Abbeys in Yorkshire (such as Bylands, Fountains, Jervaulx and Rievaulx) reveals the remarkable commitment, energy and organisation of these communities, which were dissolved by Henry VIII. However, from the 12th century monasticism was in decline. Perhaps some monasteries were victims of their own success. They had civilised some of the wildest areas of Europe and good management brought great wealth. At the same time, other institutions such as schools and universities were developing. In these, *the friars* played a crucial role.

Monasticism was a truly European movement. Before the dissolution of the monasteries under Henry VIII from 1536 there were more than 500 abbeys and priories in England. But only one order could be described as 'purely English' (ie founded by an Englishman). The Gilbertines were founded by Gilbert of Sempringham (1083–1189) but even he borrowed ideas from the Cistercians!

In 1131 Bernard of Clairvaux sent monks to found the Cistercian Rievaulx Abbey in Yorkshire. In its heyday Rievaulx had 140 monks and more than 500 lay brothers. At its dissolution it had only 22 monks.

TWO MONKS TELL THEIR STORY

'Everything here and in my nature are opposed to each other. I cannot endure the daily tasks. The sight of it all revolts me. I am tormented and crushed down by the length of the vigils, I often succumb to the manual labour. The food cleaves to my mouth, more bitter than wormwood. The rough clothing cuts through my skin and flesh down to my very bones. More than this, my will is always hankering after other things; it longs for the delights of the world and sighs unceasingly for its loves and affections and pleasures.'

'Our food is scanty, our garments rough, our drink is from the stream and our sleep often upon our book. Under our tired limbs there is but a hard mat; when sleep is sweetest we must rise at a bell's bidding. Such unity and concord is there among the brethren, that each thing seems to belong to all, and all to each . . . To put all in brief, no perfection . . . is lacking to our order and our way of life.' (From: Walter Daniel's *Life of Ailred*)

St Francis and the Friars

From the 11th century onwards there was an economic recovery. With this went the growth of towns and the emergence of universities. The institutional Church was ill-equipped to deal with the challenges of a new, freer, less respectful, more uncertain society. **Francis of Assisi** (1181/2–1226) embraced poverty and renounced everything else, including learning. He was fresh and spontaneous and gathered a group of 'Friars' around him. Unlike monks, friars were not tied to one monastery by a vow of 'stability'; they were able to move more freely.

In '*showing how the destitution of the towns could be accepted with joy and made serviceable for salvation, he touched some deep emotional springs in an urban society.*' (R W Southern). Francis believed in the importance of preaching and in engagement with the world rather than retreat from it. He was not a good organiser and after his death the *Franciscans* soon lost their simple lifestyle. They became clericalised and as much involved in the university world as were the *Dominicans*.

St Dominic (1170–1221) was a less charismatic figure than Francis. Like Francis, he stressed the importance of preaching and involvement with the world. In contrast, however, he was convinced of the place of learning. His followers soon included some of the foremost theologians in Europe. They were particularly influential in the new university centres of the West, which provided a major catalyst for the study of theology. Many of the great names in medieval theology until the mid-14th century were friars. By the 14th century both movements declined sadly from their early ideals – but they had been important new instruments for ministry.

Intellectual developments

The 11th century saw the beginnings of a revival in theology, which was to continue for centuries. Anselm (c 1033–1109), Archbishop of Canterbury, pointed the way to a new confidence in reason, based on faith. His phrase 'fides quaerens intellectum' *(faith seeking understanding)* is a good guide to what he sought to do.

Peter Abelard (1079–1142) was a brilliant scholar. He was confident enough to use his intellectual skills to question received ideas on key concepts such as the Atonement and the Trinity. His fundamental principle – *'by doubting we come to enquiry, by enquiring we perceive the truth'* – indicates the distance that had been travelled from the simple, received theology of the earlier period. He is also remembered for a famous and tragic love affair with Heloise, who later became a nun. Abelard lectured to large audiences in Paris, playing an important role in the emergence and growth of universities in 12th century France, Italy and England.

Ancient Greek ideas, particularly those of the pre-Christian philosopher Aristotle (384–322 BC), became very influential. To some, Aristotle represented such a threat to orthodox belief that they burned copies of his works. To others, he was an intellectual challenge. Was it possible to reconcile reason and faith? St Thomas Aquinas (c 1225–74), a Dominican theologian, brilliantly achieved this synthesis. He wrote extensively ('Thomism') and set out a series of 'proofs' for the existence of God.

Throughout this period, *mystics* were influential in the life of the Church. They were less concerned to analyse theological ideas than to describe religious experiences. One famous example from England is Mother Julian of Norwich who, in 1373, had a series of 'revelations' or 'shewings' (see Chapter 6).

Inspired by a rediscovery of Graeco-Roman art and literature, intellectual interest turned to artistic, literary and historical questions. The *Renaissance* (a 'Rebirth' of classical culture and learning) started in Italy and spread northwards. There was a flowering of artistic creativity.

Scholars returned to the Hebrew and Greek texts of the Scriptures. They began to see the Bible in its historical context, rather than as a collection of proof texts for particular doctrines. Thus they were able to compare their own world with previous historical periods: the age of the apostles for example. Their own times did not emerge with credit. The greatest scholar in this respect was the Christian 'humanist' Erasmus (c 1469–1536). Himself a priest, he was also a powerful satirist. In his writings the corrupt, self-seeking, clericalised Church emerged in a sorry and often ridiculous light.

Movements for change

As we have seen, the medieval Church had many low points, often followed by movements for reform. Sometimes such movements were on the edge, or were forced out, of the mainstream Church. Some were remarkably similar to the Reformation of the 16th century – looking to Scripture rather than tradition for their authority.

In southern France the Waldensians (followers of Peter Waldo – d 1205/11) wanted reform. They emphasised poverty, rejected the doctrine of purgatory, engaged in lay preaching and survived to be incorporated into Zwinglianism (see Chapter 17). In Bohemia, John Huss (c 1369–1415) was put to death (despite being promised safe conduct) for challenging the Church. His followers survived to be linked with the Lutherans (see Chapters 12 and 17). In England, the followers of John Wycliffe (1329–84) became known as Lollards. They:

- stressed the place of preaching
- attacked corruption in the Church
- rejected papal claims to authority over the secular ruler
- encouraged Bible reading in English

A deep, unquiet spirit

Throughout this period the Church acquired vast power, far exceeding its previous, or subsequent, influence. Nobody doubts that this corrupted the Church; but how extensive was this corruption? Vigorous debate persists about the spirituality of the late medieval Church.

Certainly there was immense vision and energy – as the beautiful, large and rich churches built during this time testify (see Chapter 19). Certainly too, there was deep spirituality; particularly among those who sought to develop an 'inner' personal spiritual life. But many of the laity were restive, increasingly disinclined to accept the power and privilege of some clergy, increasingly hungry for a richer spiritual diet. Their 'deep, unquiet spirit' (A G Dickens) was to bring a momentous transformation.

17

THE REFORMATION

'The religion of the late Middle Ages was a rich and complex thing. Decline is evident in many of its institutions, but more striking are its vitality and diversity.' (Eamon Duffy)

In *Atlas of the Christian Church*, he lists some of the corruptions:

1 An inefficient Church riddled with inequalities

Of 670 European bishoprics, 300 were in Italy; Germany and central Europe had only 90. The Bishop of Winchester received 1200 florins; the Bishop of Ross in Ireland received 33 florins.

2 Uneducated parish clergy

Many priests were unofficially 'married' and poor.

'Concubinage was widespread: impecunious clergy with a house-hold of children, presiding over a half-coherent liturgy on Sundays . . . as they worked their farmland for the rest of the week, were common all over Europe.'

3 Monastic decline

'In England comfortable mediocrity prevailed. Elsewhere, as in Italy and part of France, there were many openly scandalous houses. There was everywhere a decline in numbers, and hand-fuls of monks lived in luxury on incomes intended to maintain hundreds. Sexual laxity was not uncommon.'

But there were good things too:

1 Reform groups

These existed within all religious orders and there were some saintly bishops. Some individuals practised a meditative piety based largely on the Gospels. This movement (the *Devotio Moderna*: 'Modern Devotion') found classical expression in *Imitation of Christ* by Thomas à Kempis (1380–1471).

2 Preaching

Preaching was popular and sermons by Fransiscan or Dominican friars drew large numbers.

3 A strong communal element among the laity

Every parish had a least one 'confraternity' – a religious brotherhood of lay people. In Italy in particular, the brotherhoods were concerned with works of mercy: help for the dying, the poor and prisoners. They provided orphanages, hospitals and almshouses. Above all – driven by a belief in purgatory (see Chapter 9) – they organised and funded masses and prayers for the dead.

It is against this background that we must understand the struggles of a young German monk which found an echo in the deep feelings of thousands throughout Europe.

—— Martin Luther (1483–1546) ——

Martin Luther's dominating concern was to find peace with God. To this end he became a monk. Luther did penance, sought indulgences, read the mystics and theologians of the Church. A wise Vicar-General directed him to the Bible. The Bible was *'the most studied book of the Middle Ages.'* (Beryl Smalley) But it was often regarded as a source book to support doctrine, rather than a resource book for living. Martin studied it with an intense, thirsty immediacy as he prepared to lecture at Wittenberg University. He came to see that he did not have to *become* righteous in order to find peace with God.

The all important breakthrough came as he read St Paul's words, 'the just (or righteous) shall live by faith.' (Romans 1:17) It was, Luther came to understand, through faith in Christ and what Christ had done for him, that he could know that his sins were forgiven. *Salvation was a matter of divine grace and not of his good works.* It was a free gift, resulting from the love, life, death and resurrection of Jesus. 'Justification' was by faith alone.

Luther had no desire to break with the Catholic Church. He *did* have a desire to preach, teach and apply his fresh understanding of the gospel. So he attacked the whole elaborate system of 'indulgences'. Originally seen as tangible rewards for signs of penance, these had become a commercial racket – selling pardon for sin, with proceeds going to the material welfare of the Church. Such an approach obscured the richness of the Christian understanding of forgiveness through Christ, so clear in the Bible. All this drove Martin Luther, in 1517, to publish his famous *Ninety-Five Theses* on the doors of Wittenberg Cathedral. In a quite unexpected and extraordinary way, this document lit a great fire.

There was a remarkable response from many ordinary people to this obscure monk. Luther had expressed *their* feelings. There were several reasons for this groundswell:

- many people were better educated
- they had new economic, social, national and political aspirations
- they increasingly disliked foreign Italian interference
- they were disillusioned with the Church hierarchy
- the road to salvation seemed to be complex, expensive, arduous and Church-centred
- most important of all, many were spiritually hungry

The Church was taken aback. It sought to debate. It tried to suppress. It miscalculated at every stage. By the time it made up its mind to oppose Luther, he was in effect protected by his popularity in Germany. At the Diet (Council) of Worms in 1521, he refused to recant unless his position could be disproved from Scripture. He was excommunicated but the movement grew very quickly. This was partly because the Emperor, Charles V, had his mind on the threat to Europe from the Turks. In 1453 they had taken Constantinople; in 1529 they were at the gates of Vienna.

Martin Luther had an unusual brilliance with words. The evidence for this can be seen in:

- his great translation of the Bible into German (1522–34)
- his liturgy (1526) and catechism (1529)
- his prolific theological output
- his hymn writing

Luther wanted to reform the Church from *within*. He remained convinced that his teaching was true to the Bible; and indeed to the Creeds and the Fathers (the early teachers) of the Church. He was protesting only against later additions and corruption. But once the break came, he had to face the question of how to restructure the breakaway Church. For this, he enlisted the secular rulers.

In the reforms, much was swept away (the Latin mass, monasteries, all but three sacraments and in some places, bishops). But Luther was instinctively conservative, so much remained. He continued to hold a high doctrine of Christ's presence in the eucharist (see Chapter 8). Consequently, elaborate ritual and vestments often remain in Lutheran Churches today.

The Lutheran reformation spread rapidly, particularly in the north of Germany and Scandinavia. *In this way the Church in the West was divided*. This resulted, very largely, from the failure of the medieval Church to reform itself. Nor did it come to terms with the emerging new world of cities, commerce and better educated, independent citizens. It was in this context that the next stage of the Reformation unfolded.

—— Other reformation leaders ——

Ulrich Zwingli (1484–1531), reacting to the same spiritual crisis as Luther, reached very similar conclusions. He worked them through in a very different setting: the city state of Zurich. Zwingli was more strongly influenced by 'humanist' forces than Luther. *Humanism* in the 16th century was a Christian movement, made up of those who were concerned with the literary and historical heritage opened up by the Renaissance. The outstanding humanist figure was *Desiderius Erasmus* (1466–1536). He wanted to uncover the heritage of the past and allow it to criticise the present.

Erasmus used this weapon to improve understanding of the Bible, by producing a Greek version of the New Testament in 1516. For centuries, the New Testament had been known only through the Latin edition – the *Vulgate*. As people came to the text through the original Greek, their eyes were opened to all sorts of nuances which the *Vulgate* had obscured. For example, they realised that it was not correct to translate Matthew 4:17 as 'do penance', but rather 'be penitent' or 'repent'. Erasmus (a priest) never left the Catholic Church. But in many ways, his critique of its practices (as opposed to its theology) was even more radical and devastating than that of Luther. And there were others who thought as he did.

Zwingli admired Erasmus greatly. The reformation he led in Zurich in the early 1520s was more radical and rationalist than that of Luther. Zwingli rejected any idea of Christ's physical presence (the 'Real Presence') in the elements of the eucharist (see Chapter 8). Reflecting this, Zwinglian churches were as simple as possible: ideally with plain, whitewashed walls. Many of his followers were newly wealthy merchants and artisans. They were attracted not only by the theology but also by the opportunity of challenging the status quo. Zwingli became embroiled in Swiss city-state politics, and died in a battle between Catholic and Protestant cantons.

Like Zwingli, the Frenchman **John Calvin** (1509–64) was heavily influenced by humanism and was converted to a Protestant understanding of God's grace. He was called to help in the reformation at Geneva and, amid much opposition, he created a Church with clear and definite structures and a sharp separation from the State. He was a systematic theologian of great lucidity and profundity. His writings (*The Institutes* and Bible commentaries) are lengthy but remarkably readable. Calvin established an Academy which sent out many leaders to other parts of Europe. He provided a Church structure which was readily exportable and which was able to survive (as Lutheranism was not) within hostile states. *Calvinism* was often narrower and less tolerant than John Calvin himself. It spread to France, the Netherlands, Scotland, parts of Germany, Poland, Hungary and, in some measure, to England.

———— The radical reformation ————

All these leaders took the Bible as their prime authority. They established churches which were very different from the medieval Catholic Church. They stressed the importance of an educated ministry and, as far as possible, worked closely with the State. In contrast, the more extreme 'radical reformation' claimed to depend on the Holy Spirit and on God's capacity to speak to ordinary, uneducated believers. Its leaders tended to be anti-intellectual, to be suspicious of secular government and to be 'restitutional'. This means that they wanted a complete, literal restitution of New Testament Christianity as they understood it:

- all things to be shared
- an itinerant ministry
- the baptism of adult believers

Some even preached from the rooftops and tried to develop a precise replication of the New Testament structure of ministry. In contrast, the mainstream reformers were concerned with *reformation* – the reform of the Church according to principles which were grounded in the New Testament and worked out in the history of the Church. They tolerated a range of practices, for they saw that the all-important principles might be applied in different ways, depending on the historical, cultural and social setting.

Under the umbrella of 'radical' there was, in fact, a cluster of movements. These ranged from those which were comparatively orthodox (the *Anabaptists*) to those which were decidedly unorthodox (the *Rationalists*). The latter abandoned central Christian doctrines such as the Trinity. These groups were never numerically strong but they were feared as dangerous by both Catholics and Protestants, and many paid with their lives. They were seen as a threat to the State, to civic order and to good government. Some were, as can be seen by the involvement of radicals such as Thomas Muntzer (c 1490–1525) in the Peasant Revolt (1525) in Germany, and by the take-over of the German town of Munster in 1534 by radical extremists. They declared that it would become 'New Jerusalem' with Christ's imminent return in glory. They ruled the city in a highly authoritarian, fanatical style, introducing communism and polygamy.

The Reformation in England

The Reformation everywhere was a mixture of spiritual rediscovery, political and national self-interest, economic factors and social forces. But in England it took a unique path, nurtured by the presence of:

- the Lollard tradition (going back to John Wycliffe: d 1384)
- Christian humanism
- the influence of Lutheran ideas in the universities
- anticlericalism – dislike of an often unspiritual clergy
- the growth of 'Erastian' convictions (the belief that the State should have greater control over the Church)

In 1521 Henry VIII wrote against Luther, and the Pope entitled him 'Defender of the Faith' (a title still held by British monarchs). Henry's enthusiasm for the papal office was such that Thomas More – later executed by the King for his loyalty to the Catholic Church – warned Henry to remember that popes were not only spiritual leaders, but also Italian princes. But when the Pope refused to dissolve his marriage to Catherine of Aragon, Henry proclaimed himself Head of the Church of England (in 1534) and was excommunicated by Rome. Henry then set about dissolving the monasteries to raise funds and to establish his supremacy in ecclesiastical affairs.

His Act of State plunged England into bloody turmoil (see Chapter 11). His heir (the young Edward VI) was Protestant, but he was succeeded by the strongly Catholic Queen Mary. Her successor, Elizabeth I, had no wish to make 'windows into men's souls' and the Church of England eventually emerged as both Catholic *and* Reformed.

Henry VIII remained Catholic in theology but he had around him some key people who were driven by strong Protestant convictions. Among these were Archbishop Thomas Cranmer (1489–1556) and the statesman Thomas Cromwell (1485–1540).

The end result of all this turmoil within the Anglican Church, was an interesting mixture. It had:

- some members with a strongly Protestant theology
- some who emphasised Patristic theology (the early Church Fathers) and tradition
- a liturgy and church structure (bishops, vestments and church government) which retained many links with the past

The stronger Protestants (often called Puritans) resented this 'compromise' and some eventually departed for America. The Pilgrim Fathers sailed from Plymouth in 1620 in *The Mayflower* (see Chapter 18). Others became 'dissenters' or nonconformists within England.

The Catholic response

Meanwhile, Catholicism began to reform itself in a Counter Reformation. In part this was prompted by the emergence of Protestantism. In part it was a continuation of a process of reform and renewal which had often been evident before. A commission was set up to advise on reform and it produced the *Consilium de Emenda Ecclesia* (Advise on the Reform of the Church) in 1537. It was devastatingly critical of abuses in the Church and its recommendations led to significant reforms.

Earlier, *Ignatius Loyola* (1491–1556) had found his solution to spiritual crisis, by way of devotion to Christ and the Church. He wrote his *Spiritual Exercises* in 1541. These provided a guide to spiritual discipline and became the basis of the Order he founded in 1534: the *Society of Jesus* (Jesuits). The Jesuits were modern, practical and world-centred; they were concerned to live in the world, not to escape from it. They were prepared to be involved in politics and intrigue. The Order came to be a most effective instrument for countering Protestant advances – helping to win back Poland for Catholicism.

There were still some hopes of a reconciliation with the Protestants. Some Catholic theologians such as Cardinal Contarini (1483–1542) and some Protestant theologians such as the Lutheran Philip Melancthon (1497–1560), were able to agree on justification by faith. Sadly, they were unable to carry their constituencies with them. The Council of Trent (1545–63) marked a distinct hardening of Catholic attitudes. Its declarations were anti-Protestant:

- justification was not by faith alone
- tradition was given equal place alongside the Bible
- the *Vulgate* (the Latin version of the Bible) was declared to be *the* canonical text
- the Mass was to continue in Latin

The Council of Trent made the Church narrower than it had been before. It marked '*the end of the old, universal comprehensive Latin Church and the emergence of modern Roman Catholicism as one Christian denomination among several.*' (G R Elton) One example of the new narrowness, rigour and intolerance was Pope Paul IV (Pope

1555–1559). He was as far removed from the Renaissance humanism of popes earlier in the century, as he was from Protestantism. He drove his views forward, using the full force of *the Inquisition* in a way which destroyed opposition. This was ruthless but it created a Catholicism which could survive. Indeed, it was able (sometimes despite leaders like Paul IV) once again to inspire loyalty, passion and devotion, and to produce:

- saints such as St Philip Neri (1515–95)
- great mystics such as St John of the Cross (1542–91) and St Teresa of Avila (1515–82)
- people with a passionate concern for the needy such as St Vincent de Paul (1580–1660)
- martyrs like Margaret Clitherow and Edmund Campion (see Chapter 11)

But, by the path it had chosen, it had ceased to be the Church of more than one section of Western Europe.

——— The wars of religion ———

Wars of religion raged from the mid-16th to the mid-17th centuries: in France (1562–98), in Germany (1618–48), in England (1642–1662). Religious difference was only one factor among many, but it did sharpen divisions. In France the Edict of Nantes (1598) gave tolerance to Protestants. This was revoked by Louis XIV in 1685 and hundreds of thousands of French Protestants (*Huguenots*) were forced to flee.

The Peace of Westphalia (1648) recognised Protestantism in Germany. The Act of Uniformity (1662) reasserted Anglicanism as the established religion in England. The Church of England took severe action against Roman Catholics and nonconformists such as John Bunyan (1628–88). This Baptist tinker from Bedford wrote *Pilgrim's Progress* and the hymn '*Who Would True Valour See*' from his prison cell (see Chapter 20). The 'Glorious Revolution' of 1688 brought William and Mary to power in England and gave Protestant dissenters, but not Catholics, a measure of religious tolerance.

Conclusion

Reforms were inevitably mixed up with social forces, politics and a growing sense of nationalism. All this produced conflict, sometimes prolonged and savage. It is not surprising that people grew weary and frustrated. Some moved their allegiance in other directions. Sometimes they embraced a *rationalism* which marginalised or excluded religion. *Pietists* emphasised an experience of a relationship with Christ, which largely disregarded or dismissed the perceived formalism of the established churches. Others embraced a 'broad church' *inclusiveness* which seemed in danger of incorporating so much, that it said nothing that was distinctive.

But the young Luther had represented many in his despair at a Church which seemed to block the way to a joyful, liberating faith in the living God. The need to rediscover the message of the New Testament had been urgent. The Reformation helped to split Europe apart; but many regarded this as a price worth paying.

18

TO THE PRESENT DAY

The age of reason

The spirit of *the Enlightenment* can be summed up in the famous words of the philosopher René Descartes (1596–1650): '*Cogito, ergo sum*' (I think, therefore I am).

Reason was the starting place. All problems could be solved by its application. In particular, there was a growing confidence in scientific objectivity – the capacity to isolate any part of our world, to find out the principles on which it works, and to harness these to our advantage. Earlier scientific study had been driven by a concern to reveal more fully the glory of the Creator, and to glimpse his purposes through the Creation (see Chapter 10). In contrast, in the world of the Enlightenment, *man* was the measure and centre of all, and the notion of purpose was marginalised.

There was *great confidence in progess* and the mastery of the world that this would bring. All things were possible. Knowledge, as the English philosopher John Locke (1632–1704) maintained, was derived from the five senses – that is, from our experience. Furthermore, humanity (which was capable of knowing all) was, or should be, autonomous and free. Freedom of the individual was, in sharp contrast to any previous age, more important than communal solidarity. Thus Voltaire (1694–1778), the brilliant French writer, constantly sided with freedom of thought against any 'orthodoxy', particularly that of the Church.

This new way of viewing the world gradually emerged in the second half of the 17th and throughout the 18th centuries. It had no necessary place for a Christian God who had taken human flesh and who remained in a close, intimate relationship with his people through the Holy Spirit. God could easily be excluded altogther. Or he could be regarded as a remote 'watchmaker', who had set Creation in motion and then removed himself from any active involvement – an absentee Deity.

David Hume (1711–76), the Scottish philosopher, argued that if nature is uniform, and if human reason is able to provide all the answers, there is no place for miracles. This presented a great challenge to the Christian faith which is based on belief in the incarnation and resurrection of Jesus.

The Enlightenment and the Church

Some within the Church came to terms with Enlightenment thinking by more or less removing the supernatural. *Deism* (the belief that there is one, rather remote, Supreme Being) became very popular. In 1736 Bishop Butler (1692–1752) complained with irony that Christianity *'is now at length discovered to be fictitious.'*

Uncertainty entered the hearts of the denominations. Many English Presbyterians became Unitarians (that is, they rejected the doctrine of the Trinity). Within Anglicanism it became possible to hold high office and lean heavily towards Unitarianism, as did Richard Watson (1737–1816), Regius Professor of Divinity at Cambridge and later Bishop of Llandaff. The mainland European Protestant churches became defensive and strongly rationalist. As a result they lost the power to rouse emotion, to convert and change people. They retained their Anglican, Lutheran and Reformed identities, but their links with the State became a rather formal reminder of an earlier spiritual and political reality.

Revival!

As so often happens in the history of the Church, it seems that the Holy Spirit breathed life back into a body which desperately needed it. One of the first signs of this was the Pietistic movement in Germany in the second half of the 17th century. The Pietists returned to basic beliefs: a sense of sin, the work of Christ in winning salvation on the Cross, the place of faith and forgiveness. Whereas orthodoxy had become cold, cerebral and lifeless, Pietists were warm, immediate and intensely devoted to the crucified Christ. They had little time for the institutional Church.

Their most famous representative was Count Zinzendorf (1700–60), a leader of the Moravian Brethren who traced their origins back to John Huss (1369–1415). They in turn influenced John Wesley (1703–91) whose heart, he recalled, was 'strangely warmed' when he attended a Moravian meeting in London in May 1738. This happened as Wesley listened to a reading from the preface to Martin Luther's commentary on *Romans*. In that moment he came to a fresh understanding of what Christ had done for him.

Although he had a fine intellect and wide interests, Wesley's was essentially a religion of the heart. As he and other evangelicals – such as the great orator George Whitefield (1714–70) and, in America, the theologian Jonathan Edwards (1703–58) – preached, there was an immense response. Often this came from ordinary working people, more or less outside the Church. Sadly, the Anglican Church was not sufficiently imaginative to find ways of keeping Methodists (as the followers of Wesley were called) within the Church. Gradually, they formed another denomination.

This revival came about as a reaction against certain consequences of the Enlightenment. At the same time it was an expression of Enlightenment, in that it depended heavily on 'evidences' which were grounded in experience – especially transformed lives. It was the Church's response to the challenge of a new culture; or, as those involved would have claimed, it was *God's* response.

Some Christians came under these influences, yet remained in their own churches. One clear example of this is the Clapham Sect, a group of distinguished politicians, business and professional people. They were evangelical Christians within the Church of England, and they remained there. They sought to win the middle and upper classes for Christ and to attack social abuses. The MP William Wilberforce (1759–1833), the Cambridge clergyman Charles Simeon (1759–1836) and Lord Shaftesbury (1801–85) were outstanding leaders of a movement which:

- helped to bring the slave trade to an end
- did much to improve working conditions in factory, field and mine
- pressed the need to regulate working hours for children
- together with Methodism, helped transform Britain from the lax moral and religious conditions of the late 18th century

In this way they laid the foundations for the higher moral and religious tone of the Victorian era (1836–1901); an era often (with some justice) accused of hypocrisy, but which saw many major reforms. Some historians argue that the evangelical revival was a major factor in explaining why Britain did not have an upheaval similar to the French Revolution (1789–1795).

Romanticism

Jean-Jacques Rousseau (1712–78), the French writer, was an early romantic, as was William Wordsworth the English poet (1770–1850). They were prepared to celebrate the heart as well as the head. The Romantic Movement became a force in the early 19th century. It emphasised emotion, intuition, nature and history. As far as religion was concerned, it gave '*a new appreciation of the dramatic, the extraordinary and the otherworldly.*' (D W Bebbington)

This was a factor in reviving Catholicism in Europe, after the setback of the *mid-century revolutions*. In 1846, 38 out of 59 Spanish dioceses had no bishop. Two years later Pope Pius IX fled from Rome in disguise when a mob fired on his palace, killing a priest. Romanticism provided a rationale for returning to the authority of the papacy, which had been derided in the high days of the Enlightenment. It was now seen increasingly as part of the Church's defence against the onslaught of revolutionary rationalism and atheism.

Looking back

The medieval Church no longer appeared to be a disaster to be avoided. Rather it was seen as a model to be followed. The immense popularity of all things *Gothic* (such as medieval buildings) is one example of this. Another is the movement known as *Ultramontanism* (literally 'across the mountains') which pressed for a strong papal role. The most important exponent of these views was Pius IX (Pope 1846–1878). He denounced nearly all modern or non-Catholic ideas in the fiercely conservative *Syllabus of Errors* (1864). He also convened the first Vatican Council (1869–70) which defined *papal infallibility* for the first time. In contrast to the evangelicals who met their challenges by returning to the Bible and the experience of the Holy Spirit in daily life, Catholicism sought to return to a very high view of the Church and the authority of its representatives.

There was a similar revival of interest in the authority of the Church within Anglicanism. Some leaders felt the need to learn from the courage and clarity of the early, and even the medieval Church. The *Oxford Movement* which was led by John Keble (1792–1866), E B Pusey (1800–82) and John Henry Newman (1801– 90), returned constantly to these themes. It is also called the *Tractarian Movement* because its leaders issued a series of tracts. This was essentially a return to a more Catholic emphasis, with a high view of the Lord's presence in the eucharist and the central role of the priest.

These emphases were disliked and combatted by some other Anglicans. Controversy was robust and sometimes ended in the courts. But liturgy and theology within Anglicanism were gradually transformed. The Tractarians looked back to the medieval church and introduced many features which are recognisable today, such as robed choirs, coloured vestments, ornaments and candles. Some Anglicans converted to Roman Catholicism – notably Newman and Henry Edward Manning, both of whom became Cardinals.

In the same century, famous preachers filled some of the large churches which were built then – sometimes in a spirit of competition – by the various denominations. Most famous was the Baptist, C H Spurgeon (1834–92). Called 'the prince of preachers', he filled London's Metropolitan Tabernacle, established children's homes and a theological college (which continue today).

Historical and scientific challenges

The challenge of the Enlightenment was sharpened by the application of the tools of historical and critical scholarship to the Bible. These treated the Bible as if it were any other human composition. They appeared to challenge not only questions of authorship, but the whole supernatural undergirding of the Bible. If the Scriptures told of miraculous events which were not part of the experience of modern people, then there must be some other explanation for those events. So ran the argument. It was taken further by the apparent challenge of science. In particular, Charles Darwin's (1809–82) *Theory of Evolution*, gave a very different account of creation from that in Genesis (see Chapter 10). *Doubt* became a problem for many thoughtful Victorians, for whom religion was a vitally important matter. *'The ship of faith rocked gently at its moorings.'* (Owen Chadwick)

The response of many liberal Christians was similar to that in the early 18th century. They jettisoned large tracts of traditional belief (miracles, much of the Old Testament and any belief in hell). They saw Jesus primarily as a supreme human teacher and example – and revealer of God in word and deed. Sin tended to be seen as error rather than evil, and salvation as sacrificial living.

Particularly after the First World War, scholars such as Karl Barth (1886–1968) came to see that it was *un*historical and *un*scientific to reject all possibility of the supernatural. Certainly the evidence has to be weighed, but there should be no *assumption* that such things are impossible. Furthermore, the sheer power of the Bible to transform those who listened to it, was once again realised. All this became urgent as people faced:

- the challenges of war
- Godless totalitarianism in Nazi Germany (see Chapter 14)
- atheistic Marxism in the Communist states of Eastern Europe

Notions of unstoppable progress and human goodness were destroyed by the Great War (1914–18). Bible doctrines of sin and salvation were seen to be relevant – though the immense suffering of the War severely challenged Christian faith. The scientific challenge was in one sense more easily dealt with, as theologians came to see that much of the Bible was not addressing *how* questions but *why* questions (see Chapter 10). Nature has come to be seen, not as a machine, but a delicately balanced organism of which we are part. Some would argue that Nature is in danger of being destroyed, precisely *because* religious questions of purpose (the 'why' question) have been marginalised.

Expansion

The Church in the West declined before the forces of the Enlightenment. But there was fresh energy for Protestant missionary expansion from the late 18th century, with the advent of a new instrument: the voluntary missionary society (many of which still flourish in today's very different climate). The motivation for this missionary work was complex but leading factors were:

- the increasing colonial expansion of Protestant countries – especially Britain and Holland (although some missionaries spoke against the policies and practices of colonial powers)
- a burning evangelical desire to preach the Gospel

Catholic overseas missionary work, which had been substantial – particularly in the Americas – declined in the 18th century. In the early 19th century, Roman Catholic commitment to missionary endeavour began to return. The cumulative results in Africa, Asia and South America were immense. Though the Church has declined numerically in the West, Christians represent about one third of the world's population because of this growth.

The *ecumenical movement* arose partly out of the missionary movement. Some leaders in the 'sending' churches came to believe that it was foolish and wrong that young churches should reflect church controversies and divisions from another continent. Other factors which gave rise to ecumenism were a deeply spiritual vision for unity and the weakness of the churches in some parts of the world. These churches felt the need to stand together (see Chapter 13).

The Church in society

The Industrial Revolution brought prosperity to some; it brought poverty, suffering, dislocation and rootlessness to many others.

Thousands moved from the country into the new, monochrome, hastily built industrial towns and cities. The response of the churches was patchy; indifference was mixed with committed concern. The latter gave rise to massive church building programmes and engagement with social, moral and educational issues. Christians became involved in a host of ways, as they sought to alleviate some of the problems. Founded by William Booth (1829–1912), the Salvation Army has become famous for its practical, and musical, Christianity. Others began to challenge the economic theories which gave rise to the suffering.

F D Maurice (1805–72), an English Anglican, was particularly influential in questioning:

- the cult of individualism
- the glorification of competition as an unavoidable law of economics
- the uncritical acceptance of the notion of *laissez-faire* (non-interference by governments in the workings of the market)

Christianity, Maurice argued, is about *co-operation* and it has a duty to persuade people of the relevance of its view of being human. To this end, in 1848 he founded a movement called *Christian Socialism*. This was shortlived but his ideas live on and have influenced many, including some leading politicians. Maurice started a tradition of questioning capitalism and some of its practices. Among those who took the same path was Charles Kingsley, advocate of 'muscular Christianity' and author of *The Water Babies*. This novel highlighted the terrible plight of chimney boys and child labour in general.

Leo XIII (Pope 1878–1903) issued an encyclical (*Rerum Novarum*) in 1891. This was a landmark. While it attacked Socialism, it also maintained that employees had rights and employers had obligations – which included paying a sufficient wage.

Throughout the 20th century there was pressure from some for capitalism to be replaced or radically modified. One landmark was the Conference on Politics, Economics and Citizenship (COPEC), held in Birmingham in 1924. COPEC challenged economic individualism. William Temple, Archbishop of Canterbury 1942–44, was a leading participant. He laid down important principles of equality and the need to subordinate the 'profit motive' to the 'service motive'. All this was important for the emergence of the Welfare State in Britain in 1948.

The gospel of personal redemption and the call to social action are both clear in the Bible. Concentration on the former can lead to indifference to poor social conditions. Equally, there is a danger that the so-called 'Social Gospel', with its concern for questions of political and economic structure, might replace the spiritual challenge of Christ to the individual. This undoubtedly happened at times. At a World Council of Churches conference in Bangkok in 1972, salvation was debated as if it were a concept wholly related to the structural sins of societies, rather than the personal sins of individuals.

But there is widespread agreement that the churches must seek to apply the principles of the gospel to the whole of life in society. One example of this is the Church of England report entitled *Faith in the City* (1985), which challenged politicians and the Church itself to combat urban deprivation. The report was strongly criticised by some Conservative politicians but it gave rise to the *Church Urban Fund* which continues to sponsor a wide range of projects. A sequel entitled *Staying in the City* was published in 1995.

RELIGION IN THE USA

One striking feature of the USA today is that it is a very religious culture. Many different faiths can be found: from the new ideas which bubble from California to the large Jewish community in New York. However, Christianity, in its wide diversity, is the religion embraced by most Americans, with some 42 per cent attending church regularly. There is, however, no 'State religion'; the writ of private enterprise runs here too.

The story of American Christianity is too complex to chart here. (A readable account within brief compass can be found in the *Atlas of the Christian Church*: see Recommended Reading). Colonisers sought to establish the Church of England in North America as early as 1619 (in Jamestown, Virginia). Most famous of the early English settlers are the 149 who set out from Plymouth on the *Mayflower* in 1620) to escape the straight-jacket of the English Church.

Over the years, a wide range of churches has found a place in American society; for example, there are 60 million Roman Catholics and a large number of Independent, Fundamentalist and Pentecostal Churches. Churches from the USA continue to exert world-wide influence through a large number of overseas missionaries.

Post-modernism

Both the Enlightenment and the Romantic Movement had confidence in our capacity to discover Truth. *Modernism* and especially *post-modernism* (the cultural movement of the late 20th century) have lost this confidence. Some doubt that there is any objective reality which can be known. On this view, all that is left as important is to express one's inner feelings and experiences and to relate to others. Significantly, in this climate a spiritual approach to life has enjoyed something of a resurgence in the late 20th century. This has been strong among some who are outside, or uneasily on the edges of, the traditional churches. It tends to be private rather than corporate and easily degenerates into superstition and bizarre practice, under the umbrella of 'New Age'.

Society has not become atheistic and rationalistic. In most Western countries a large majority believe in God and many people claim to be members of churches, even though they do not attend regularly. Modern Western society is sometimes described as *secular*, because organised religion has declined and because faith in God is not often a factor in decision making – in contrast to Islamic nations. But Western society could equally well be described as *superstitious*. In Europe and in the USA, horoscopes have never been more popular. This presents the Church with an opportunity to show that reasoned faith in the Living God is a far better way of dealing with an unknown future.

Into the 21st century

Writing a few decades ago the trappist monk Thomas Merton could say: '*We are living in the greatest revolution in history, a huge, spontaneous*

*upheaval of the entire human race . . . This is not something we have
chosen or are free to avoid.'*

At the beginning of the 21st century our world is both exciting and
daunting. The rate of change is extremely rapid. In our 'global village',
communication and trade are trans-national. New and exciting developments mean greater affluence and opportunity for many. But life is
very hard for many more. Millions of children are homeless or in bond-
ed labour and there are 23 million refugees, 80 per cent of whom are
women and children. 25,000 – mainly civilians – are killed or maimed
by land-mines every year. Millions of deaths from tuberculosis are pro-
jected by 2050 AD. About 1.3 billion live in abject poverty and 12 million children die annually because of this. One million children are HIV
positive.

Given such enormous problems, the call of Jesus Christ to love our neighbour as ourselves has never been more urgent. Such love needs to be
worked out in many political arenas of tough debate and informed decision-making, as well as in simple good neighbourliness. *Social justice* is
'agape' love painted on a large canvas. Non-governmental organisations,
some of them Christian (such as CAFOD, Christian Aid, Tear Fund,
World Vision) play an important part in the alleviation of suffering, and
in long-term strategic thinking. Many churches and Christian charities
have responded to the need for medical supplies in Eastern Europe, especially Romania. Nearer to home, soup-runs and night-stops for hungry
and homeless people in British towns and cities, are organised by churches working together ecumenically.

A future for the Gospel?

Within the churches there has been a movement away from a hierarchical, priest or minister-dominated concept of the Church, to an understanding of the *Church as the whole people of God*. This was given
impetus by the enormously influential Second Vatican Council (1962–5)
convened by Pope John XXIII. Other significant emphases were discussed in Chapter 13, such as the *Charismatic Movement* with its
stress upon renewal in the Holy Spirit and *Liberation Theology* with its
insistence on God's bias towards the poor. In a world of rapid change,
the churches continue to communicate the gospel and they contribute
vigorously to current debates and to social and ethical issues.

As the world population explodes so does the Christian Church, which welcomes more than 100,000 new members daily (see page 161). It grows rapidly in Africa, Asia and Latin America, as it struggles to hold its own in Europe. The world Church of the 21st century will be increasingly young, energetic, poor, non-white and Pentecostal. In some places it will be made welcome, in others it will be persecuted. Sadly, Christian martyrs do not belong only to the past.

The certainties of the past, particularly those of the Enlightenment, no longer hold sway. Uncertainty brings danger and opportunity. 'Post-modernism', with its stress on personal choice and experience rather than objective truth, may mean that the Christian viewpoint will be increasingly disregarded in the West. Bishop Lesslie Newbigin's experience of 'cold contempt for the Gospel' may become more common. Much in post-modernism is contrary to Christianity and there is a danger that sections of the Church will simply seek to ignore the problems posed by this new way of viewing life and truth. But it cannot be ignored – for ideas are in the air we breathe, the newspapers we read, the television programmes we watch, and the assumptions we share.

A community of hope

Throughout its history, the Church has shown great energy in crossing boundaries of culture and class. And it has engaged with many ideas, some of which have been hostile to a Christian understanding of life. At such times, the Christian calling is difficult and exciting. Reflection on the past can give courage to face the future.

There is much that is ambiguous in the history of the Church, which is a patchwork of shame and glory. The Church has been corrupt, compromised and weak: standing in need of God's forgiveness and strength. It has also ministered to the needs of the deprived, inspired hope and positive action, spoken for the voiceless and stood by the powerless. It has preached the good news of Jesus Christ and made disciples of all nations. It has survived fierce persecution, often emerging stronger, as in modern China.

But perhaps the word 'Church' is too general, for the Christian faith is lived and shared in tens of thousands of local congregations and by millions of individual Christians. Popes, Patriarchs, Archbishops,

Moderators, Councils and Synods exercise great influence and eventually wend their way into the history books. *But the effectiveness of the Church stands or falls with the quality of fellowship and outreach to be found in churches on a thousand street corners and in ten thousand fields and forests.*

'The church is a community of hope, which looks with humble confidence to the future.' (John Stott) Through glory and shame, the eye of faith can discern that 'our God reigns.' Time and again he has breathed life into what appears to be dead or dying lives and communities (see Ezekiel 37). Sometimes God works in hidden and obscure ways, but Christians believe that he never lets go and always beckons us on to his future. In that same God, Christians throughout the 21st century can continue to have confidence, as they reflect upon the promise of Jesus concerning his Church: *'the gates of Hades will not overcome it.'* (Matthew 16:18)

— 19 —

HOLY PLACES, ART
& ARCHITECTURE

———— The earliest days ————

Jesus' ministry took place mainly in the open air. Neither his little group of followers, nor the crowds who flocked to hear him, required a building or needed any visual magnificence. From time to time this has also been true for later Christians, and a meeting for worship in the open air – perhaps beside a lake – is often a treasured memory. But this does not mean that Jesus rejected all holy places and buildings, or their splendid decoration. Indeed, after his resurrection, his first disciples met daily in the Temple precincts.

Jesus' ministry rested on the Jewish religion. He and his first followers had been brought up in this, and they remained practising members. Judaism was, and is, intensely corporate. Private or group devotions were viewed against the background of the worship and obedience offered by all Jewish people. In Jesus' day that included the daily sacrifices offered according to the law of Moses in the Temple at Jerusalem. This had been newly restored and lavishly decorated by Herod 'the Great' (a brilliant tyrant whose building feats, sometimes in the desert, were breathtaking).

Some Jewish sects were violently against the Temple and its priesthood. That was not because of the building or its liturgy as such, but because Jerusalem had become tainted in their eyes by too much co-operation with the Roman occupying forces. This represented, for these groups, compromise with pagans, who worshipped many gods.

But Christianity soon became separated from its Jewish roots. The early believers soon realised that Jesus' life, death and resurrection had made both temple and animal sacrifices redundant. The early Christians came to see that on the cross, Jesus had become our Great High Priest who had offered the one perfect sacrifice: his own life. So Christian worship took place in *people's homes* or in *the open air*, as during the days of Jesus' ministry.

That did not last long. Any movement which passes into a second and third generation, tends to become an institution. This happened to the Church. As it increased in numbers and spread through different countries and cultures, it developed an organisation with identifiable 'places'.

The best known early places are the *catacombs* (burial chambers), where people could meet underground for worship and to commemorate their dead. This invisible meeting place was ideal, for the Church was intermittently persecuted for the first 300 years. As soon as specific places became identified with Christianity, art was employed to beautify and to instruct. The catacomb paintings are the earliest known form of Christian art. They often show Christ as:

- the Good Shepherd
- the King who promises salvation
- the giver of the Communion meal

Some of the more wealthy Christians were buried after the Roman manner in ornately carved stone coffins. These carvings show Jesus and his disciples with Christian symbols instead of the gods of Greek and Roman mythologies.

Not all Christian worship had to be secretive, even during the first 300 years. *The earliest known Christian church* is a house adapted soon after AD 200, in Dura Europos in Syria. Two rooms were turned into a baptistry and decorated with wall paintings. A similar house church has been found in Britain from two centuries later, at Lullingstone in Sussex.

Christians begin to build

Christianity was eventually 'permitted', and then almost immediately adopted as the official religion of the Roman Empire, early in the fourth century. So church buildings were not only allowed; they were required. But because there had been no specific form of church building before, the first churches were copied from two different types of building already popular in the Roman Empire. These were:

• the mausoleum
• the meeting hall or basilica

Mausoleums were round or octagonal in shape. This enabled people to gather round a tomb for commemorations and worship (an obvious 'coming out into the open' of the catacomb tradition).

The basilica was a rectangular pillared hall where hundreds, or even thousands, could gather to listen to speeches or witness ceremonies.

Both shapes could be either large or small and both have been used ever since by Christians the world over. The round shape became more common in the Eastern Empire, and this is the form commonly associated with the Eastern Orthodox churches of Greece, Russia and those of the Middle East generally. The rectangular shape, with nave and aisles, became more general in the West – so much so that many Western people today think of it as *the* shape for a church.

The holiest and the grandest

Some of these early fourth-, fifth- and sixth- century church buildings still exist today. As soon as the public building of churches was possible, a longing to locate the sites of central events in Christ's ministry made itself felt. The most holy place in all Christendom is the *Church of the Holy Sepulchre* in Jerusalem. This vast building stands over the place where Jesus was crucified – and where the tomb of Christ was located, according to fourth-century Christians (a claim which has been supported by recent archaeology). Round the remains of the rock tomb of Jesus, there still stands a huge octagonal shape built by Constantine the Great in the fourth century. He also built a basilica over the site of *the Nativity* in Bethlehem, although the great basilica now standing there, over the cave where Jesus was born, dates from the next century. (Caves were, and are, used as stables.)

The grandest early church still standing is the *Church of the Holy Wisdom* (Hagia Sophia) in Constantinople (Istanbul). Built in the fifth century it is decorated all over with mosaics in gold and other colours. It is huge enough to hold thousands at a time, magnificent even today after centuries as a mosque and now just as a museum. The mosaics show bishops and saints, and the emperors and their courts, as God's servants clad in priestly garments. The Eastern Emperors were the 'popes' of church and state. They were contemptuous of the claims of the bishop of Rome to this position.

The round, or centrally orientated, church was not totally confined to the East. Those which survive in Britain were built by the Order of Knights Templar as copies of the Holy Sepulchre in Jerusalem. Examples can be found in London (the *Temple Church*), in Northampton, Cambridge, and Little Maplested in Essex. This influence is seen today in those churches where a central tower dominates.

The most memorable churches are grand buildings in cities and towns, built under the patronage of a king, bishop or other wealthy person. But, of course, most churches were humble buildings in villages. The vast majority of these were of timber, built in the same way as huts and barns. Few have survived from earlier than the 13th century. The earliest in Europe is in Greensted, Essex, from the 11th century. There are 20 or so stave (timber) churches in Norway which survive from the 12th century onwards.

In the early days, stone churches were rare and reserved for wealthy patrons (royal, episcopal, cathedral, civic or monastic). A large stone church was sometimes called 'the white church' (hence *Whitkirk* or *Whitchurch*), because it stood out from all other buildings.

Open-air sites

Although the Church of the Holy Sepulchre is nearby, Christians still gather for worship in their thousands in the 'garden tomb' in

Jerusalem. This is not the actual site of Jesus' burial but it is a *garden* (not a huge building!) and helps modern pilgrims to visualise the events of the first Easter morning.

The desire to visit open-air holy sites as well as buildings has grown in the late 20th century, partly as a result of renewed interest in Celtic Christianity. Lindisfarne, Iona, Glendalough and St David's welcome an increasing number of pilgrims, many attracted by the stories of Columba, Cuthbert, Aidan, Dewi Sant, Kevin, Patrick and Brigid. Stone crosses from the days of the Celtic Mission (see Chapter 16) may be found in many places in Britain. They served as a gathering place and the characteristic Celtic decoration is often still visible. Some holy places have no strong associations with the past. Taizé in the Burgundy region of France has become a place of ecumenical pilgrimage for thousands of (mainly young) people since the 1960s.

Focal points

Church buildings were influenced by the Christian ceremonies that took place inside them and for which they were built. The basilica, or the great octagon or circle, held the people, but the focal points for worship were:

- the altar – the necessary table for Holy Communion
- the lectern, or desk – from which the Scriptures were read and sermons preached
- the throne (the 'cathedra') for the bishop

These were placed together so that the people faced them. The fourth essential focal point was the font for baptisms. Originally a great basin of water, this was sometimes placed in a separate building nearby. In later church buildings it is usually found at the back, near the entrance – to symbolise that it is through baptism that we come into membership of the Church.

The mosaics which covered most of these early churches usually had a gleaming gold background and depicted prophets, saints, bishops and Christian emperors. Presiding in the centre were Mary holding the child Jesus, or Jesus reigning in majesty as King of the world. In the early period Christ was never depicted as suffering on the cross. It was his humble friendship or his power and glory as resurrected Lord that made believers want to worship him, not his dying.

—————————— **Decoration** ——————————

Other visual arts were employed as well. Carvings in stone became a feature of Christian decoration from the beginning. These often depicted scenes from the Bible and the lives of saints. Carvings in wood were also made but fewer have survived, since wood is more vulnerable than stone. Work in textiles (including embroidery), gold, silver and jewellery was also commissioned by the Christian Church. The clothes worn by the ministers – and the carpets, draperies and other furnishings – should be, it was felt, the finest possible. Altar frontals, episcopal and priestly vestments, and the vessels for use in the celebration of the eucharist became very fine – at least the equal of any to be seen in the palaces of kings and emperors.

Monasteries became centres for the production of *books* – many of them beautifully scripted and illustrated. In Chapter 16 we noted the *Lindisfarne Gospels*. These were written on Holy Island in Northumbria around 700, 'in honour of St Cuthbert.' In 950, a priest called Aldred wrote an Anglo-Saxon translation between the lines of the Latin text.

From the early days in the catacombs, Christians expressed their faith through paintings. In the East this took a unique form – the icon – which has recently become known, admired and copied in the West and world-wide. *An icon* is a stylised painting on wood of a Christian subject, usually Christ or a saint. Icons are painted according to strict rules which are devotional as well as artistic. The resulting icon (which means 'image') is regarded not just as a picture to inform the mind or excite the emotions: in some ways it is seen as an embodiment of what it depicts. So it can be revered and gazed upon in prayer, for it was created in prayer. There is no more powerful assertion of the place of art in Christian worship, than the tradition of making and using icons.

The cross

In medieval Europe the Church was, at first, the only patron of the arts. So all the early examples of painting, carving and work in stained and painted glass are of Christian subjects. Almost all the great paintings of medieval and Renaissance times are of biblical or church events or people.

In the late Middle Ages the earlier dislike of portraying Christ's cruci-fixion in agony had vanished. Instead, there was a concentration on the human suffering that he, as God's Son, underwent to bring salva-tion to the world. There were frequent representations of episodes from Christ's final days: the whipping, the crowning with a wreath of thorns, and the jeering crowds. The nailed body on the cross was no longer robed in majesty but almost naked, writhing and with blood streaming down. In this tradition there is a strong appeal to the emo-tions. Perhaps the most famous early example is *The Crucifixion* by Grunewald, painted in 1515–16. In the 20th century, Salvador Dali's painting of Christ on the Cross became equally famous.

Colour and height

Art performed another function; it helped to teach an illiterate popu-lation the basic elements of the Christian faith. This is why scenes of Christ's birth, life, suffering and resurrection were so frequent – together with Old Testament figures, saints and bishops. The finest display of original *stained glass* in situ is probably in Chartres Cathedral in France. In Britain, York Minster has more than a third of the nation's surviving medieval glass. Wall paintings are much more vulnerable and few remain, although Pickering in Yorkshire and Chaldon in Surrey retain impressive examples.

The medieval age produced the most splendid churches in the *Romanesque* (round arch) and *Gothic* (pointed arch) styles. It pro-duced and furnished them in such numbers, that in many parts of Europe the local church is more likely to be medieval than of any other period. Some buildings are huge. The cathedrals in Seville, Milan and York are the largest – in that order. Some are very large (most cathedral, collegiate and abbey churches). Even the smaller ones are often the largest building in the town. And there are little country churches by their thousand all over Europe.

The Gothic style aimed at *height*. Most British builders went for width as well as height. But all Gothic churches aimed to dominate the town with tall towers and spires, pointing to heaven. This was an inescapable sign of the ultimate Power to whom all must give account. The cathedral in Ulm in Germany has the highest medieval spire at 161 metres. Britain's tallest spire is that of Salisbury Cathedral, at 123 metres. Many who have never visited Salisbury are nevertheless familiar with the cathedral through the painting by John Constable (1776–1837).

These great buildings were much more beautiful than any other human construction that medieval people saw. The first glimpse would cause them, as it does us, to gasp in wonder and to feel both lowliness and exaltation. We modern people marvel at the superb medieval craftsmen and their physical ability to shift huge stones. We wonder too at their willingness to work for years on a building which they would not see completed. Some medieval cathedrals, York Minster for example, took more than 200 years to complete.

Art

Art and architecture have been first cousins from the earliest days. Christian churches have been adorned by artists and craftsmen in every possible way. But a great deal of art, though sponsored by the Church, flourished outside these buildings.

A walk around any of the great European art galleries reveals the importance of the Bible as a source of inspiration for painters and sculptors. Supreme among subjects are the annunciation to Mary of the birth of her son, the shepherds and wise men visiting the infant Christ, the last supper, the crucifixion and the resurrection. But we instantly think also, of numerous great works on other biblical themes: Michelangelo's *David*; Masaccio's *The Expulsion of Adam and Eve*; Rembrandt's *Jacob Wrestling with the Angel* . . . The list is endless.

In every generation there has been an attempt to make Christ contemporary. Styles of clothing, buildings and landscape, often refer to the time of the artist rather than to the time of Christ. This is an attempt to say that, in a profound sense, that ancient event is happening *here* and *now*.

For example, in a 17th-century painting in Peru's Cuzco Cathedral, Jesus and his disciples eat guinea-pig (an Andean Indian delicacy) at the Last Supper.

This sense of enduring significance is also captured powerfully by Stanley Spencer, who painted Christ carrying his cross through the English village of Cookham in 1920.

Simplicity and destruction

From time to time in the 2000-year history of Christianity, there has been a reaction against prevailing artistic trends. Sometimes an attempt has been made to create Christian art and architecture which reflects the humility of Jesus Christ rather than the glory of God the Father. Occasionally, Christians have tried to do without holy places or, more often, to do without elaborate art or architecture (or music: see Chapter 20).

In the eight and ninth centuries, in the East, there was a movement against icons. Many were smashed or defaced. The protesters became known as *iconoclasts* or image-breakers. They argued that icons of Christ showed only his humanity. And they feared that people were tempted to worship the icons rather than God himself.

In the 12th century a movement for greater austerity in the monastic life spread through the Benedictine houses, and the Cistercian movement was started. As well as protesting against laxity in lifestyle, Cistercians also argued for greater simplicity in the art and architecture of abbeys. Their leader, St Bernard of Clairvaux wrote,

> 'Tell me then poor monks, what is gold doing in the holy place? For the sight of these sumptuous and amazing vanities encourages man to give rather than to pray . . . the poor are allowed to groan in hunger and the money they need is spent in useless luxury.'

Such accusations have often been levelled against elaborate buildings and extravagant acts. We are reminded of Mary's extravagance in pouring expensive perfume on Jesus' feet. Judas rebuked her but Jesus defended her action. (John 12:1–8)

In the Reformation of the 16th century, some movements, particularly those of the Calvinist tradition, felt so strongly against pictures and statues that they destroyed or beheaded them. But these destructive phases were intermittent and represent the extremism which occasionally strikes most religious traditions. This Protestant influence sometimes improved the medieval buildings. By removing a clutter of statues and altars, they allowed the simple dignity of the architecture to stand out.

The new churches built by these Reformation groups often introduced another form of church architecture. The main focus was on *the pulpit* rather than *the altar*. The seating was arranged so that as many as possible could see the preacher; galleries were often built at first-floor level. This did not mean a complete change, for the other focal points of Christian worship – the communion table, the font, and the seats for the president and his assistants – were retained.

Many of these churches are very beautiful in their simplicity. Examples abound in churches erected during the 17th and 18th centuries for the Protestant denominations, with somewhat more emphasis being given to the Holy Table within Anglican churches, such as the Wren churches built in London after the Great Fire of 1666. (Christopher Wren designed 53 churches, including St Paul's Cathedral.) In these buildings, art is still in evidence, if not in statues and vestments, then in monuments and painted patterns around biblical texts and other inscriptions.

Contrasts

During the Middle Ages, the Church was so dominant that we think of all contemporary art and architecture as 'ecclesiastical'. Gradually, during the 16th and 17th centuries, power and wealth moved to the royal houses and the aristocracy. The kind of art and architecture favoured in their palaces and public buildings was copied also in the churches.

In southern Europe, a highly elaborate style known as *Baroque* produced some fantastic churches similar to theatres or opera houses. Huge canopies with angels and rays of the sun towered over the altars. Pulpits were between 10 and 20 metres high, with so many curtains and saints and trumpet-blowing angels, that the preacher could hardly be seen! The best examples of this exuberant style of decoration are to be found in Austria and southern Germany, although most countries in Europe were touched by this fashion.

There was also at that time an almost opposite enthusiasm for everything in the classical style of ancient Greece and Rome (producing the word *'Gothic'* as a term of contempt for the 'barbaric' styles of the Middle Ages). So churches, as well as great houses and public buildings, were built like ancient temples: rectangular, with graceful lines and Doric, Ionic and Corinthian columns. This was the style exported by empire-builders and missionaries to the New World. So most of the older buildings in Canada and the USA are in this 'colonial' neo-classical style.

Back to the future

Then in the 19th century there was a reaction against simplicity and Gothic once again became popular. Not only churches, but other public buildings and even houses, started to sprout pinnacles, traceried windows, stained glass and all the other features of medieval art and architecture.

The great increase of population in Europe at that time led to thousands of new churches being built. Most of them are in this medieval style, although 19th-century skills in mass manufacture were fully employed and not much was handmade. Because of the survival of so many medieval churches in Europe, and the number built in the last century in that style, many people still think that the only 'proper' church building is 'Gothic' (ie one that looks 'medieval').

In the 20th century there have been many changes in fashion, in building and in decoration. New technology and materials have become available, such as fibre-glass, concrete, plastic, aluminium. It has been a century which has *felt free from dominance of the past*. There is much greater diversity in today's buildings, as people experiment with different styles and try out new combinations.

In recent times there has been a greater emphasis on symbolism than on pictorial art. This can be seen most clearly in contemporary stained glass, in textiles for church use and in paintings (and to a lesser extent in sculpture). There has also been a conscious attempt to adjust church architecture afresh to 20th-century patterns of worship. One of the disadvantages of the 19th-century enthusiasm for the building styles of the Middle Ages, was that church buildings were not always suitable for styles of worship then evolving. They exercised a retrograde influence, for worship had to adjust to the building, rather than the other way around.

Several contemporary churches have abandoned the basilica pattern with its eastward-facing focus, so dominant in the West for 17 centuries. Architects have experimented with the centralised plan of the Eastern tradition where the focus is nearer the centre, with the congregation ranged around, such as the Roman Catholic Cathedral in Liverpool. This freedom from tradition has been expressed in some very unusual churches, of which the *Holy Family Church* in Barcelona, Spain, (yet to be completed) is probably the best known.

—— Glory to God in the highest! ——

In one sense Christianity has no holy places. Unlike a Muslim or a Hindu for example, a Christian is under no obligation to make a pilgrimage. God can be experienced with equal power and worshipped with equal validity in every place.

But it is a universal human need, which Christianity in no way denies, that people need a place, usually a building, which is set apart (the word *holy* means this) for the worship of the Creator and Sustainer of the universe. These places remind us of the claims upon us of that which is greater than ourselves. In building and decorating such places, we offer the fruits of our best and most precious gifts, as tokens of our worship. In recent years, interest in church buildings has grown. Many – especially cathedrals – have become extremely popular with tourists. For example, York Minster welcomes more than two million visitors each year.

The church buildings of these many centuries, with their architecture and their artistic contents, witness to the immense contributions that Christianity has made to this universal human need for sacred places. They bear witness to the billions of hours that have been devoted over the centuries, by thousands of unknown people – in planning, building, carving, painting, weaving .... The exercise of these skills has produced some of the most beautiful works of human achievement.

Why such massive endeavour? Partly because of the God-given creative drive within human beings. Partly, no doubt, to bring glory to the town, the clergy, and the architect. But there is another motive too – a desire to glorify Almighty God, and to raise human hearts in worship, adoration and thanksgiving.

20
MUSIC AND
LITERATURE

Continuity

Jesus came, he said, not to destroy the Hebrew scriptures ('The Law and the Prophets') but to fulfil them; to *'bring out their full meaning.'* The Old Testament *Law* (or *Torah*) is itself rich in poetry, from the spectacular rhythms of its opening drama – the Creation story – to the song of Moses near its end. Among the volumes of later history, *Chronicles* goes into enthusiastic detail about the specialised music of the temple. Elsewhere the prophets, impatient as they are with empty rituals and meaningless songs, themselves soar to heights of lyrical writing as they deliver the Word of God for good or ill.

The highest peaks of Israel's praises are found between the Law and the Prophets, in 'The Writings'. *Job*, the *Song of Songs* and *Ecclesiastes* are outstanding literary works. But the best-known, and best-loved, of all Bible poetry is the collection of *Psalms*. These 150 Hebrew songs in many moods were sung in the synagogue and temple; they were adopted by Christians from the earliest days of the New Testament Church.

Those who travelled with Jesus for his three public years, repeatedly heard him use these already ancient verses as inspired pointers to himself. The singing of a Psalm concluded the last meal before his death; at least two others were on his lips as he hung dying on the cross. After the resurrection they were part of his final teaching, and after Pentecost the widening circle of his followers took up the song. With few exceptions, their successors have kept such music echoing around the globe.

Slip into Evensong in an Anglican cathedral and you will hear the appointed Psalm(s) for that day. Touch down in the Western Isles of Scotland and, in tiny chapels clinging to rocky hillsides, the people will be working through their own rugged metrical forms. In the lively meetings of the less formal 'Community Church', you may clap hands to songs with phrases lifted freely from the same Bible source. And in their different forms, Psalms introduce weddings ('Praise, my soul, the King of heaven'), are sung at funerals ('The Lord's my shepherd') and accompany national remembrance ('O God, our help in ages past').

These Hebrew songs have become part of a totally international body of praise. They adapt to plainchant: Gregorian, Anglican or Taizé chanting; solemn Genevan paraphrase; exuberant hymns; and the music of flute or guitar, synthesiser or whatever is to come. In the monastic stream, notably among the Benedictines, each of the day's services has its own mood and music, with the rotation of Psalms as a fundamental element of their song.

FROM THE RULE OF ST BENEDICT: SIXTH CENTURY

'The Psalmist says, "seven times a day have I praised you." We will fulfil this sacred number of seven if we satisfy our obligations of service at Lauds, Prime, Terce, Sext, None, Vespers and Compline. Concerning the Vigils the same Psalmist says, "At midnight I rose to give you praise." Therefore we should praise our Creator for his just judgements at these times.'

Transformation

But from its earliest days Christianity had to repudiate the idea that it was simply a new sect or subdivision of Judaism. In worship as in teaching, the dying and rising again of Jesus the eternal Son of God was central. His coming marked not simply a new direction, but in some ways a total contrast with what had gone before. Continuity and contrast are found in perfect balance in the New Testament *Letter to the Hebrews*.

The New Testament has nothing like the musical detail, or even the poetry of the Old. What it does have, apart from encouragements to sing (Ephesians 5:19 and Colossians 3:16), is an apparently random sprinkling across its pages of some of the new songs (e.g. Ephesians 5; Philippians 2; 2 Timothy 2). They sparkle within their prose context mainly by vocabulary and rhythmic structure. The climax of all such writing comes with the sequence of poems in the last book of the Bible (*Revelation*), which opens the door an inch or so to catch the sound of singing in heaven. In all these songs, the focus is different from the Old Testament Psalms. The centre of praise is now Jesus Christ the Lord: specifically the Lord once crucified, now living and reigning in the glory of the Father.

A singing faith

The pre-eminence of Jesus in the New Testament is matched exactly in one of the earliest pieces of evidence about the Church, from a writer outside its membership – even outside Judaism. '*On an appointed day*', writes Pliny the Younger to the Roman Emperor Trajan in about AD 112, the Christians '*had been accustomed to meet before daybreak, and to recite a hymn antiphonally to Christ as to a god . . ..*'

Having gradually transferred some of the Sabbath (Saturday) traditions to the first day of the week in honour of Christ's resurrection, Christians went on singing this kind of hymn for the next 19 centuries. One of the finest survivors from the Church's youth, inevitably undated and anonymous, is the Latin *Te Deum Laudamus*: 'We praise thee, O God, we acknowledge thee to be the Lord . . . Thou art the King of glory, O Christ!'

English-speakers can still enjoy the flavour of the ancient Greek and Latin hymns in the paraphrases of John Mason Neale, a Victorian pioneer in their recovery, and some more recent versions. Medieval Christendom leaned heavily on the Psalm tradition, and Miles Coverdale added 'spiritual songs' to his 16th-century translation of the Psalms. After the Reformation it was the 'Old Version' of paraphrases by Sternhold and Hopkins which held sway in parish churches – true to the Hebrew but harsh to the ear.

Martin Luther, the father of the European Reformation, was a keen singer, a gifted musician, and a strong believer in the power of hymns (not just psalms) in his vernacular German (not just Latin). *'Next to the word of God'*, he said, *'music deserves the highest praise.'* Not only Germans but most English-speaking Christians still sing his tunes and themes: *Ein' feste Burg: A safe stronghold our God is still*, as well as much gentler music and the secular melodies he adapted for sacred purposes. John Calvin, by contrast, combined his positive appreciation of culture with a determination to stick to Psalms in church.

By around 1700, however, there was a new version of the Psalms by Nahum Tate and Nicholas Brady – more poetic and soon popular enough to be bound alongside the *Book of Common Prayer* (1662). This practice continued for a further hundred years.

Also around 1700, a young Southampton man named Isaac Watts (1674–1748) complained about the version of the Psalms sung in his dissenting chapel. His father challenged him to do better, and the English hymn as we know it was born. Just turned 30 years, Watts wrote with a scholar's discipline, a communicator's clarity, a preacher's passion – and sometimes a patriot's idiosyncrasy. He pioneered original hymns (*'When I survey the wondrous cross'*) as well as transforming *the Psalter* – an alternative name for the Psalms.

A generation later, Charles Wesley (1707–88) greatly extended the range of hymnody. His hymns were enlivened by the direct freshness of his evangelistic travels on horseback, informed by his encyclopedic memory of the Bible, and constructed with amazing speed. His soaring verse still dominates most major hymn books and adorns many literary anthologies as poetry in its own right. Charles was uniquely assisted by his elder brother John, who also wrote hymns and translated others from German, as well as promoting and publishing Charles' hymns. To this day, the Methodist Church is renowned for its hymn singing.

> *When I survey the wondrous cross*
> *On which the Prince of Glory died,*
> *My richest gain I count but loss,*
> *And pour contempt on all my pride.*
> Isaac Watts

Hark! The Herald-angels sing
Glory to the new-born King,
Peace on earth, and mercy mild,
God and sinners reconciled . . .
Charles Wesley

Technically, the Wesleys were lifelong Anglicans and other Church of England writers continued where they left off. From a long list we may select John Newton (1725–1807) – a converted slave-trader – and William Cowper (1731–1800), a poet of the first rank. Distinguished Victorian writers include Catherine Winkworth, Frances Ridley Havergal, and (Mrs) Cecil Frances Alexander. In their hymns we hear a clearer call to world-wide mission. Meanwhile, James Montgomery and Philip Doddridge led the Free Church stream. Reginald Heber, Christina Rossetti and Robert Bridges were genuine poets whose gifts were also used in hymn-writing.

To the present day

The 20th century saw some falling-off in writing, and the consolidation of *Hymns Ancient and Modern* (which began in 1861) as the archetypal English-speaking hymnal. But recent decades have seen a world-wide explosion of hymnody, still too close for evaluation. Two of today's most popular writers of hymns and songs are Bishop Timothy Dudley-Smith and Graham Kendrick. The Taizé and Iona communities also produce music which is sung world-wide.

With increasing technology and mass communication, Christian songs and hymns have crossed confessional and national boundaries more quickly than ever. American, Afro-Caribbean and Australasian tastes may not be the same, but styles overlap and mingle in recent hymnals and song-books. However, it is possible to move from one church to its next-door neighbour and find an entirely different pool of favourites.

Spirituals

The *Spiritual*, whose mood and rhythms have crossed the Atlantic twice over, has proved to be an enduring art-form. Its roots are in

black Africa; its main development was among the slaves of the
American continent. Its more genteel flowering adopted by white
North Americans and Europeans, has found ready affinities with folk-
song and gospel hymns.

Oppressed peoples of many nations still find in them a vehicle for
their cries to God for help in this life and the next. But it is not only
the persecuted and poor who enjoy and appreciate them, and Gospel
choirs have never been more popular.

Music versus words

The art of written musical notation was developing around 1000 AD.
The choir could now sing a tune its members had never heard, simply
by reading the marks on the page! For the first time, a melody could
be fixed and even attached to a composer's name. The art of harmony
grew and musical decoration became increasingly complex. Reformers
like John Wycliffe in the 14th century sounded a warning which was
repeated four centuries later by John Wesley and is still heard today.
What is the point of lovely music, he asked, if it obscures the sense of
the words and is produced by those who neither mean nor believe
what they sing?

● In 1519 Erasmus expressed a trenchant criticism of ornate music
  that obscured the text:

  *'Modern church music is so constructed that the congregation
  cannot hear one distinct word. The choristers themselves do not
  understand what they are singing . . . Words nowadays mean
  nothing.'*

● At the Reformation the emphasis changed markedly from long,
  intricate lines and harmonies with Latin words, to simple settings
  in English, which had to be comprehensible to the listener.
  Archbishop Holgate's injunction in 1552 to the Dean and Chapter
  of York Minister reveals this tension:

  *'We will and command that there be none other note sung or used
  . . . saving square note plain, so that every syllable may be plainly*

and distinctly pronounced, and without any reports of repeating which may induce any obscureness to the hearers.'

- The Council of Trent (1545–1563) added its plea for liturgical words to be clearly heard, and for music to avoid profane origins and associations. Both of these proved something of a losing battle.

- In 1550 John Merbecke produced his 'noted' version of the main church services in line with Reformation ideals, and with free rhythms matching the natural flow of the words. His acclaim came much later in the revival of his work, for different reasons, nearer our own times. The work of Thomas Tallis and William Byrd in the 16th century, and Henry Purcell in the next, retains its power and attraction for many.

Magnificent music to wonderful words

The decades from 1600 onwards saw a magnificent flowering of church music, notably in Italy, and the beginnings of oratorio. But it was the Lutheran J S Bach (1685–1750) who emerged as possibly the greatest composer ever produced by Western culture. As an organist he was breathtaking, as a composer, unequalled; but his work grew slowly in public esteem. He set Bible narrative to music as none before or since. His contemporary G F Handel wrote many oratorios, including *Messiah* (1741) – possibly the most popular of all religious compositions. This work retains its wide appeal, and has given rise to many choirs formed to sing it. Haydn's *The Creation* (composed in 1798), is another great work from the oratorio repertoire by a devout Christian.

Applause for popular oratorios like *Messiah* was not universal. Was it right to make the person of Jesus Christ the subject of what looked like, and was promoted as, popular entertainment?

Similar questions have greeted recent shows and films. Critics argue that shows like *Jesus Christ Superstar* create an entirely new 'Jesus' and wrap him up in the pop music of its day. Others argue that musicals like *Godspell*, plays like Dennis

Potter's *Son of Man* and films like *Jesus of Nazareth* contain substantial material from the Gospels. They can and do speak with a fresh voice to those outside the community of faith.

Haydn, Schubert, Verdi and Brahms are among a number of first-rank composers who wrote a Mass (sometimes more than one). This is a musical setting to five lyrical and significant passages from the Latin service. Among the greatest are Mozart's *Requiem Mass* (1791), Bach's *Mass in B Minor* (completed in 1738), and Beethoven's *Mass in D* (1825).

The Passion Narratives, using the words of the New Testament Gospels, have also been a fruitful source of musical inspiration. Two of the greatest examples of this form are the *St Matthew Passion* and *St John Passion* by J S Bach.

Composers continued to be inspired by the Scriptures, the Liturgy and Christian poetry. Still popular with choirs is Stainer's *The Crucifixion* (1887). Other works of note include Edward Elgar's setting of Cardinal Newman's poem *The Dream of Gerontius* (1900); William Walton's *Belshazzar's Feast* (1931) and Leonard Bernstein's *Chichester Psalms* (1965). Many of today's composers – such as John Rutter, John Tavener, James MacMillan, Andrew Carter and Philip Moore – find inspiration from Christian themes.

⸺ Music in the local churches ⸺

The above are essentially 'performance' works requiring great skill, talent, and hard work in rehearsal. Back in the English parish church in the 19th century, music was again on the move . . .

Thomas Hardy's novel *Under the Greenwood Tree* (1872) reflects the sadness of villagers in his father's time, at losing their gallery orchestra and choir as the organ took over. Parish churches began to imitate a style more appropriate to the cathedral; this initiative was driven forward by the spirit of the Oxford Movement (see Chapter 18). Less affluent churches opted for harmoniums or even a barrel organ. The chanting of Psalms, in Coverdale's Prayer Book version, came to appear characteristically Anglican, but chanting is losing ground today except where a strong and older musical tradition is maintained.

In our own day the pendulum has swung again as other instruments are commonly heard, including drums, guitars and synthesisers. Christian worship continues to inspire creativity. Many local church organists and choir directors, such as Phil Redding and Meurig Watts compose musical settings and other musicians write and sing Christian songs in a more popular style – for example David Casswell and Sharon Winfield.

Top of the pops

The Second Vatican Council in the 1960s gave encouragement to Roman Catholic writers and composers alike. New responsorial settings to the Psalms have been one outcome. But the older monastic music continues to be popular – Gregorian chant topped the charts for several weeks in 1995! The Bible is no stranger to the pop scene. In recent years passages from Scripture heard by millions include *Ecclesiastes* ('a time to weep and a time to laugh, a time to mourn and a time to dance . . . a time to love and time to hate') and *Psalm 137* ('By the rivers of Babylon we sat and wept when we remembered Zion').

Some Christian singers are firmly established as popular entertainers (for example Cliff Richard, Van Morrison, Amy Grant). The number of Christian bands playing contemporary music (often written by band members) is enormous. The annual *Greenbelt Arts Festival* gives many of these an opportunity to be heard by the thousands (of mainly young people) who attend. Other art forms flourish too; some examples are poetry (Steve Turner), drama (The Riding Lights Theatre Co.), mime (Geoffrey Stevenson) and dance ('Springs'). This is my personal selection from a wide range of possibilities.

——— The literature of faith ———

Caedmon (seventh century) is the earliest known English Christian poet; he is credited with the earliest surviving Christian hymn in the English language. The prose of King Alfred (848–99), like much of the whole corpus of Old and Middle English, clearly comes within the same tradition of faith.

The *Mystery Plays* of the 13th to 16th centuries have enjoyed a new lease of life in our own day. Following the *Miracle Plays*, they probably took their name from the 'mysteries' or trade guilds who performed them. They vividly presented great Bible events from the Creation onwards, developing strong local styles and texts, especially in the north of England.

The most popular survivor of all is the *Nativity Play* accompanied by Christmas carols. The huge number of Christmas carols in use reflects the pre-eminence of this festival in folk-religion, greatly reinforced by Charles Dickens and other Victorians. The Cambridge service of *Nine Lessons and Carols* (a 20th-century invention) has by contrast become a media event of professional excellence, rather than the boisterous local celebration in which everyone joins. Both ends of this spectrum are valued by many millions around the world.

The writing of Geoffrey Chaucer (c 1342–1400), together with his near contemporary William Langland and his successors, Spenser, Shakespeare and other Elizabethans, reflect their Christian heritage. Two masters of English prose who paid for their writings with their lives were Thomas Cranmer (1489–1556) the liturgical reformer and William Tyndale the Bible translator. The former enabled English speakers to pray in their own tongue; the latter made it possible for them to read or hear the Scriptures in English (see Chapter 11).

The poet George Herbert (1593–1633) and the satirist Jonathan Swift (1667–1745) were clergymen and Samuel Johnson (1709–84) was a devout layman. John Donne, appointed Dean of St Paul's Cathedral in 1621, is remembered for both religious and erotic poetry and for his powerful and original sermons.

'All mankind is of one author, and is one volume. When one man dies, one chapter is not torn out of the book, but translated into a better language; and every chapter must be so translated . . . No man is an island, entire of itself. Every man is a piece of the continent, a part of the main. If a clod be washed away by the sea, Europe is the less, as well as if a promontory were, as well as if a

manner of thy friends or of thine own were. Any man's death diminishes me, because I am involved with mankind. And therefore never send to know for whom the bell tolls; it tolls for thee.'
(John Donne: *Devotions upon Emergent Occasions*)

Two other Johns, Milton (1608–74) and Bunyan (1628–88), the scholar-statesman and the tinker-preacher, both stand in the Puritan tradition. Each produced several works of enduring worth and one masterpiece; in order, *Paradise Lost* and *Pilgrim's Progress*. Both created unforgettable images in verse and prose respectively, one from his study, the other largely from a prison cell. Each used his powerful imagination to illuminate eternal truth and practical living, from the enticement of temptation in the garden of Eden to the trials and triumphs of Christian pilgrims in this world's Vanity Fair.

Among the more committed but less predictable authors was William Blake (1757–1827) – visionary poet, painter and engraver. His poem *Jerusalem* has become a popular and rousing hymn. Blake is one of those who would be surprised to find their prophetic verses adopted and domesticated in this way.

To the present day

Many 19th-century poets explored questions of religious faith and doubt, including Samuel Taylor Coleridge, William Wordsworth, Robert Browning, Lord Alfred Tennyson and Matthew Arnold. Among 20th-century Christian poets we note T S Eliot (a key figure in the transformation of poetry), Gerard Manley Hopkins (undiscovered until the 20th century), Jack Clemo, Norman Nicholson, R S Thomas and W H Auden (in later life). David Adam and others have popularised a revived Celtic culture. *The river wanders, varies in pace and depth, but never runs dry.*

The desire to explore and explain the Christian faith has prompted apologetics (the defence of the faith), novels, poetry, essays and drama from 20th-century believers such as Dorothy L Sayers, C S Lewis, G K Chesterton, J R R Tolkein and Charles Williams. Three Catholic writers – Anthony Burgess, Graham Greene and Evelyn Waugh – were powerful novelists, whose religious background and faith strongly influenced their work. Novels and plays by Christians and unbelievers continue to explore great themes such as the existence and nature of God, suffering, meaning and purpose.

Biblical vocabulary and Christian concepts have become part of our cultural heritage and have found their way into everyday speech:

- 'It's the eleventh hour.'
- 'She's the salt of the earth.'
- 'He passed by on the other side.'
- 'I wash my hands of the matter.'
- 'She's a good Samaritan.'
- 'He's a Judas.'

Words and phrases from the same sources spill over into literature of various kinds, on a range of themes; for example, Aldous Huxley's novel *Eyeless in Gaza* (a phrase based on the story of Samson in the Old Testament), Arthur Miller's play *After the Fall* and P D James' thriller *Original Sin*.

In this brief note we have concentrated on English literature, but the Christian legacy is to be found in many languages. Many Christian writers look for inspiration to one short passage in the Greek language: a passage which reminds us of the power of words – and the significance of 'the Word made flesh.'

> *'In the beginning was the Word, and the Word was with God, and the Word was God . . . In him was life, and the life was the light of men. The light shines in the darkness, and the darkness has not overcome it . . . And the Word became flesh and dwelt among us, full of grace and truth.'* (John 1:1, 4–5, 14 RSV)

'Christian truths, Christian images, resonate more widely than the boundaries of Christian belief. Jonathan Miller, for example, who comes from a secular Jewish background, has said that Christian imagery constantly reinforces his sense of human tragedy.

'The tragedy of being human, and the idea of the Incarnation is one of the great imaginative inventions of the moral imagination. I would find it very hard to think forcefully and properly without in fact being stocked with such images.'

To a Christian, such a positive affirmation of Christian imagery should not be as surprising as at first glance it might appear. For Christian truths are not just beliefs which a select body of believers happen to hold. They are the reality in which the whole universe is grounded. So works of art can awaken faith, or at least the longing for faith. Van Gogh said he could not look at a picture by Rembrandt without believing in God. At the very least art, in all its forms, keeps the possibilities of faith alive. Christian art makes the faith explicit.' (*Art and the Beauty of God*: Richard Harries)

'For many today, art has replaced God. The answer is not to turn art into Christian propaganda which all too soon passes its sell-by date, but for the church and the Christian community to allow art to speak as it should – to the imagination which, along with the conscience, is the only path for God to break through our shell of self-sufficiency. Art must delight or shock us before it can teach us and, if we honestly aim at the first we may well achieve the second; if we try for the second we shall nearly always miss the first.' (Nigel Forde: see Recommended Reading on page 291)

21
MODERN LIVES

St Paul described members of the Corinthian Church as *'a letter from Christ . . . written not with ink but with the Spirit of the living God.'* (2 Corinthians 3:3) In the first letter of St Peter believers are described as 'living stones' who together make up a 'spiritual house' (1 Peter 2:5)

Important as buildings, works of art and literature are, the greatest heritage bequeathed to us by the Christian centuries are people whose lives have been touched by Christ. It is *people* who believe in, or deny or ignore, the Christian faith. It is *people* who encourage and inspire us to follow Christ – or who put us off.

To end on a personal note – this has certainly been true for me. It was a fellow student who lived the Christian life with sensitivity and integrity, who set me thinking about questions of the Spirit; questions about:

● the existence and nature of God
● whether life has purpose and meaning
● whether prayer is valid, or superstitious nonsense

Since those early days I have been fortunate to meet a number of stimulating, intelligent Christians who have encouraged me in my discipleship. Of course I have met bigoted, off-putting believers, too. And I am acutely aware that others may choose to use similar words about me. But I take heart from the fact that the first disciples were a very mixed bunch, too.

I think it was the Jewish writer Martin Buber who suggested that, concerning belief in God, *'there are no evidences, only witnesses.'* As this book has attempted to show, this is an exaggeration. But it is a helpful exaggeration. So it will be appropriate to end by glimpsing a few Christians' lives from around the world – people who are living witnesses to Jesus Christ.

Sister Sarah is an Indian Roman Catholic nun. Sisters from her religious Order are scattered around the world; the headquarters are in London. For some years Sister Sarah worked in India, where she was born and brought up. She became expert in primary health care in rural areas. Her success in raising standards gave rise to invitations to speak at International Health Conferences. Now she lives and works in rural Peru. Her aim is to show the love of God in practical ways – through health care and feeding programmes. By means of a simple 'come and collect' system, she and her American colleague, Sister Antonia, provide a daily breakfast for 1000 Peruvian farmers – in no more that 30 minutes! The intention is not to make these families dependent; rather to help provide the necessary energy required for long hours of survival-farming in arduous conditions.

Sarah does not usually wear a nun's habit. She wears scruffy trousers and a worn sweater like most of the farmers. Two things remain in my memory from our conversation: her tranquillity and her chuckle.

Jonah Lomu became a household name in June 1995 when he represented New Zealand in the Rugby Union World Cup. He weighs 16 stones and moves at the pace of a top sprinter. In full flight he is awesome on the television screen, let alone the rugby pitch! An article in the *Independent* newspaper (June 12th, 1995) picked this up: *'As he thunders down the wing his opponents could be forgiven for dropping to their knees in prayer. He would be delighted if that happened. The brightest star of the World Cup may run at the opposition like a charging bull, but off the pitch the All Black is a shy young man and a devout Christian.'*

Jonah Lomu is one more name in a line of top 'personalities' to make public their Christian faith. The same article lists several other sportsmen, including Bernard Langer (golf), Va'alga Tuigamala (rugby league) and Gavin Peacock (soccer).

Coping with fame and wealth is not easy and Christians may find extra problems in relating these to their faith. But lack of a competitive spirit is not one of these. When British athlete *Kriss Akabusi* came to faith in Christ through reading the Bible (see Chapter 5), some onlookers expected him to lose his will to win. He responded, *'It gave me an added edge, an added motivation . . . I began to believe that my talent was God-given.'* He went on to point out that faith is not a magic wand, nor a guarantee of success: 'God gave me the right to work, not to win.' But win he did: 10 medals from top competitions, including Olympic bronze in 1992.

The link between Christianity and sport is strong.

- The YMCA (Young Men's Christian Association) was founded in London in 1844 and the YWCA in 1855. Both have become international movements and have produced some fine sports teams, especially in the USA.

- Some of Britain's famous football (soccer) clubs started as Sunday School or Church teams!

Mehdi Dibaj is an Iranian Christian. His story illustrates that religion can be oppressive as well as liberating, evil as well as good. As we have seen, this is tragically true of Christianity, which is scarred by movements like the Crusades and the Inquisition. Islam too, has its dark side. It is a noble religion, with a distinguished history; and some deep scars, as Mehdi's story shows.

For several years he has been a follower of Jesus Christ who seeks to share his faith with other people in Iran. This has brought him into sharp conflict with the rulers of that totalitarian Islamic country. He has been imprisoned for nine years and threatened with hanging. An effective campaign – involving Bernard Levin of the London *Times* – brought about his release. While in prison, Mehdi wrote a moving final testament, addressed to his jailors. It ends with these words:

'Among the prophets of God, only Jesus Christ rose from the dead, and He is our living intercessor for ever. He is our Saviour and He is the Son of God . . . I have committed my life into His hands. Life for me is

an opportunity to serve Him, and death is a better opportunity to be with Christ. May the shadow of God's kindness and His hand of blessing and healing be upon you and remain for ever.' Amen.

With respect, Your Christian prisoner. Mehdi Dibaj

Eileen is a teacher from England who was forced to take early retirement because she suffers from multiple sclerosis. She continues to lead an active life although her mobility is severely limited. Two particular interests are music and enlisting support for the Save the Children Fund – which she does very effectively.

Eileen has a quiet faith. She doesn't feel angry at God for 'allowing' this to happen to her. She recognises that illness and accidents are facts of life. Instead of asking, 'Why me?' she asks, 'Why not me?'. She realises that suffering is a problem which makes belief in God difficult for some people – but not for her. Eileen feels supported by friendship and by prayer. She retains her sense of humour and her peace of mind, as the following extract from one of her letters makes clear:

'I've had to give up driving. The fatigue is rotten, but not such a worry now that I've stopped working. The blurred and double/triple vision is a nuisance, but curiously interesting – for example the Cathedral has had two spires for a couple of years, there are three moons in the sky and an awful lot of eight-legged cats about! I am quite used to it now and it's not a worry. I've made no retirement plans, confident that something will emerge for me, when the time is right.'

These brief sketches make it clear that following the Christian Way means much more than 'going to church' or belonging to a cultural group. When it is true to itself, Christian faith engages with real life. It brings challenge and inspiration; it gives strength and comfort in trouble.

GLOSSARY

Abba Father
'Abba' is one of the few Aramaic words found in the New Testament (Aramaic was Jesus' first language). It is an intimate family word – the nearest English equivalent is probably 'Daddy'. Jesus addressed God the Father in this way – so did the first Christians. The word, and the close relationship to God which it describes, was the gift of Jesus to his disciples.

Canon
A Greek word meaning *rod* or *rule*, which came to signify a list or catalogue. In Christian usage it denotes the list of books regarded as Holy Scripture (Chapter 5)

Creed
A definition or summary of Christian belief. The earliest creeds are found in the New Testament, for example Romans 10:9 ('Jesus is Lord') and 1 Corinthians 15:3 (see page 42). Later Creeds include the *Apostles' Creed* and the *Nicene Creed*.

Eternal Life
A new quality of life to be entered into, by God's grace, through faith in Jesus Christ. It starts in this world and continues beyond death – into eternity. The phrase is found frequently in John's Gospel and first letter.

Evangelism
Proclaiming or sharing the good news of God's love revealed in Jesus Christ.

Evangelisation
Sometimes this means the same as 'evangelism'; sometimes it refers to the permeation of human relationships and cultures with gospel values. This word – rather than 'evangelism' – tends to be used by Roman Catholics.

The Gospel
'Glad tidings of great joy' (Luke 2:10) William Tyndale wrote: 'Evangelio (that we cal gospel) is a greke word, and signyfyth good, mery, glad and joyfull tidings, that maketh a mannes hert glad, and maketh hym synge, daunce and leepe for joye.'

High Priest
A title given to Jesus in the New Testament (especially in *Hebrews*), signifying the fact that he has dealt with human sin. The offering he made was the perfect sacrifice of his own life.

Holy Spirit
In the New Testament the Holy Spirit has many titles: the Spirit of God, the Spirit of Christ, the Spirit of Jesus, the Spirit of Truth, the Counsellor . . . Many of these titles convey the notion of the closeness (the 'immanence') of God, as opposed to the 'transcendence' of God the Father.

Incarnation
The Christian belief that in Jesus, God became a human being in order to save the world. (This is quite different from *Reincarnation* – see page 126).

Liturgy
Literally in Greek, 'the work of the people.' It came to be applied to the services of the Temple and, later, to Christian worship – especially the eucharist.

Mission
Mission is a wider concept than evangelism, though it includes this. It embraces *all* that God calls his Church to do in the world: the pursuit of justice, peace and care for Creation, as well as praying for the world and spreading the gospel of Jesus Christ. The Swiss theologian Emil Brunner declared that 'the Church exists by mission as a fire exists by burning.'

Monotheism
Belief in one God. The three great monotheistic faiths are Judaism, Islam and Christianity.

Myth
In common speech this is usually a 'bad' word, referring to something which is untrue – a fabricated story, perhaps even a lie. In theological language it is usually a 'good' word – referring to something *so* important and profoundly true that it can *only* be conveyed in the form of a story.

New Age
'The fastest growing spiritual movement in the world today'. (Margaret Brierly) It is a movement without hierarchy or central organisation. It stresses *spirituality*, which in this context means 'doing your own thing' – anything from meditation to hugging trees. *'In one sense the New Age Movement is a religion without being a religion, with its emphasis on self-realisation rather than upon God.'* (Graham Cray) See *Post-modernism*.

Polytheism
Those religions which, like Hinduism, honour many Gods.

Post-modernism
'Modernism' was the child of the *Enlightenment* (Chapter 18). *Post-modernism* is a 'buzz' word suggesting a time of rapid transition – a new way of viewing the world. *'Post-modernity is a flux of images and fictions . . . truth is human, socially produced, historically developed, plural and changing'*. (Don Cupitt) Truth is viewed as relative not absolute, and insights from various places may be pulled together to form a view of life – a 'pick and mix approach' (see *New Age*).

Salvation
The activity of God which – supremely in Jesus Christ – brings healing, wholeness and reconciliation with God to human beings.

Son of Man
The title which, in the Synoptic Gospels, is used by Jesus to refer to himself. Scholars have debated its background and significance, and whether Jesus did in fact use the phrase. Its likely origins can be found in two Old Testament books. Throughout Ezekiel, God addresses the prophet as 'son of man' – ie *as a human being*. In Daniel 7:13–14 the phrase refers to an awesome *heavenly* figure.

Synagogue
A Jewish meeting place for worship. Unlike worship in the Temple, Synagogue worship did not (and does not) include animal sacrifice but is based on prayers and readings from the Hebrew Scriptures. At the time of Jesus, as now, synagogues were established in every town with a Jewish community.

Tabernacle
A portable sanctuary (an elaborate 'tent') in which God 'dwelt' among the Israelites in the desert. It was a fore-runner of the Temple.

Temple
The first Temple was built by King Solomon. (2 Chronicles 3) At the time of Jesus, the Temple in Jerusalem (built by Herod the Great) was the focus for national worship – including animal sacrifice. Herod's great Temple was destroyed by the Romans in AD 70.

The Trinity
The Christian doctrine that there are three 'Persons' in one God. The doctrine developed over the first few Christian centuries and is found in the Creeds hammered out at Church Councils: (Nicaea AD 325), Constantinople (AD 381) and Chalcedon (451). But the building blocks are found in the New Testament and in the experience of the disciples. As they reflected on *the significance of Jesus* they became aware that he was 'the man Christ Jesus' (1 Timothy 2:5) *and* 'My Lord and my God' (John 20:28). On the day of Pentecost they were *filled with the Holy Spirit*. They understood these experiences as three actions or manifestations of the One True God – Creator and Redeemer of the World (see page 14).

Virgin Birth
The belief that Jesus Christ had no human father, but was conceived by Mary through the power of the Holy Spirit (Matthew 1; Luke 1). More properly called 'the virginal conception'.

Wish Fulfilment
The view of Sigmund Freud and others that Christians believe in God because (unconsciously) they find reassurance in the notion of a 'Father in heaven'. This criticism can be turned against itself; for example Aldous Huxley admitted that for years he believed that the world was without ultimate meaning and moral purpose, because he wished to be free of irksome moral constraints.

RECOMMENDED READING

From the Bible, *Luke's Gospel* and *Paul's letter to the Philippians.*

Modest-sized books

If you wish to read one other book I recommend:
Polkinghorne, John; *The Way the World Is*, SPCK
(In this book a scientist explains his faith) or Wright, N T; *Who Was Jesus?* (SPCK).

Likewise, I recommend:
Anderson, Sir Norman; *Jesus Christ: the Witness of History,* IVP
Dunn, James; *The Evidence for Jesus,* SCM
Huggett, Joyce; *Listening to God,* Hodder and Stoughton
Hughes, Gerard; *God of Surprises,* DLT
Maitland, Sara; *A Big – Enough God,* Mowbray
Robinson, John; *Can We Trust the New Testament?*, SCM
Schillebeeckx, Edward; *I am a Happy Theologian,* SCM
Tutu, Desmond; *The Rainbow People of God*, Transworld

Paperbacks by C S Lewis are still popular (eg *Mere Christianity, Screwtape Letters*).

Biography

From a long list, I recommend:
Bethge, Eberhard; *Dietrich Bonhoeffer*, Collins
Colson, Charles; *Born Again,* Hodder and Stoughton
Cruz, Nicky; *Run Baby, Run,* Hodder and Stoughton
Garrow, David; *Bearing the Cross* (on Martin Luther King), Vintage
Gordon, Ernest; *Miracle on the River Kwai*, Fount
Montefiore, Hugh; *O God, What Next?* Hodder and Stoughton

Christianity and literature

Adam, David; *Rhythm of Life*, SPCK (Celtic Prayers)
Forde, Nigel; *The Lantern and the Looking Glass*, SPCK – in preparation
Harries, Richard; *Art and the Beauty of God*, Mowbray
Mayne, Michael; *This Sunrise of Wonder*, Collins

Larger books and reference works

Anderson, Sir Norman; *Christianity and World Religions*, IVP
Bosch, David; *Transforming Mission*, Orbis
Chadwick, Owen; *History of Christianity*, Weidenfeld-Nicolson
Chadwick & Evans (Eds.); *Atlas of the Christian Church*, Equinox
Geoffrey Chapman; *Catechism of the Catholic Church*
Edwards D L & Stott J R W; *Essentials*, Hodder and Stoughton
Küng, Hans; *On Being a Christian*, Collins
Küng, Hans; *Christianity*, SCM
McGrath, Alister; *Christian Theology: an introduction*, Blackwell
McGrath, Alister (Ed.); *The Blackwell Encyclopedia of Modern Christian Thought*, Blackwell
McManners, John (Ed.); *The Oxford Illustrated History of Christianity. Oxford Dictionary of the Christian Church* (1997 Edition)
Stott, John; *The Cross of Christ*, IVP
The Bible, A Lion Handbook
The History of Christianity, A Lion Handbook
The Mystery of Salvation, Church of England Report
Yates, Timothy; *Christian Mission in the Twentieth Century*, Cambridge University Press

Teach Yourself books (Hodder & Stoughton)

McConville, Gordon; *The Old Testament*
Stone, David; *The New Testament*

Books by John Young

Know Your Faith, Hodder & Stoughton (for group study)
The Case Against Christ, Hodder and Stoughton
Live Your Faith, CPAS (for group study)
Jesus: the Verdict, Lion
Creating Confidence in Evangelism, CPAS

INDEX

Pentecost 39, 75, 99, 208-9
Pentecostal Churches 174, 188
Peter (apostle) 76, 165, 209-10
petition 91
Pietist movement 244, 247
Pliny the Younger 12, 272
Polycarp, Bishop of Smyrna 146
post-modernism 254, 256
prayer 81-2, 87-93
Presbyterian Churches 169
Priestland, Gerald 81-2
Prodigal Son parable 6
Protestant Churches 167-8, 241
Psalms 270-1, 273
purgatory 122-3
Quakers (Society of Friends) 94, 114,
    174
Rahner, Karl 206
Ramsey, Michael, Archbishop of
    Canterbury 16-17, 96-7
ransom 27
Ratushinskaya, Irina 81
reconciliation 27, 113
Redhead, Brian 47
reductionism 137
Reformation 167-9, 235-44, 266
    church music 274-5
    martyrs 150-1
relics 146-7
Renaissance prince-popes 228
repentance 122, 123
Resurrection 33-46, 124
    of the body 127-8
Revelation 57-8, 69, 76
Robinson, Bishop John 11
Roman Catholic Church 149, 165-7,
    172, 176, 180, 193
    and contraception 202-3
    and the Reformation 242-3
    revival 248, 249
Romanticism 248, 254
Sabbath 10, 51, 272
Sacraments 94, 101-17
St Luke's Gospel 2
saints 146-50, 151-2
    canonisation of 151-2, 153
salvation 23-4, 26, 253
Salvation Army 114, 173-4, 252
Samaritans 197-8
Sarah, Sister 284
schism 213

Schweitzer, Albert 46
science 131-43
scrolls 59-60
Sea of Faith movement 187
Sermon on the Mount 4, 10, 54, 70
sexuality 192-3, 214, 220
Shelter 198
Simpson, James Young 133
sin 22, 153-4, 250
social justice 255
Solzhenitsyn, Alexander 80-1
South Africa 200
spirituals 274-5
statistics (Church) 160-1, 172-3
Stephen 145
Synagogue 51, 59
Tacitus 12
Talmud 12
Teresa, Mother 111, 153, 186
thanksgiving 90
Toronto Blessing 188-9
transubstantiation 109-10
Trinity, doctrine of the 15, 55, 87-8,
    95, 216-17
Trinity Sunday 99-9
Tutu, Archbishop Desmond 7, 182,
    200
Tyndale, William 150-1, 278
Uganda 152-3
Unitarianism 246
United States 253-4
Vermes, Geza 13
Virgin Birth 149
virtues 154-6
wars of religion 243
Watts, Isaac 273
Wells, H.G. 13
Wesley, Charles 173, 273, 274
Wesley, John 83, 247, 273, 275
wish-fulfilment 135
Wolfendale, Arnold 133
women
    Jesus and 192
    in the Middle Ages 227-8
World Council of Churches (WCC)
    179-80
worship 93-7
Worsley, Malcolm 77, 79, 187
Wycliffe, John 275
Young, Frances 80
Zwingli, Ulrich 238-9

Other related titles

THE OLD TESTAMENT

Gordon McConville

The Bible has had a profound effect on the whole of Western culture – through the religions of Judaism, Christianity and Islam, and also through literature and art. It has been the often unrecognised inspiration behind many of the values by which a large proportion of the world's population chooses to live today.

This book introduces the background and contents of the Old Testament, together with the methods used in its study and the ways in which it is read, both traditional and contemporary. It offers the student and the general reader a straightforward approach to this rich source of religious and cultural inspiration.

Gordon McConville teaches at the Cheltenham and Gloucester College of Higher Education.

Other related titles

ty **TEACH YOURSELF**

THE NEW TESTAMENT

David Stone

The Bible has had a profound effect on the whole of Western culture – through the religions of Judaism, Christianity and Islam, and also through literature and art. It has been the often unrecognised inspiration behind many of the values by which a large proportion of the world's population chooses to live today.

For both the student and the general reader, this book gives a sound basis for an understanding of the New Testament. It introduces the New Testament books, their background, the approaches taken to them by scholars and the ways in which the New Testament is used today.

David Stone is Vicar of St Jude's Anglican church, Courtfield Gardens, London, as well as an author and broadcaster and has a wealth of experience in preparing study guides to the New Testament.